The Big Tax Lie is a searing indictment of our nation's tax system and the IRS written by a successful, patriotic entrepreneur who spent $6 million of his own money in battling against an incompetent, unethical, and out-of-control IRS investigation—and won. William Kilpatrick's provocative plan for the major restructuring of our tax system, as well as the shocking disclosure of IRS collection procedures and practices, will revolutionize the American tax system.

Kilpatrick contends that today's problems of welfare, unemployment, $200 billion annual deficits, and a $2 trillion debt are all symptoms of a totally ineffective and counterproductive system of taxation. His "battle plan" is ingeniously simple: a direct consumer tax combined with a Truth in Taxation law (similar to Truth in Lending, Truth in Advertising, and so on) that would make it mandatory for all hidden taxes to be labeled on all products and services. This would lead to making the entire present tax apparatus obsolete and ultimately solve virtually all our worst and most pervasive economic problems, including balance of payments and national debt.

Kilpatrick's legal battle and eventual victory over the IRS, involving numerous documented abuses of civil liberties by IRS agents and prosecutors, was twice featured on *60 Minutes* and was publicized nationally and prominently throughout the legal profession. Kilpatrick also goes beyond his own case to demonstrate how the

IRS has become not only a law unto itself, but the most feared, powerful, and seemingly immune agency in government.

There's a madness to the present method of taxation, and William Kilpatrick is determined to right the wrongs our government has imposed on the American taxpayer. For any man or woman who has felt like the little guy going up against the vast, impersonal bureaucracy that is the IRS, here finally is a book that makes a thought-provoking case for a new route toward our country's economic future.

William A. Kilpatrick is President and Chairman of United Financial Operations, Inc. He lives with his wife and family in Littleton, Colorado.

THE BIG TAX LIE

William A. Kilpatrick

87·674

SIMON AND SCHUSTER
NEW YORK

SIMON AND SCHUSTER and colophon are registered trademarks
of Simon & Schuster, Inc.
Designed by Irving Perkins Associates
Manufactured in the United States of America

10 9 8 7 6 5 4 3 2 1
Library of Congress Cataloging in Publication Data

Kilpatrick, William A.
  The big tax lie.

  1. Taxation—United States. 2. Taxation—Law
and legislation—United States. I. Title.
HJ2381.K55 1986 336.2'00973 86-13903
ISBN: 0-671-63109-8

Acknowledgments

Jim Reeves, the first elected official who, in my case, took a stand against the IRS and who continues to stand as tall today.

Rick Reeves, who converted my illegible handwriting to readable type.

Doug Vaughan, who edited for content.

Christine Barker, whose preliminary verb-tense and punctuation editing brought order to chaos.

Bill Waller, who did the initial legal reading of the manuscript.

Rick Rufner, Bill Waller, and *Dennis Mark,* defense attorneys whose legal work prevailed in *U.S.* vs. *Kilpatrick* against all the "hired guns" Washington could muster.

Declan O'Donnell, tax attorney *extraordinaire* whose tax planning and legal opinions proved to be correct and to reflect the intent of Congress throughout the nine years of intense scrutiny, and *Bob Grossman,* who shares the *Tax Attorney Championship.* Together, they come closer to understanding our unfathomable tax laws than all the rest of the legal profession combined.

Megan and Tyson, for their special support and constant confidence and for being my kids.

All the Friends and Relatives who never wavered in their faithfulness although the world promised me they would and the bureaucrats depended on it. Especially *Nancy Stanley,* who because of her special courage, initiated a letter to Judge Winner, which led, in large part, to the finding of the 102 violations. Last, but far from least, my hundreds and hundreds of *investors and partners* who individually refused to knuckle under to the power and threats of all the government agencies that the IRS directed also against them.

*To Marita for all the reasons
that all who know her know so well*

Contents

Foreword

CONGRATULATIONS! The simple commitment to read the foreword of a book about taxation proves you have overcome the inherent fear of addressing yourself to a subject often regarded as too complex to warrant the attempt.

Taxes are not complex. They are simple. Understanding taxation is easy: All you need is the truth.

Once you know the truth, it will be as clear to you as it has become to me that the only barrier to understanding is lies—lies we have told ourselves and lies told to us by others. These lies are totally believable because we want to believe them. As Sir Walter Scott warned, "O, what a tangled web we weave, when first we practice to deceive"; and my, have we got ourselves a tangle! We've been at it a long time, practically our entire history. In the epic manner of all lies, the first lie required a second to support the first, and each subsequent lie has required others to sustain it.

Actually, you know the truth already. It's just difficult to discern through that tangled web.

My one purpose in this book is to brush away that web. Prepare yourself to feel the same thrill I felt when I first cleaned my own house. It's an absolutely marvelous feeling to stroll through a clean abode with all those jewels of truth shining in the light, unencumbered by a lifetime of dust-collecting webs.

You may rebel at first. I did. I'd look at a "truth" and say, "That's ridiculous." I, too, had a lifetime of lies to

11

overcome. I, too, was comfortable with what I had always taken for granted. I had built my life on these lies. I had learned them at my father's knee, as he had at his father's knee. They'd been reinforced in formal education, and then I had earned a fortune and built a multimillion-dollar company based on them. It was a nice feeling; I wanted to keep it.

But then I was forced to face the truth. I had to be indicted on twenty-seven criminal counts—facing 140 years in prison, the loss of my family, my business and everything I held dear—before I would face the truth.

I'd like to make it a little easier on you. Just read this book. You'll have some difficulty. For a while you'll probably read a statement I call a "truth" and say, "That's ridiculous." But soon a transition will occur. You'll read some equally "ridiculous" statement and say, "I know that. I've always known that. It's so obvious!" When that happens, go back and reread the earlier ridiculous statements; you'll find them now to be equally obvious.

The truth is funny that way. Whether we like it or not, it is absolutely irresistible, and no lie can stand the brilliance of its light once we remove the shade and let it shine. And it had better shine, because economically America is in trouble, deep trouble.

The list of problems is almost endless. They are not small, and they are not diminishing. To the contrary, they are growing at an alarming rate, with no solution in sight. There is no solution because the so-called problems themselves are lies, and all the proposed solutions are greater lies yet. Let's take stock of ourselves.

We have a national debt of over $2 trillion.

We have an average annual deficit of $200 billion to add to that debt.

Yet people feel that they are already overburdened by taxes. Their weight is so oppressive that ordinary, law-abiding citizens have lost faith in their government and hope for the future. They face a crisis that seems incom-

prehensible, and they throw up their hands in exaspera-
tion, withdraw in cynicism or apathy, or, in desperation,
are driven to desperate acts.

No greater proof exists of the failure of our current tax
system. Even if the myriad other problems with the current tax system were tolerable, the fact that the system is
incompetent to accomplish its *only* purpose, which is to
generate sufficient revenues to run the government,
proves it to be a failed system of taxation. A lie. But there's
more.

We have a negative balance of international trade and
payments that drains us of billions each year.

We have a growing unemployment problem that is
made worse as our industries slip farther behind in international trade competition.

Our agricultural community is going bankrupt, while
the bounty it produces cannot be bought by the hungry of
America, let alone the starving masses of the world.

It's as if an economic vampire stalked the land, sucking
the lifeblood from farmers and steelworkers, nurses and
clerks, salesmen and janitors. The federal budget absorbs
an ever-greater share of the gross national product, while
burgeoning deficits absorb capital, drive up interest rates,
and inflate prices.

Most dangerous of all, the freedoms that we hold dear
are being lost, neutralized, or subverted at an alarming
rate. Yet these very rights and liberties are our only means
of salvation.

All of these problems are a direct result of our system
of taxation—not the amount or degree of the tax, but the
method. Even if the system were successful in generating
sufficient revenues to balance the budget, any system in-
flicting this type of pain on the people it is supposed to
serve must be eliminated.

Not one of these problems has shrunk in the past fifty
years. Each has grown. And every solution proposed for
any one problem has only worsened the others.

We are the richest, most productive, most creative nation in the history of the world. There is no excuse for our apparent helplessness in the face of catastrophe. Every previous crisis has crumbled in the wake of our determination, our drive, our ingenuity, and our well-deserved confidence.

So why do our current problems seem so intractable? The agony of the Great Depression, the threat of Nazi Germany, the secret of atomic energy, the conquest of space—all these challenges were faced in the living memory of we same Americans who now seem so perplexed and paralyzed by what is nothing more than an economic phantom.

The reason we have been unable to resolve our current problems is our absolute refusal to face the truth. Not one of these perceived problems is the true problem. They are all symptoms of the problem. To attempt to treat a symptom while ignoring the disease is futile.

Yet our underlying syndrome is treatable; we may need painkillers for the symptoms, but there is a cure for the disease once we recognize the cause. And the cause is a fatally flawed system of taxation. It is a lie, and there is no way to "fix" a lie. Whether trying to support or correct that lie, we have posted hundreds of deceits on top of it. Thus, we have enlarged the original lie and, ultimately, we have aggravated the very problems we have attempted to resolve.

Without truth, there is no solution. With truth, there is no problem. The choice is ours. We have the right, and we have the power. If we demand the truth, we will get the truth. We must demand "Truth in Taxation," for it is our only salvation.

PART ONE

THE RIGHT TAX

CHAPTER 1

The Wrong System

LET'S UNDERSTAND ONE THING at the start: I am not now nor have I ever been a "tax protester," not by any definition of the term.

I love and worship this nation, and I am prepared to make any sacrifice necessary to ensure its preservation. I have served voluntarily in its armed forces not once, but twice.

I am equally prepared to make any tax contribution necessary for the nation's social, economic, or military requirements in order to assure its perpetuation as the greatest and most dynamic in the history of the world. I love this nation and its people for what they are: the most benevolent society ever known.

This nation has taken into its fold the races, creeds, and colors of the world. It blends the best of each into the bounty of its blessing. No other nation can begin to lay claim to even the most minute part of its magnificence. Therefore, I will pay, and have always gladly paid without protest or regret, my share of any and all taxes required for its maintenance. Nothing that follows should be construed as a desire on my part to avoid such taxation. My entire premise is that the necessary tax should be paid by the citizens of this nation, its beneficiaries.

My sole objection is to the system currently in effect to collect these taxes. The system is ineffective. It is counterproductive. And it is parasitic, for it destroys the host upon which it depends for nourishment. The system is fatally flawed and must be replaced. Not reformed, but replaced.

The worst part of this system was initiated in 1913. At that moment, this nation became afflicted with an economic cancer of the most insidious type. Not the kind that instantly announces its virulence by the host's early demise, but the type that eats slowly and without warning, unnoticed but with an ever-growing ferocity. It gradually attacks every organ of society, leaving each mortally wounded before that organ is even recognized as diseased.

This cancer is the Sixteenth Amendment to the Constitution—the amendment that attempts to bestow respectability upon a tax that the framers recognized would be an economic disaster, and so prohibited in Article I, Section 9, Paragraph 4, of the original document. It is a tax on wages and income.

There is no doubt of the intent of the Constitution's authors to forbid an income tax. As late as 1908, the U.S. Supreme Court declared any such tax to be unconstitutional. The following year Congress proposed and the state legislatures thereafter agreed to "repair" this defect[1] in the Constitution with the Sixteenth Amendment. Making the income tax constitutional in no way makes it palatable, repairs its fatal flaw, or renders it any more

---

[1] Bill Benson and M. J. "Red" Beckman, *The Law That Never Was* (Holland, Ill.: Constitution Research Assoc., 1985). This book raises considerable question as to whether or not the Sixteenth Amendment was ever passed by any vaguely legal requirements of constitutionality. It is well documented and worth reading, but not pertinent to my arguments. If the Sixteenth Amendment worked, the flaws in its passing could be repaired or ignored. The fact is that it has failed on every element of every function it was enacted to achieve, and therefore its repair is not warranted.

effective economically. This system of taxation did not fail to work because it was unconstitutional; it was made unconstitutional by the Founding Fathers because they knew it would fail to work and that it had the potential to destroy the entire economic structure they were erecting.

How right they were. We have very nearly undone all their good work. Our failure to recognize that fact prior to imposing this impossible law of an income tax on ourselves permitted the initiation of the cancer I have described. That cancer has grown slowly but surely until it now infects our entire society with its malignancy. After over seventy-two years, the symptoms are obvious:

1. We have a $2 trillion national debt that is growing by over $200 billion a year. We have become a debtor nation, and at the current rate we will be the world's biggest debtor nation by 1989.

2. Unemployment officially is above 7 percent of the work force (that is, those willing, able and actively seeking work, but excluding those who have been unemployed so long they have given up). It is twice that average for minorities and four times that average for minority youth. Clearly, the economy grows too slowly to provide jobs to all who want and need them.

3. Far too many of those who are working fail to earn enough to rise above the poverty level. Even if one accepts the official definition of poverty (which many experts regard as too low), the figures indicate a decisive trend toward more "working poor," reversing twenty years' painful progress toward elimination of poverty.

4. Our basic industries—steel and metals, automobiles, machine tools—are failing at an alarming rate. Even in electronics, computers, and communications—the three-legged stool upon which the megatrendy priests of high tech propose we base our "service-oriented" economy in this "information age"—American manufacturers are losing whatever edge they once had.

As a result of these failures, we are taking on the classic attributes of an underdeveloped country, shipping our raw materials to faraway lands where they are fashioned into finished goods that we must import—if we can afford them. This has led to a negative balance in international trade, grown from $72 billion in 1983 to $108 billion in 1984 to $117.7 billion in 1985.

When the government has to borrow money to cover its expenditures, interest rates increase and American businesses are squeezed for credit they need to innovate in order to remain competitive; also, the value of the dollar expands, making our exports less competitive in overseas markets and imports less expensive here. High interest rates also attract foreign investment, which may help our balance of payments but leaves us working for absentee landlords whose profits eventually will flow out of the country.

The conventional approach to these problems, as reflected in the last two presidential elections, has been to debate whether to raise taxes, cut expenses, or both. Republicans correctly predict that raising taxes will leave the economy more stagnant, while Democrats rightly criticize further shredding of the "safety net" that cushions the fall of the victims of that stagnation. Both parties are right—yet both completely miss the point: The tax system itself is fatally flawed. Not only does it fail to raise sufficient revenues to cover expenses, it generates the very problems the politicians propose to address by "fine-tuning" the system. The result is paralysis, while the malignant tax continues to consume everything it touches.

Perhaps most insidious, the freest nation the world has ever known is rapidly losing the rights that made it great. And this crisis of liberty, a far greater danger than our economic crisis, is also directly attributable to the imposition of a fallacious system of taxation.

"Repairs" have been attempted, but they amount to nothing more than killing some of the cancer, and it's too late for that. The smallest residual cancer is as deadly as the largest, and we have already played with this cancer for over seventy-two years.

There is a system that will work. It is a proven system that has worked in every instance of its implementation, and it will work for us. This magical but maligned system of taxation is *a direct tax on consumption to the exclusion of all other taxes.*

But there's a catch. In our society, this system is a pariah. It is possessed of an unfounded but hideous reputation, and it will never be implemented until this reputation is overcome. It doesn't matter that such a tax could resolve all our perceived problems. It will never be given that opportunity until its value is proven in advance. Something I call "Truth in Taxation" will do this, but that's getting ahead of ourselves.

Interestingly enough, our system of taxation on income *is* a tax on consumption. It's an *indirect* consumption tax, but a consumption tax nonetheless. Whether we recognize the fact or not, the final purchase of a product is the point in the economic process at which *every* tax is collected. Regardless of the point of imposition, all taxes have been, and always will be, collected from the consumer. Why? Because there is no one or nothing else from whom the government can collect. There are impositions of taxes at other points in the economic system, but these taxes are simply passed on as a cost of production or cost of doing business to the next purchaser/reseller of the product, until they reach the only party who makes no resale, the consumer. The consumer then absorbs all the prior hidden consumption taxes as a part of the purchase price of the product.

This is a basic economic fact, and it has nothing to do with greed or wealth on the part of the manufacturers or merchants. It is a law of economics. All merchants must collect sufficient funds from the purchasers of their wares to cover all their expenses or they will go broke. Any tax, other than a sales tax on the end product, becomes an expense. It then makes the product more expensive and less competitive in the marketplace. All the supposed problems of our society are traceable to our refusal to recognize this one fact. If taxes were imposed at the point of collection from the consumer, our problems would be resolved automatically. The problems would cease to exist because they have never been *the* problem. They are merely symptoms of the problem: our attempting to tax transactions that are not taxable at the point we impose the tax. All nonconsumer "taxpayers" are mere conduits. At best, they are tax collectors; but they are not taxpayers.

I readily admit that taxes must be paid; and we, as citizens, must pay them. Moreover, we should pay them in sufficient quantity to support the governmental services we demand and/or permit on a pay-as-you-go basis. The only question is how these taxes will be paid.

I am advocating that we impose on ourselves a tax that would not be self-destructive or even self-injurious. The only law that requires us to commit suicide in order to support ourselves is the law that established the income tax.

All taxes in a republic are supposedly collected for the betterment of the payers of those taxes. They are supposedly collected in order to permit the government to perform such services as it collectively can perform more efficiently than the citizens themselves. A tax is not a penalty on the citizens. It is their payment for services, insurance, defense, safety, and their society's welfare.

The first consideration in designing any tax must therefore be, "Will such a tax provide sufficient revenues to pay for the desired services?" The second consideration must be, "What tax can be imposed that is least injurious to the people?"

The answer to the first question, in the case of a tax on income, is obviously no. We can't deny this. We have over seventy-two years of proof of insufficient revenues. And to make matters worse, the gap is not closing; it is widening. Each year, the difference between government collections and expenditures grows greater.

Given the failure of the income tax to meet the first requirement, we should not have to bother with the second. Yet the very insidiousness of a tax on income calls for some such analysis. For the fact is that every dollar the income tax takes from society for the purpose of solving a problem will exaggerate that very problem:

> A dollar collected to aid the existing poor will create more poor.
> A dollar collected to reduce the deficit will increase the deficit.
> A dollar collected to pay off the national debt will result in greater indebtedness.
> A dollar collected for unemployment relief will cause more layoffs.
> A dollar collected to aid a troubled industry will leave in its wake more empty factories with boarded-up windows and more declining cities.
> A dollar collected to subsidize a negative balance of trade will reduce exports and increase imports.

Even if none of these problems existed, a dollar so collected would create them.

Any tax has the potential to do damage to the individual. It deprives the individual of the economic benefits that would have been available to him had that amount of tax not been paid. Taxes are therefore inherently a burden, a burden bearable by degrees depending, more or less, on how the tax is collected, the manner or the transaction on which it is imposed, and the gross amount. Normally the amount is least important. When we cash our paychecks or try to meet a payroll, we can, in fact, pay the amount currently being collected and probably more, possibly considerably more. So it is not the amount of tax that is the problem, it is the system of collection that we cannot tolerate.

A direct tax on consumption, on the other hand, avoids these problems. It can, and will, collect the revenues required to meet governmental expenses. It is easily adjusted to meet extraordinary expense. It is identifiable and controllable. And most important, it does not injure its economic system; it supports it.

We have pointed out how, under our current system of taxation on income, the tax is already a consumer's tax. But it is hidden. The consumer still pays all the taxes just the same, whether he realizes it or not. With an admitted and open consumption tax, such as a sales or value-added tax (VAT), the consumer also pays all the taxes. But there is a very significant difference, a difference entirely created by the attempt to hide the consumption tax from the consumer. The deception makes every producer of goods and services in our economy noncompetitive in the world market, and this noncompetitiveness in turn creates all our other problems.

We will have an open consumption tax, however, only after we destroy the myths that create its bad reputation.

My proposal for "Truth in Taxation" can do this. "Truth in Taxation" will prove to every citizen that consumption taxes are the only taxes there ever have been, or ever will be. "Truth in Taxation" will provide the clarity that any truth has always provided, and it will permit the instituting of the only correct tax: an open and admitted consumption tax.

CHAPTER 2

Types of Taxes

THERE ARE TWO TYPES of taxes, direct and indirect. Both are ultimately taxes on consumption, and no rationalization can change this irrefutable fact. Our attempts to avoid this fact are the root causes of every problem we face as a nation. This will become apparent as we examine the effects of indirect consumption taxes on various elements of our society and economy.

To resolve our problems, we must:

1. Admit that a tax must be paid to support the government services we accept;
2. Define the costs of these services;
3. Agree to pay that amount proportionate to our ability to pay; and
4. Pay that amount by openly and admittedly imposing a tax on the item to be taxed.

Since all taxes are ultimately collected from the consumers of products and services, why not impose the tax directly on consumption? It's easy to do, everyone understands it, and it eliminates the greatest complaint about our current system. The most constant complaint, and the centerpiece of every reform program, is a cry for simplification.

Good, let's simplify it. Let's impose a flat-rate sales or use tax on a service or product that is for sale. Let's tax it right here.

Cost of item	$1.00
Sales tax	+ .07
Total	$1.07

You pay $1.07, and the merchant keeps the $1.00 and conveys $.07 to the government. It's over with, it's done, it's complete.

This is the beauty of a *direct* consumption tax. You don't have to fill out Internal Revenue Service (IRS) form 1040, detailing how many other dollars you earned that year, what you spent them on, the amount of your house payment, how much you gave to your church, or how many children you are supporting. There is no need for an IRS agent to check your receipts, determine your truthfulness, or pry into your personal and financial affairs.

Have you ever heard of any state revenue agent of the sales-tax division going to a home and placing a seizure notice on the owner to collect the $.07 tax on a $1.00 purchase? Of course not. You can't leave the store with your purchase until the tax is paid. The entire transaction is complete before you receive your purchased item. The merchant got his, the government got its, and you paid your share.

There are currently three types of direct consumption taxes in vogue. In the U.S., we have sales and use taxes. In most other countries, the tax is imposed as an ad valorem, or value-added, tax. The VAT is nothing more than an extremely complex system of imposing a simple sales tax. It makes poor sense to collect in this way, but it beats the devil out of the way we do it in the U.S.

An oversimplified example would be a loaf of bread. Suppose the VAT is 25 percent of the "value," that is, the sale price.

Suppose a farmer sells 100 bushels of wheat to a granary for $100. If the VAT is 25 percent, the bill to the granary would be:

Wheat	$100
25% VAT	+ 25
Total	$125

The farmer would pay $25 to the government and retain $100 for his efforts, expenses, and profit.

Suppose the granary mills the 100 bushels and sells the flour to a baker for $110. The baker would be charged:

Flour	$110.00
25% VAT	+ 27.50
Total	$137.50

The granary would pay the government $2.50 cash and present the $25 receipt from the farmer as payment in full for the tax bill of $27.50. In other words, the granary would pay the percentage of tax on the value it added to the wheat by milling it into flour.

The granary would retain $135. One hundred dollars would be its recapture of costs for the wheat, $25 would be its recapture of the cost of payment of the tax paid by the farmer, and $10 would be for the services and the costs of storage, processing, and grinding.

Suppose the baker makes $400 worth of bread from the 100 bushels. He would charge the grocer:

Bread	$400
25% VAT	+ 100
Total	$500

The baker would pay to the government $72.50 cash and convey receipts from the granary of $27.50 as proof of payment of the balance of the VAT. He would retain $400 for recapture of his actual costs and profits. (Obviously, he would also have costs and tax receipts for yeast, eggs, milk, and other ingredients, but for simplicity, let's assume that only flour is required to make bread. Therefore, only the tax on the flour is deducted from his value-added tax liability.)

The grocer proceeds the same way as the others. Suppose he is selling 1,000 loaves to 1,000 customers for $1 each. The grocer would charge his customers:

$$
\begin{array}{lll}
\text{Bread} & \$1.00 \times 1000 & = \$1000 \\
25\% \text{ VAT} & +\ .25 \times 1000 & = \ \ \ \ 250 \\
& & \\
\text{Total} & \$1.25 \times 1000 & = \$1250
\end{array}
$$

The grocer would pay $150 cash and present the prepaid tax receipt of $100 from the baker as payment in full to the government.

In total, the government would receive $250 in taxes in the grocer's transaction. *This is exactly the same amount it would have received if it had simply imposed a retail sales tax of 25 percent,* without all the foolishness of having other people (hundreds if we counted the sellers of yeast, eggs, milk, and other ingredients) exchange all sorts of receipts to figure out what happened.

In reality, the VAT is a stupid system of sales-tax collection, with absolutely no excuse for all its confusion. Let the grocer collect the tax and pay it.

It is sad for nations to come so close to an honest, fully disclosed, open system of taxation—an admitted tax on consumption and a simple tax within the comprehensible grasp of every citizen—and then make it so ridiculously complex.

According to the bureaucrats and politicians with whom I have discussed the VAT, the reasons it is made so complex are manifold:

1. "It permits the citizens to see that the merchants are paying their fair share."

The truth: It permits the politicians to bamboozle the citizen into believing that the merchant is paying the consumer's taxes for him. This is done to obtain votes. In the previous example, the purchaser of the bread paid $1.00 for the bread and $.25 in tax. The consumer actually reimbursed every merchant for every cent the merchants paid. Keep this thought in mind as we analyze our own tax system.

2. "The receipts and payments at each level of production make the system self-policing, reducing the propensity for cheating."

The truth: Bureaucrats cannot stand the idea that they might lose the power to meddle in everyone's business; this way, they retain the excuse to inspect business's private affairs. If the retail merchant is licensed to collect and hold in trust the funds of the government, it is a crime to fail to convey these funds to the government. This is called theft. Prosecute the criminal, leave the rest of us alone, and let's get on with the business of enjoying our freedoms and whatever else we have left after paying our taxes.

3. "Since the tax is collected from numerous transactions, the burden is not so great on any one party."

The truth: Since the tax is collected from the farmer as soon as the grain is grown, from the granary as soon as the wheat is ground, and from the baker as soon as the bread is out of the oven, the politicians don't have to wait for those oafs, the consumers, to buy the bread in order to get their hands on some money. There is not one iota less burden on the only party that pays the entire tax bill, the consumer. The total tax on the loaf he eats is $.25. He pays the entire $.25. He probably also pays another $.20 out of the $1.00 for all the merchants' bookkeeping needed to figure out who owes what!

4. "Many products are made for export, as well as for local consumption. This country doesn't tax exports. At

whatever point a product is exported, the bureaucrats need to determine a refund of the previous taxes, as they should not have been collected on nontaxable exports."

The truth: By collecting taxes on every step, the money is collected early. It can be held for three, six, ten, fifteen months before the refund. This is a continuous process that creates a continuous float. Sometimes the float is in the hundreds of millions, even billions of dollars. This is not the government's money, yet the government can use the float without the people's knowledge. If the taxes aren't collected at the wrong place, there is no need to ascertain a refund.

Not surprisingly, the majority of proponents of the consumption tax in the U.S., particularly those in elective office, favor the VAT over the simpler sales and use taxes. They point out that more nations, which have finally seen the wrong of hidden consumption taxes, have been able to get the VAT implemented rather than the sales or use taxes. Or they assert that the VAT is 100 times better than the continuation of what we now have. Better it may be, but it still tries to tax *all* the wrong transactions.

The fact remains, the VAT is fraught with the same lies that underlie our present dilemmas. And it creates much more confusion than the sales or use taxes.

If we can divest ourselves of our present lie-ridden system, why reinfect the new system with the old system's lies? We already have sales- and use-tax systems. Our people know how to use them, they are trouble free, and the laws are already written.

The VAT at least is open and disclosed, and it is relatively simple to understand. So let's apply it to you the wage-earner.

The farmer, in the aforementioned example, was perfectly satisfied to receive $100 for his wheat, but he had to collect $125 in order to keep the $100. He never considered charging the granary $115, because he knew he must pay $25 to the government, which would leave him only $90. He needed $100. That is all the farmer received, $100. He didn't receive $125 and pay a $25 tax. He received $100 and collected $25 for the government.

The same is true of your paycheck.

When you supposedly receive a $1,000 paycheck and $250 is taken out for income-tax withholding and FICA, you don't receive $1,000. You receive $750, and you collect $250 for the government.

Your employer is in the position of the granary in the example above. The wheat costs the granary $125, $100 for wheat and $25 for taxes. Both are expenses, and both must be considered a cost to the granary. The granary must add these costs to the price it charges the baker, and the baker must pay or the granary will go broke.

And so, when we Americans accept the *lie* that companies, corporations, merchants, and businesses pay taxes, we make fools of ourselves. These entities don't pay the tax. They *can't* pay the tax. They don't have any money to pay the tax until they collect it from us—exactly like the granary collected the tax from the baker, who collected it from the grocer, who collected it from the consumer.

Suppose the granary were willing to pay the tax. It has paid the farmer $100 for the wheat, $25 for the tax, and, if it charges $110 for the flour, it owes $2.50 more in tax to the government. That is a total of $127.50 the granary has paid or will pay for the privilege of making the flour, for which it receives only $110. Where is it supposed to get the $17.50 difference? It has only one source from which to get the money, the baker. The granary could be General Mills, one of the richest corporations in America, but if it continued to pay out $127.50 for the privilege of collecting $110, it would soon be the poorest. The corporation would go into bankruptcy, and its officers would go to jail (maybe) for not collecting the tax.

The only difference with the $250 withholding and FICA on your paycheck is this: The fact is, you receive

$750, and the employer *loans* the government $250 for the privilege of your presence. The entire $1,000 must be added to the price of whatever you produce. You don't pay that tax, nor does your employer. You both collect it from the purchaser of your product, your "flour." The tax cost is passed on, just as is the VAT, until someone buys and eats the bread. Since this consumer has no one else to whom he can pass on the tax cost, he ends up paying it.

All taxes are paid by the consumer. Whether the tax is printed on the sales slip, hidden in your paycheck, or transacted among suppliers, the consumer of the product pays the tax.

It is of no importance to the consumer how the tax bill is presented, he will pay it. There is no difference in his cost if bread is priced $1.25 or $1.00 plus $.25 VAT. The total is still $1.25. The fact remains, he will pay the taxes because only he can pay the taxes. Everyone else is a middleman, whose costs must be passed on to the customers.

The obvious question is, since it works out to be the same result either way, what difference does it make? None at all to the consumer! At least not in this oversimplified scenario. Except that someone must do all the accounting and the cost of the accounting must be added to the price of the product. In our system, that cost is appreciable.

But the big difference is the cumulative effect of the indirect, hidden tax on the competitive position of goods so taxed in the world market and the political ramifications for our rights and freedoms. More on that later, but for now the important point to grasp is that *All taxes are consumption taxes.* They are consumption taxes on the products we produce.

The license plate on your car is a tax that the consumer of your product pays. Doubt it? Where do you get the money to pay for a car license? Your employer. Where does he get the money? From the purchaser of your product. That purchaser pays the tax, as surely as he pays "your" $250 withholding and FICA. Similarly, he pays your real estate taxes, your property taxes, your entertainment taxes, and your hunting and fishing license taxes.

Your employer is aware that you have all these needs. He must pay you enough to permit you to pay for them. He must add the cost of the payment of these needs to the price of the product.

What would the price of the product be if you didn't have these costs? What if your employer paid only the $750 you receive in wages after taxes? What if he could reduce your salary another $100 a month because there were no property or real estate taxes? What if . . . ? You'd still be making the same amount to cover all your expenses other than taxes, but how much cheaper would your product be?

Hold that thought, keeping in mind as well that all taxes are consumption taxes. What we are going to do next is look at the huge difference between *hidden* and *open* consumption taxes.

CHAPTER 3

Anatomy of the Lie

TAX REFORM. If there is a more consuming subject in the country today, you won't hear of it from the Congress, the President, the public, or the media. And our income tax system *should* be our highest priority, for there is no greater problem before us.

Virtually every candidate in every election campaigns for tax reform. Each makes strong commitments, and each is bound to perform—unless we, their constituents, let him or her off the hook. Immediately after election day we hear, "If not this session, then the next."

This has been the pattern for over fifty years: fervent promises followed by equivocation, or at best more patchwork on the current system.

The reason the patches fail is because the underlying fabric is rotten. None of the political promises we've heard has yet offered an overall solution because none has recognized the real problem. To the contrary, each promise is or would be simply one more patch on a decrepit system that was fatally flawed at birth. It's like putting Band-Aids on a stillborn child. And you can't blame the voters, even when they forget the campaign promises, because they, too, are focusing on the symptoms, unaware of the real problem.

The problem with our tax system is that it is based on

an absolute lie. We do not tax what we claim to tax. Our entire system of taxation is based on an attempt to tax those things that are not taxable, to the exclusion of the one thing on earth that can be taxed: consumption. All other taxes are passed on as cost of production and are ultimately paid by the consumer. That is the truth. Any claim to have levied a tax on any other transaction in the market structure is a lie. The purpose of the lie may be for any number of noble reasons, but it is a lie nonetheless. The perpetrator of the lie may be conscious of the lie or a victim of it, but either way it is still a lie.

There is only one tax, a consumption tax. There is not now, there never has been, and there never will be any other. The simple reason is that no other transaction is an end purchase. All taxes on any other transaction become an expense; and like all other expenses, they are passed on to the next purchaser, who adds his expenses and taxes to his customer's costs. Only the ultimate consumer has no one to whom to pass the burden. The consumer pays all of the expenses of all the contributors to the good's pro-duction as a part of the purchase price. Otherwise, the seller couldn't afford to sell.

Virtually every other nation on earth, certainly most of the free world's industrialized nations, have recognized this fact. Only we have not.

Perhaps it should not be surprising that we refuse to believe this truth. We were founded in a revolution against it. Everyone beyond the sixth grade is aware of the Boston Tea Party, a rebellion against the excessive consumption taxes imposed by the British. Now, of course any tax can be excessive and justify rebellion, but Americans seem to have forgotten the word "excessive" and concentrated on "consumption."

For over two hundred years, we have refused to face the fact that only consumption can be taxed. With no small amount of aid from our elected officials, we have at-tempted to hide our taxes behind other names and claim them to be collected from other sources. The consumption tax is now so well hidden, it is so difficult to identify, that we actually believe we don't have one (other than negligible city, county, and state sales taxes).

The mere mention of a sales or value-added tax drives liberal politicians into a frenzy, with their dramatic cry, "That is a tax on the poor, it's regressive, and we'll never permit it."

Our largest party, the Democratic, is to a large degree based on that very precept, and the precept too is a lie. Whether the hierarchy of the party actually believes its party line or whether it is perpetrating a gigantic fraud is not relevant. The fact remains, it is a lie.

> When we are told we pay income taxes, it is a lie.
> When we are told that the corporations pay tax, it is a lie.
> When we are told that we pay tax on real estate, it is a lie.

They are all lies because none of these things can be taxed. Other than by expropriation, none of these entities have any money with which to pay any tax until money is collected from the end-user of the product, the consumer. He pays the tax because it is hidden in the purchase price. If the assets of any of these entities were expropriated to pay a tax, the entity would cease to exist.

Since the taxpayer must pay the tax in the form of money, he pays out of current income by including the tax in the price of the product as a cost of production, or out of savings from sales of past production, or out of future income by converting income-producing assets to cash. If the individual taxpayer cannot embody these tax costs in past, present, or future production (in order to recapture them when that production is sold), he will be reduced eventually to a level of subsistence. If the process continues long enough, he will be reduced to the situation of the

Chinese peasants who were forced to pay a levy of grain to a warlord until they had to eat the seed grain for next year's crop. The choice is yours: You can starve now or starve later.

The corporate taxpayer is in the same leaky boat. Unless his firm can pass on the tax burden as a cost of production embodied in the sales price, it will sink. Stockholders may bail out the firm with new infusions of capital, but the leaks have to be plugged sometime or other for the corporate ship to stay afloat.

Partial expropriation of income-producing assets by means of an income tax simply delays the death of the tax base. A tax on a percentage of income may not immediately kill the tax base, but it does, at the very least, cripple it. The following year's tax cripples it further. And if the tax percentage is increased, the crippling proceeds further and faster.

Don't take my word for it; look at 1960–85. Every single decrease in income tax rates has resulted in an increase in productivity and tax revenues. Every single increase in tax rates has accomplished exactly the opposite. John Kennedy's tax decreases of the early 1960s not only rejuvenated the entire economy, *they created more tax revenues than were being collected with the higher rates that were in effect before the reform.*

For the next nineteen years, through 1980, every tax reform was either a direct increase with higher rates imposed or an individual increase as the result of the infamous "bracket creep" (in which a taxpayer receives a higher income, which forces him into a bracket with a higher percentage; if the increased income does not keep pace with inflation, the taxpayer's purchasing power is reduced by both the increased price of goods consumed and by the higher rate of tax paid). Each of these tax increases resulted in a decrease in revenues relative to either the gross national product, expenditures, prior years' collections, or all of the above.

In 1981, Ronald Reagan managed by virtue of great personal popularity to push through at least a part of the Kemp-Roth Bill. His Economic Recovery Act revealed some of the cancer of income tax. It was recognized by Kemp, Roth, Reagan, and the Congress that economist Arthur Laffer's "Laffer Curve" was valid. The curve demonstrated that the only way to increase income-tax revenues was to reduce the *rate* of taxation. The program worked for almost one whole year.

The gigantic deficits we now face are not the result of that reduction. The reduction accomplished exactly what the Laffer Curve predicted it would: It increased tax revenues. The deficit is, to no small degree, the result of considerable increases in expenditures stemming from previously legislated entitlement programs (Medicare, social security) and military expenditures, along with interest payments on the national debt. But even more, it is the result of Congress refusing to let well enough alone and allowing the tax-abated, invigorated economy to do its job. In less than a year, Congress passed the largest tax increase in history: a tax that totally negated the benefits of the Kemp-Roth Bill. The increase took its historic and predictable toll: It decreased tax revenues and assured our current deficit.

Perhaps the most amazing part of this scenario is how we can continue to ignore the truth. It is not necessary to analyze the entire economy to reach the conclusion that something is fatally wrong with a system that attempts to tax income. We need not depend for our conclusion solely on the fact that any system that decreases tax revenues when tax rates are raised, and increases tax revenues when tax rates are lowered, has a flaw.

Look at any individual industry. The second an industry gets into financial difficulties, what do we do? We say that it has problems with labor, competition, tooling, debt structure, management, or equipment. Then, we instantly give it tax relief. It gets tax credits on new equipment, accelerated depreciation, or government loans. Why not labor relief? Why not management relief? Why not raw material relief? Because, as we know, if only subconsciously, these are not the problems. Tax relief does the job because it is nothing more than a refund of the taxes that should never have been collected, or imposed, in the first place. It is a refund, or forgiveness, of that part of the wrongful tax that is more than a particular industry can bear and still remain internationally competitive. The tax on income causes the problem, and tax relief alleviates some element of it without overtly admitting the failure of the entire system of taxation. To further prove the connection, try to recall one instance in which the most desperate and failing company ever even suggested the need for sales tax relief.

It's only a short step from this recognition to the admission that, if the small concession of income tax relief to industry can take it from bankruptcy to viability, then the total relief of all such taxes on all of our industries would return this nation to the awesome stature it once enjoyed in the world's economic community. This is, however, a step we have steadfastly refused to take for over seventy-two years.

No amount of rhetoric will ever change the basic economic fact that *all* taxes are consumption taxes. The continuation of our failure to admit this fact has led to a perpetuation of the lie that is destroying our nation.

The perpetuation of this lie does the greatest harm to the very group it is supposed to protect, the poor. It forces them to pay a greater percentage of their available funds for taxes than any other group because *all* of their funds are spent for sustenance. Therefore, all their funds are taxed at the prevailing hidden consumption rate. Meanwhile, at the other end of our society, our industries are hobbled with hidden costs that make them uncompetitive in world trade. The industries close, and the already unemployed poor become more unemployable. Robbed of the possibility of rising above their current status, they are joined in their dilemma by those most recently laid off. Thus, those who have always paid the greatest share of their income in hidden taxes on their means of subsistence become "burdens on the tax rolls," and the reduced tax base is less able to support the level of subsistence provided under welfare programs to the expanding number of eligible recipients. And so we are forced to cut back the level of consumption permitted under the program or redefine eligibility to purge people from the rolls.

The U.S. is the most powerful industrial, economic complex ever known, and it is being brought to its knees by a lie. Worse yet, it's our own lie! And worst of all, in the compulsive manner of all liars, we are reinforcing our original lie with hundreds of supporting lies. Lies such as the ones that our industries' problems are caused by labor, management, capital formation, and unfair, subsidized foreign competition. All lies to support the original lie that we can tax the nontaxable and, thus, avoid the tax ourselves.

The world doesn't care. We are not tricking them. We are only deceiving ourselves. The rest of the world is reaping a bonanza from our deceit. There is only one solution for us. We must expose our own lie to the light of truth. We must admit we are not taxing what we claim to be taxing and commence to tax directly that which we have taxed covertly all along.

It's time to confess! Confessing not only cleanses the soul, in this instance it can cleanse a nation. It can turn America into a "Born Again" economy.

CHAPTER 4

Economic Laws of Taxation

We are ignoring some fundamental economic laws. Until we recognize these laws our problems will increase, and existing problems will be compounded and aggravated.

Economic Law #1—*A tax on income is not a tax on income; it is a hidden sales tax.*

In order for an employee to be able to survive, he must receive sufficient net pay, after all withholding and all payment of every tax, to procure his necessities and sustain his life-style. Failure to receive this amount will result either in his inability to work or in the loss of his incentive to do so. In the extreme he will starve. In the lesser instance, he will find other work, which pays enough to permit the maintenance of the standard of living he believes he deserves.

The gross salary, as we recognize it today, is sheer codswallop! It means nothing to the employee—the only salary meaningful to him is his net salary after taxes. That portion deducted from the gross for FICA or withholding is not available to him for rent, clothing, food, or amusement. It is not his money and will never be available as such. The employee who supposedly earns $30,000 per annum, but nets $23,060 after deductions, will work as happily for $23,060 gross with no deductions as he does for the fake $30,000.

Therefore, the employer's actual computation for the value of an employee is the amount he must pay the employee in order to net the employee enough to warrant expending his efforts.

The employer lumps FICA, withholding, and the net salary together and calls it a wage. It is not. The wage is the net to the employee. The balance, together with the employer's contribution, is paid to the government as a tax on the employee. The check is made payable to the Treasury of the U.S. and is as surely a tax charged to the employer as was the $5.00 head tax on slaves. To claim that the employee receives the total salary is as economically absurd as saying that the old Southern slaveholders "paid" their slaves food, clothing, shelter, and $5.00 per annum. The $5.00 was not the slave's to spend, and neither are the withholding and FICA the employee's to spend. They are a tax collection requirement imposed on the employer and become an expense that, like all others, must be added to the cost of his product. Mailing the check to the Treasury, instead of handing the money to the employee, does not reduce by one cent the expense the employer must assign to the product.

The employee does *not* pay income taxes, any more than the slave paid a $5.00 head tax. The slave never had the $5.00 with which to pay it, and the employee never has the withholding, nor the FICA. The tax is paid in exactly the same manner in both instances. The slaveholder added the $5.00 onto the price of cotton, and the employer adds the withholding and FICA onto the price of his product. The consumer pays the tax, which is hidden in the purchase price. He pays not only the "slave tax" of the original processor, he also pays the "slave tax" of all other processors, wholesalers, and retailers who handle the product. Each absorbs the costs of his suppliers (including their tax costs), adds his costs (including taxes), and passes all costs on to the next purchaser. The purchaser who uses up the product has no one to whom to pass the costs and, thus, he absorbs all prior costs and taxes. This purchaser is called a consumer, and no matter how carefully we hide the taxes, it is he who pays them all.

The occasional employee who obtains a refund on withholding in effect receives a bonus. This extra wage, or addition to his purchasing power, does not decrease the price of the product because the earlier addition of the tax already increased it. The employer who pays the tax doesn't care who gets the money—the only fact pertinent to him, and the price of his product, is that he collects the tax. It is a cost to him either way, and he must add it to the price of the product. It is a hidden sales tax.

Economic Law #2—*A tax on profits is not a tax on profits; it is a hidden sales tax.*

Capitalism allows a corporation, or a business owner, to try to make a profit on his production. No proponent of the free enterprise system will deny this: The incentive of profit is the organizing principle upon which production is based.

But the question remains: "How much profit?" In a free market, this decision will be made by supply and demand, and will be controlled by competition between producers and consumers. A producer who produces more efficiently (more cheaply) than his competitors, who reduces costs per unit of production, will make a higher rate of profit than competitors selling at the same price but producing at higher costs. Or he will make more total profit with the same rate of profit as his competitors, by cutting the price in order to sell more. Either way, the profit may be used by the business owner to increase his own income and consumption, or reinvested in the business to produce more product more efficiently; or it can be invested in some other line of business. Profit is both the motive and the reward for taking the risk of putting time, effort, and money into production.

But profits are also subject to the laws of supply and demand for investment capital, and to competition in the marketplace between different profit-making enterprises. Once costs are determined, a desired rate of profit is added, and price is established, the business will receive no more and no less than this marked-up percentage on its production—provided, of course, that the product is sold at this price. Whatever costs are, this amount (percentage) will be added to the price of the product in order to achieve the appropriate return on investment.

The percentage will vary with alternative investments, but usually it will have a bottom line of something in excess of interest rates. In other words, no business or businessman will enter into a risk investment that pays less return than a passive, secure, insured savings account, Treasury bill, or municipal bond. To do so would be economic insanity, even suicide.

For the sake of simplicity, let's assume the current rate on top-graded, tax-free bonds is 10 percent, close to the actual present rate.

Any capital formation for a new business, or the sustained operation of an established one, will require a return of not less than that amount. Since no return is guaranteed or insured, as with municipal bonds, the risk is greater. Therefore, the potential return must also be greater. But let's assume the required return to be equal to the municipal rate of 10 percent. If no taxes on profits are imposed, the chief executive officer can simply add up his costs and mark up another 10-percent profit. This poses no problem.

But there is a tax on profit, or at least so it would seem. In fact, in the corporate instance, there is a double tax: one on the corporation and one on dividends paid to the corporate owners.

The business must remit to its investors 10-percent net

return on their investment from profit after taxes, or lose those investors to the tax-free municipals which return 10 percent virtually risk free. Therefore let's take a hypothetical corporation which requires a 10-percent markup on its product in order to achieve a 10-percent return of its shareholders' investment. In order to net 10 percent after taxes, the company, with a 50-percent corporation tax levy, must add to its costs a 20-percent markup. This is 10-percent net only to the corporation, however, not a 10-percent net to the investor. In order to achieve a 10-percent net after tax to the investor (assuming the investor to be in a 50-percent tax bracket), the business must add 40 percent to the cost of the product.

Example:

Cost of product	$1.00
Desired net after tax profit	$ .10
Sales price	$1.40
Cost	$1.00
Gross corporate profit	$ .40
Less 50% corporate tax	$ .20
Net to corporation after tax	$ .20
Corporate dividend	$ .20
50% tax on shareholder	$ .10
Net to shareholder	$ .10

Suddenly, a desire for a 10-percent return, $.10 on the dollar, the return currently available in savings accounts, causes the price of a product to be inflated 40 percent, a 40-percent inflation incurred solely by a failed system of taxation.

There are other factors computed by individual businesses, but the end result is the same. If the shareholder cannot make ten cents on the dollar, he will not invest. If he doesn't invest, there will be no business. If there is no business, there will be no product.

In reality it is a $.30 sales tax paid by the consumer of

the product. The merchant doesn't charge $1.10 for the product and create this other $.30 from thin air. The merchant possesses only one source of revenue: income from the sale of his products. If he must pay a $.30 tax, it is added to the price of the product. It is a sales tax that operates as an expense, a cost of production which increases the price of the product.

At this point, the effect of the tax on the nontaxable grows geometrically. The 40 percent must be added to all costs. And, don't forget, this transaction is burdened with other taxes hidden as expenses. As will be demonstrated later, the total hidden tax constitutes an average of 60 percent of the actual costs of production. The real costs of U.S. produced items which we purchase (less taxes) are only $.40. If the tax is not hidden as a cost and there are no profit taxes, the merchant can add 10 percent for his profit, or $.04, to his $.40 cost and charge $.44 for the product, which now costs the consumer $1.40.

The consumer is, in reality, paying a 240-percent sales tax. The fact that it is hidden does not relieve the burden. To the contrary, hiding the tax aggravates the burden.

Economic Law #3—*Any tax on any asset is not a tax on the asset: it is a hidden sales tax.*

Let's consider real estate. Be the occupant an owner or renter, the occupant pays the tax. For years, only property owners in Colorado could vote on bond issues under the theory that since only the property owners would be required to pay off the debt, only they should vote. But then the renters noticed that each time the owners agreed to pay, it was their rent that was raised. It was the end user, the renter, who made the payment. The owner is only a tax collector, not a tax payer.

The owner-occupant's tax is also a hidden sales tax. In order to pay the tax, the owner-occupant must earn enough to pay the mortgage and the tax. Sufficient amounts must be added to the product of the occupant's production to pay the tax. The occupant must have food, clothing and shelter. He needs certain excess funds for amusement and amenities. This requires that he receive $A. If he must pay a real-estate tax, he must receive $A plus the real-estate tax dollars.

The real-estate tax he pays becomes a cost of production added to the price of his product. Real-estate taxes are hidden sales taxes. They must be because the real estate has no money, only its owner occupant has money, and he receives his money from the sale of his product.

Similarly, inventory taxes, auto taxes, license fees and all other property taxes are sales taxes. Some are hidden deeply, others more overtly, but all are sales/consumer taxes. The same analysis of any tax will produce the same results.

Economic Law #4—*The attempt to deny or hide sales taxes creates artificial inflation and economic chaos.*

The producer's costs are set. He pays $A for wages, $B for tax on wages, $C tax on his profits and $D for the wage earner's real estate, license fees, and so forth. $A, $B, $C and $D must be added to the cost of his product.

The producer needs only the labor, $A. The balance is taxes hidden in his costs, which artificially inflate his product's price. $B, $C and $D may be refunded to the supposed payer of the tax, but the refund does not reduce the cost to the producer. The same price must be charged because it is an expense, in that amount, to the producer.

At some point, when $B, $C and $D become sufficiently burdensome, the producer's product is priced out of the market and chaos results. His real costs, $A, may be less than a less-efficient foreign competitor who escapes the $B, $C and $D expenses, but the fact remains, he will not be able to compete. A producer so burdened will close.

This is the status of U.S. industries today. Their foreign competitors escape the $B, $C and $D hidden sales taxes and can, therefore, sell for less. Our more efficient industries are being put out of business by less efficient competition.

To summarize, all taxes are collected from the consumer of the production, directly or indirectly. Regardless of the amount supposedly collected from the ostensible payer, the cost of the tax is simply passed on as a cost of production to the next buyer, until it reaches a consumer, who has no one to whom to pass the cost.

The worker has only one source of revenue: his employer. The worker must collect all revenues necessary to maintain himself and dependents, plus all taxes he is expected to pay from that employer.

The employer has only one source of revenue: the buyers of his products. He must pass all prior costs, his and his employees' taxes included, to the buyer.

If *the product buyer* is a processor, he adds his taxes to the previous producer's taxes; and he passes all costs, including his taxes, to his buyer.

The consumer of the end product pays the total of all prior costs, all taxes included. Because he has no buyer, he consumes the product.

The problem with our system of taxation is our refusal to recognize the consequences of hiding the tax. An open, announced sales tax on all products of all manufacturers would place an equal burden on all producers. The more efficient would survive, with the benefit of the lowest possible prices accruing to the public. The tax would be known, computable, nonrefundable, and controllable with no artificial inflation.

This is the tax we need to the exclusion of all others. It is, however, a tax we will not get until the four economic laws above are recognized. This is why we need "Truth in Taxation." The truth will expose the validity of the laws and force the implementation of a true, open system of taxation on consumption.

CHAPTER 5

Benefits to Industry

THE MOST VIRULENT EFFECT of the lie that we tax other than consumption has been on our industries.

Through most of our history, we have led the world economically to the extent that we could choose the areas in which we wanted to compete. Now, for the first time, our industries are unable to compete with those of other countries. The fault lies not with management or labor, nor with any lack of innovation, desire, or determination. The problem is simply that our products are overpriced. And they are overpriced solely because we have secretly imposed an illegal and unconstitutional 150-percent tax on every export, and a hidden 150-percent tax expense on our own domestic sales, an expense our foreign competition escapes.

Article I, Section 9, Paragraph 5, of our Constitution states:

> No tax or duty shall be laid on articles exported from any State.

The courts have consistently held that "State" in this paragraph also be defined as "the nation."

Whether or not this provision proves our forefathers

49

had astonishing insight on this point, it clearly indicates their recognition of the fact that no state's citizens would be willing to pay another state's taxes; they saw that countervailing taxes on exports from one state to another would artificially raise prices and limit trade. They knew from the restrictions on colonial trade imposed by the British to preserve their monopoly that restriction of internal markets in the newly independent and not entirely united states would limit development of fledgling industries and open the door to foreign producers. They saw that our stunted industries would be unable to grow; they would atrophy and would never be able to penetrate foreign markets. Instead, we would become a nation exporting raw materials to absentee landlords and importing the goods fashioned from America's endowment of natural resources by foreign producers. We would buy from them, and eventually they would own us.

The merchants, shipowners and builders, tradesmen and planters who drew up the constitutional framework for the new nation fought bitterly over its many struts and braces, but they all had learned from bitter experience with their colonial masters that no other nation would be willing to pay for our taxes. They understood that consumers in other nations would preferentially purchase our products only as long as they were worth the price and cost less than similar products they could make for themselves or buy from other nations.

American consumers today have exactly the same attitude. Think of a product you are considering buying for yourself. You will invariably purchase the item that has the features you want at the least cost per feature, regardless of where it is made. No amount of advertising that encourages you to buy products "Made in America" will change your buying habits. How else do we explain the millions of foreign autos, televisions and other imports that we purchase annually to the ruination of our own industries and the loss of our own jobs?

Nor are the would-be purchasers of our products in foreign nations any less intuitive and cost-conscious. They have finite funds available and will make those funds stretch to the maximum. If our goods are overpriced for whatever reason, foreign consumers will not buy them.

Our system of taxation imposes hidden expenses on every American product. I do not question the amount of the tax, nor argue over whether government expenditures are cost-effective, or accomplish the desired goals, or even whether those goals are in fact desirable. That's not the concern of this book. My point is simply that regardless of the merits of the expenditures, the costs must be covered by taxes. When these taxes are imposed as a hidden cost on production, they become an expense that must be recovered from the sale price of the finished product. This means our products must sell at cost, plus profit, plus taxes.

According to President Reagan's budget, our federal government required $950 billion in revenues to accomplish its functions for the fiscal year 1985–86. Suppose every proposed expenditure were cost-effective, that the expenditure would achieve its goal, and that every goal was desirable. The only question remaining would be, "How do we pay it?" It must be paid, now or in the future. We will pay it from current tax revenues, or we will pay it, plus interest, from future tax revenues.

Certain delays for major capital expenditures may make sense, as they sometimes do in business and industry. The added costs of interest may well be justified for an earlier delivery of an asset, thus allowing the asset to create the revenues to pay for itself. This presumption, however, is valid only if current projected tax revenues are sufficient to cover current expenses plus the additional expense of amortizing the asset. It's a situation that no longer exists in the U.S. We have not balanced a budget in the lifetime of most Americans. Worse yet, we have absolutely no prospect of doing so in the foreseeable future. Therefore let's discard, for discussion purposes, any delayed payments. The payment of the budget must be done on a current basis, and this means we have to collect $950 billion in tax revenues for 1985–86.

We are back to the original question: "How do we (the citizens) pay it?" Under the current system, it supposedly is paid mainly by income and social security taxes on labor, wages, and profits, and by borrowing the difference.

Our income-tax collectors demand taxes of 20 percent to 50 percent of the income of every employee (management, administration, and labor); plus 15 percent of the same paycheck (up to $36,000) for FICA; plus 50-percent tax on the corporation's profits, plus 50-percent tax on the balance if any dividends are paid to investors. These taxes are costs of production and must all be added to the cost of the product, no matter whether it is sold, here or abroad. All are costs. It is not relevant to the producing firm whether it pays these costs to the employee, the owner, or directly to the government. To the company the tax remains an overhead. It is a cost that must be recovered in the sales price of the product.

The amount of the increased price incurred as a result of these hidden taxes is not an inconsequential sum. It amounts to $.60 of every $1.00 the producer charges for his products. This is a 150-percent increase in sale price for our entire gross national product. At this rate of hidden taxation, with this cost added to every product, it is astonishing that we are still able to sell anything to anyone.

No other nation on earth *even begins* to impose such a burden on its industries, nor would any dream of trying. No industry in any other nation could withstand the strain. But then, neither can we. Way back when the rate of this system of hidden tax increased from 10 to 25 percent, the majority of our industries shrugged it off; their competitive advantage was so great, they barely noticed the strain. When the weight reached 50 percent, they toughened out of necessity. At 100 percent—in effect, now carrying their own productive weight in hidden taxes —they struggled to stand up and move forward through sheer drive and determination. Somewhere between 100 and 150 percent, the necks of the majority, even some of the best, broke. The only ones remaining today are those with technology so advanced that there is no competition and, therefore, no cost comparison. But the onerous burden of hidden taxation guarantees that any such technological advantage will be temporary.

The survival of the majority of our industries through the ordeal of a 100-percent tax burden and cost increases does not imply that the tax was a good tax up to that point. To the contrary, it would be a debilitating tax at one half of 1 percent. A small hidden tax is merely tolerable in an economy with our dynamics, but it remains an abomination because its effects combine and compound.

There is something the IRS refers to as the "cash black market" in the U.S. By the IRS's own figures, the untaxed production and distribution of goods and services is estimated to be $80 billion per annum, with some estimates as high as $200 billion. The IRS's main concern over this enigma is its own inability to collect the taxes that are going unpaid, since there is no way to maintain records of the transactions. This is not our concern, however. We ought instead to see this phenomenon for what it is: as dramatic proof that *all taxes are paid by the consumer,* regardless of where they are ostensibly imposed, and as stark evidence of their devastating effect if imposed at the wrong location.

Even a cursory inspection of the participants in the black market renders undeniable proof of this truth. The IRS knows that no withholding or FICA is paid by the seller, and the Treasury is losing 60 percent of the gross receipts of the transaction. This amounts to at least a $48-billion-a-year loss in tax revenues, even at the low estimate of $80 billion in untaxed sales.

Meanwhile, the citizens who buy these goods and services are doing so mainly because they can obtain them for 20 to 60 percent less than from a legitimate merchant who *is* complying with the tax laws. The price is so much lower, the purchaser is prepared to waive the warranties and service expected from a normal merchant and to buy from a party he most likely realizes is nothing more than an unindicted, unconvicted criminal operating in violation of the tax laws.

The cash black market is doing business in the same land that supposedly cannot compete with the rest of the world. In fact, the excuses generally offered for our inability to compete abroad are all belied by the success of the black marketers.

"Labor is too expensive." Yet, the black marketer pays more; his labor costs are higher because he must reward his employees for breaking the law and maintaining their silence.

"Management is not competitive nor innovative." But, as a group, the black marketers do $80 billion a year, and they are U.S. managers, managers innovative enough to have hit upon the secret to foreign competition—the hidden tax—and avoided it illegally in order to compete in the production and distribution of presumably beneficial goods and services that are otherwise legal.

"Ownership extracts too much in profit." Yet, the cash black marketers take higher percentages of profit than any of their legitimate competitors precisely because of their illegal tax advantage.

Every excuse we give ourselves for our industries' noncompetitiveness is faced equally by the black marketer and is, in fact, more costly to him. But the cash black marketer does have one advantage. He has eliminated the single greatest *expense* that his competitors must pay, the hidden tax that, in reality, is no tax at all. As we have seen, it is not a tax on income, it is merely a function of making businessmen tax collectors, a function surreptitiously slipped into their business so that the government can pretend it is not charging a sales/consumption tax.

Simplistically stated, the cash black marketers are doing to us at home what the world does to our industries in the international market. Each time one of us accepts a cheaper service or buys a cheaper product that *must be paid for in cash,* we are a living demonstration that all taxes are paid by the consumer because, unwittingly or not, we are avoiding the tax on consumption in order to consume more with the same dollars. On a local and private basis, we are individually committing the same economic atrocity on our own legitimate, local taxpaying, tax-collecting businesses that BMW is committing internationally on Cadillac.

It is not necessary to take my word for it. Call the Department of Commerce and ask about our international balance of payments. Or better yet, let's take the example of the U.S. Cadillac versus the German BMW.

In West Germany, taxes, hidden or otherwise, are refunded on exports. The production costs of the BMW, without taxes, require an approximate $13,000 retail price on the European Common Market. On the average, a sales (value added) and/or luxury tax of about $9,000 is imposed by the importing or consuming nation. The total retail price for the BMW, plus taxes, delivered to the consumer, is then $22,000. A comparable Cadillac, with hidden U.S. taxes on profit, income, and social security, retails for about $21,000 here or abroad. But since our hidden income taxes are not recognized as a product tax, they are not refunded on our exports. After the same Common Market 70-percent sales tax is added to the Cadillac, its delivery price for a European buyer suddenly becomes $35,700. For obvious reasons, General Motors no longer sells many Cadillacs in Europe.

The sales-tax percentage rate applied by the importing nation is the same for both cars. The importing nation is not being unfair to the Cadillac, which is charged with the same tax percentage rate as the country's own products and all other imports. *We* as a nation are unfair. *We* unfairly impose a hidden, illegal, and unconstitutional 150-

percent tax on the Cadillac, amounting to 60 percent of its sales price before it ever leaves our shores. Without the tax expenses imposed on General Motors caused by the hidden profit, income, and FICA taxes, the Cadillac could sell for about $8,400, plus the 70-percent VAT of $5,880, for a total retail price of $14,280. And at this price Cadillacs could flood the European market, no other luxury car could compete. In other words, General Motors has not lost its competitive edge, but has had that edge stolen through a hidden system of taxation we impose on ourselves. It has been stolen by a lie.

Let's reverse the situation. The U.S. has no national sales tax or VAT. Instead, we hide those taxes in Cadillac's expenses. The sales price is the same $21,000 in the U.S. as abroad because it still carries the burden of the hidden tax of $12,600. And again, the Cadillac can't compete. The BMW can arrive here at $13,000 because it arrives free of its exporting nation's tax. But why should the exporter sell so cheaply? Why should BMW sell for $13,000 when its competition is $8,000 higher? BMW, like the black marketer, will also take what the market permits. And, since we have voluntarily limited imports and BMW can send over only a limited number of cars, it maximizes its profits by charging an even higher price than the $21,000 Cadillac price. BMW takes the extra profit. It can do so because a certain number of Americans desire the BMW and will pay even the increased price. The foreign importers to the U.S. are, therefore, not just availing themselves of our market, they are making our market their windfall. Their profits in the U.S. on the same car are greater than their profits in any other country.

If you have any doubt of the validity of the numbers, I refer you to the "Bitburg incident"—the furor over President Reagan's visit to a German military graveyard in the spring of 1985. I believe that the President was unaware, until it was too late, that the bodies of 49 SS troopers were buried in the graveyard because his advance men were too busy to perform a proper reconnaissance of the grave-yard. They were busy buying $13,000 BMWs (with an additional 20-percent diplomatic discount). I mention this not to imply any impropriety in these men obtaining the best deal possible on the auto of their choice: there was none and is none. It merely points up the stupidity of our system of taxation; how it rewards foreign nations' industries, while punishing our own.

By the way, it's time to put the trite old cliché about the quality of U.S. cars versus the imports to rest. Even now I'm not certain that the general run of imported autos are superior to the general run of U.S. production, but I am dead certain that if the 150-percent tax overhead were removed our automotive industry and its workers could take the 50 percent to make improvements, create a vastly superior auto and sell it for half the price of any foreign competitor. I can't imagine why there should be any doubt of our ability to do so. We did it for over forty years, and we continued doing it until well after World War II. In fact we are doing it right now, it's just hard to see behind all those hidden taxes.

The same analysis can be made of every product from shoes to steel. Other industrial nations the world over have long since recognized the futility of attempting to impose their taxes on the foreign buyers of their products. Of equal or greater importance, they have also recognized the stupidity of permitting foreign industries to enter their economy free of the tax expenses imposed on their industries. In most instances, even the nations that continue to impose some hidden taxes on their own citizens reimburse their manufacturers for the cost of any hidden tax on the product to be exported, before the item leaves that nation's borders. Thus, their manufacturers are permitted the maximum latitude in the international trade wars. Imported products are subjected to the same consumers' tax to which their industries are subjected.

Our government accuses these nations of subsidizing

their exports and, thus, dumping their production on us. This is another lie to support our original income tax lie. They are not subsidizing, they simply aren't abusing their industries. The reimbursements to their exporters are not subsidies, they are refunds of a tax that should never have been collected on exports in the first place.

Article I, Section 9, Paragraph 5, of our Constitution states *no export taxes*. It's a law that makes perfect sense, for if an export tax is added to the price, at whatever level of taxation, the product will become too expensive to compete. No one will buy it, and since no one buys it the tax will not be collected because the product simply will not be produced. Thus, no tax revenue will accrue to our government. The only result of the attempt will be either the total destruction or the severe curtailment of the viability of one of our own industries. Net, taxpaying citizens—the employees of the company—will be transformed into net welfare recipients simply because the government attempted to collect an income tax that is not, and cannot be, collected at that point in the economy without destroying the company from which it is collected.

It is all the more amazing, then, that even with this absurd and unconscionable burden of a 150-percent hidden tax expense, the majority of our surviving industries remain within 20 percent to 30 percent of being competitive with foreign producers. Of course, this proximity does not prevent their demise, but it is a tremendous tribute to our labor and management, a testimonial to their abilities.

Just imagine our impact on the world market if the entire burden of illegal taxes were removed from our industries. We could sell 30 percent to 40 percent below foreign competition. We could again assume the dominance in world trade that we had before the hidden tax burden became too great to overcome. That prior dominance was not granted by the gods; our labor and management earned it with their work and productivity. They maintained it through awesome outside impositions. That dominance was not lost to a superior competitor. It was given away through a tax system of unbelievable stupidity.

We still believe our own lie, that we can tax income and profits and remain competitive. We may trick ourselves for a while longer, but the world won't buy it. Only our hidden taxes make it impossible for our products to compete abroad, or at home. Since the "trick" isn't working, isn't it time to forget it and get on with what we do better than any other nation, producing and competing on an equal basis?

Our industrial northeast lies devastated by these ignored but inescapable economic facts. Our unemployment and welfare problems are centered directly on this problem. To the individual and his family, the agony of the lost job is horrendous. It is predictable and understandable that those so afflicted would lash out against the closest and most identifiable targets, their partners in labor, management, and capital. The resulting hate-filled crossfire of blame is both self-destructive and inevitable.

The problem is that the venom is misdirected. There simply is no longer a market for the products of our factories, either here or abroad. The job security that was earned and passed from father to son for generations has been lost to the insidious cancer of a 150-percent hidden tax on their work, a burden no amount of ingenuity can overcome.

Misdirected excuses and acrimonious accusations are wasteful, nonproductive, and noncorrective. Each element of the economy blaming the others accomplishes nothing. None is to blame. Management, labor, and capital each reason that, because they are good at what they do, one of the others must be at fault. But this will not recapture lost markets. Labor accusing ownership of greed, of failing to invest in modern equipment, and of failing to understand labor problems is an exercise in futility. The accusations of ownership and management that labor is overpriced, benefit-loaded and thus noncompetitive are simply not realistic.

None of these accusations targets the source of the problem. Both sides continue to do their jobs well, and our industries continue to manufacture more efficiently than those of any other nation. But, even if some of the accusations contained elements of truth, it wouldn't matter. Suppose one, or the other, did take more than its share. So what? All combined, they only have 40 percent of the pie they created to split up. Sixty percent goes to hidden taxes, to the government (the only participating party which contributes nothing to production), and to the income tax. Nothing that labor, management, or anyone else can take even approaches the effect of this. If any one of the contributing elements could take all 40 percent, it would have less than half the negative competitive impact of the income tax.

Current suggestions include protective tariffs, domestic content laws, extended unemployment benefits, job guarantees, retraining, government subsidies, and employee ownership. For what? Each has some merit, some potential for relief of the immediate problems, and some shortfalls. But none can solve the problem, because none addresses the problem.

Employees, as owners, immediately encounter the same tax problems that destroyed the past owners. The proposed government subsidies and benefits raise the cost of government, require more hidden taxes, and make the problem worse for those employee-owned industries still struggling to stay alive. Domestic content regulations, which require that some percentage of a product or its components be manufactured in the United States, institutionalize the foreign retention of the majority of our market. Big deal! We get to add just enough of our "content" to permit the tax-free importer the assurance that we have enough money to buy his products, which *still* enter at an advantage. Any tariffs we impose on imports are matched by the foreign nations on our exports to them, and rightly so. Job guarantees from bankrupt and nonexistent businesses are worth about as much as a loan guarantee from Continental Illinois Bank. Retraining for new jobs in new industries burdened with the same tax that killed their predecessors borders on absurdity.

The solution lies in adherence to our Constitution and, secondly, in elimination of the hidden tax costs in our products. Expose those costs as a consumers tax, impose the same percentage of sales tax on imports that we impose on our own products, and drop *all* hidden taxes that raise the price of our products. That does it! Our foreign competitors couldn't retaliate any more than they already do.

I repeat, the amount of tax is not the issue here, it is not important so long as we treat foreign competition on the same basis as we treat our industries. If necessary, keep the same tax percentage we now have, but impose it on the correct transaction, on consumption, so that foreign imports are subject to the same tax as our domestic products. Do it like it is being done to us. Don't hide the tax; don't convert the tax into a hidden expense. Expose it. Print it on the sales receipt for the world to see and announce it for what it is, an economic necessity of life, a sales tax.

> The price of this product is . . . . $ .40
> The government imposes a sales tax of . . $ .60
> PURCHASE PRICE $1.00

What's the difference? The purchase price of the product remains $1.00. There is no difference to the buyer. But there is one huge difference! Our industrial community could suddenly compete both here and abroad. And when our industry competes on the same basis as foreign competitors, we win. Take the same imaginary product that we would currently sell for $1.00 but can't because our competitors undersell us by $.30. No foreign competitor could go any lower than the current average of $.70 for this item. This is proven by the fact that not one has. If one could, he would have done so already and taken more of the market from his other foreign competitors.

If all hidden taxes were removed from our costs of production, the new sales price of our products would gross the same return to the producer as now, $.40. Net wages would be the same as today's net wages after withholding. The same employer simply mails no withholding nor FICA check to the government. The foreign competitor pays the same percentage of tax as the domestic.

Sales in the U.S.	U.S. Product	Foreign Product
Price of product	$ .40	$ .70
U.S. sales tax (150 percent)	$ .60	$1.05
Purchase price	$1.00	$1.75

Overseas Sale	U.S. Product	Foreign Product
Price of product	$ .40	$ .70
Foreign sales tax (?)	X	X
Purchase price	$ .40 + X	$ .70 + X

We win. Here and abroad, we win. And well we should. We are the most productive. We are the most cost-efficient and effective.

Certainly, the foreign nations could retaliate with an import tax. But so what? We could do the same. It's like the goose and the gander! What's fair for one is fair for the other. This is the greatest effect of the sales tax: It forces everyone to play fair.

This one change in our *system* of taxation (not a change in the tax rate, only the system) could eliminate every economic problem faced by our industries. It could create a resurgence of productivity and prosperity unrivaled since World War II.

One question remaining in your mind may be, "Does the current system truly create a 150-percent hidden consumption tax/expense burden?" The answer is a resounding *yes,* and it is easily proven by the most elementary process.

The gross sales price of any raw material delivered to the next processor contains only equipment costs, energy, transportation, possibly interest, wages, and profit. Equipment costs, energy, and transportation, although obtained from third parties, necessarily carry the very same percentage of hidden tax in their costs as are in the product we are examining. After all, they are produced in the same tax environment as the subject product. Any cost competition for them is the same percentage as the company's own direct costs. Therefore, we will not include their costs. To do so only results in the same answer, and through vastly greater computations.

We will assume, therefore, that a unit of the raw materials costs $1.00 to produce and that the entire cost is in wages. We will assume further that corporate owners desire to make a 10-percent profit and would not invest if they thought that such a return was unlikely. In the average union shop, $.22 of every $1.00 for labor is withheld for income taxes. Another $.075 is withheld for FICA and matched by the corporation. That means $.37 of the $1.00 is not wages paid to the employee, but a hidden tax that in reality becomes an expense to the employer. The worker apparently is satisfied and able to meet his needs with the remaining $.63. He'd better be, because that's all he'll get. The balance is mailed to the Treasury of the U.S.

But, for the owners to net 10 percent after taxes[1] the company must pay a 20-percent dividend because the government wants half of the dividend as income tax. So the company must charge the customer a price that includes a 40-percent profit in order to pay the 20-percent dividend, since the government wants half of the corporate profits before it will permit the payment of the dividend to the corporate owners. This means the raw material must sell to the next processor for $1.40. Thirty-seven cents of the $1.00 wages and $.30 of the $.40 markup have now been paid out as $.67 tax. This becomes an expense of production. Forty-seven percent of this sales price is now therefore a hidden tax.

The next processor has $1.40 raw material cost, which is, in reality, $.67 in previously paid taxes and $.73 in raw materials. He, too, adds $1.00 in wages and wants a 10-percent return. (His extraneous costs are also presumed to be equally tax burdened and do not warrant computation.) He, too, pays the same $.37 for withholding and FICA as the raw material supplier pays. He, too, must charge a 40-percent markup to achieve a 10-percent net profit after taxes. Forty percent of the total $2.40 cost is $.96, of which $.70 is tax. This results in a wholesale cost to the retailer of $3.36, of which $1.76, or 52 percent, is a hidden tax. So it too has become an expense. If the retailer adds $1.00 labor cost and 10-percent net profit, the product must retail for $6.10, of which $3.48, or 57 percent, is paid by the consumer as a hidden sales tax.

This example assumes only three steps from raw material to consumer, each step increasing the tax content of

---

[1] An argument can be made that the investor expects a 10-percent return on his investment, not the product. The argument is valid. However, some products require 300-percent or 400-percent markups to achieve that 10-percent. Others require only 2 percent, 3 percent, or 4 percent. An example figure must be chosen. Ten percent is used as a median markup because it coincides with the required minimum return on investment, as compared to interest rates, net after taxes.

the price by 4 or 5 percent. Any additional handlers each incur additional taxes, and each such step continues to raise the percentage of the final purchase price paid as a hidden tax. Include the normal number of brokers, distributors, and suppliers indigenous to a complex product, such as an auto or refrigerator, and the tax burden approaches 75 percent or higher. The addition of even one more intermediary in this example pushes the tax to over $.60 of each $1.00, the equivalent of a tax rate of 150 percent. Also, in the above example, only the two largest hidden taxes are computed, income and FICA. Include the hundreds of other taxes which the federal, state, county, and city governments collect and the true horror is exposed.

The time for self-flagellation is past. Not one of the excuses that we have given ourselves for the torpor of our economy can stand the first ray of light from the truth, because they are all lies! The excuses are supporting lies to reinforce the first lie that we can tax income and not consumption.

"Unions have forced pay rates too high. Their demands for benefits are too great." Garbage! American workers are not overpaid. They are overtaxed and taxed by the wrong system. They are the most productive, cost-effective workers on earth. The percentage of U.S. workers represented by trade unions has dropped from 18 percent to 13 percent in less than a decade, a lower rate than in almost all other industrialized countries. Even though union contracts continue to set the industry standard in some sectors, wage scales in basic industries, especially manufacturing industries, have declined relative to workers' purchasing power. Productivity, as measured by output per worker or by value added per unit of labor cost, has increased; only the rate of growth in productivity has slowed. Black marketers pay more for labor and still beat unionized competitors in price, but only because of the tax factor.

"Our industries have not retooled; they are inefficient. Owner-ship has extracted too much of the capital." Garbage! U.S. in-dustry has historically reinvested 20 percent or more of all profits (when it has any) into new equipment. Our indus-try was and is efficient enough to absorb all its own costs, plus a 100-percent tax expense, and still beat the socks off its competition. It remains, today, within 20 percent to 30 percent of its competition in price, with a 150-percent ex-traneous tax expense. Ownership works on 10 percent or less net profit in virtually every instance.

"Our management is not sufficiently imaginative nor innova-tive to compete." Garbage! American managers and their methods are copied by every nation on earth. Americans are sought out to manage foreign plants. Our manage-ment has no parallel. Even its castoffs, the failures who enter the cash black market, show they can whip the for-eigners once they unburden themselves of the taxes, and at that with the secondhand equipment legitimate produc-ers have thrown away.

"Our schools are no longer graduating competent engineers, scientists and creative thinkers to create new technology." Gar-bage! What other nation has walked on the moon, devel-oped a reusable space shuttle, or moved so far into the heavens or beneath the seas? Who else has come so close to inventing life in the laboratory, reproduced it in a test tube, replicated the parts of the body, unlocked its mys-teries, synthesized the processes of nature to harness the power of the atom and the growth of bacteria to repro-duce at our command, and advanced so close to the fron-tiers of defying death itself with medical technology? What other nation is so afflicted with foreign industrial spies attempting to steal its technology? We are not the "spier," we are the "spyee." We don't need other nations' technol-ogy. We threw theirs away years ago as obsolete.

"Our oil supplies are depleted; the oil companies are not finding more reserves; energy is too expensive." Garbage! We have more oil in three proven fields in Alaska than exists in all

of the Middle East, and five times that amount in the continental U.S., with more fields coming on line daily. The *only* reason energy is too expensive is that a total of $23.62 in hidden taxes is imposed on every $32.00 barrel of Alaskan oil before it even reaches the lower U.S. Without this hidden tax, gasoline could still sell for $.40 at the pump. Alternative fuels like natural gas, coal, and uranium are abundant but are burdened even more by a tax system that does not accord them the much-pilloried depletion allowance—a relief from taxes without which the oil industry would have even less incentive to drill and supplies would dwindle further. Without tax incentives that allow companies to write off more of their research and development costs faster, and that allow consumers to credit their purchases against taxes they have paid, such renewable sources of energy as solar technology remain a chimera.

Name any other excuse, it won't stand up. The only reason we have problems in industry is our absolute determination to refuse to impose our taxes at the correct point—that is, our refusal to tax consumption directly. The sum total of *all* other alleged problems—labor, management, profit-taking versus reinvestment, innovation and energy—only comprise 40 percent of the dollars cost of production. They do not represent a high enough percentage of costs combined, much less individually, to be the dominant problem. They are all symptoms of the disease. They may themselves be debilitating or deadly, but they are not the disease. To claim otherwise is tantamount to describing a terminal cancer patient's agonizing death throes as a stomach ache. Pepto-Bismol won't help.

CHAPTER 6

Benefits to the Poor and Unemployed

LABOR AND MANAGEMENT ARE so closely related and dependent on one another under the conditions and tech-
niques of modern production, it is virtually impossible for
either to do well without equivalent benefits accruing to
the other. In the early part of the twentieth century this
was not the case; industrial warfare prevailed with inter-
mittent truces until World War II. Since the mid-1950s,
however, they have worked well together. They have
learned to cooperate in mutual interest and to make
concessions, even sacrifices when necessary, to ensure not
only the survival but the well-being of the work that sus-
tains them both.

Stock options, equity participation, and profit sharing
have become more the rule than the exception. But now,
with the demise of our basic industries, acrimonious
echoes from the turn of the century come back to haunt
us. A gulf is opening between labor and management.
Each is confident it is doing its job in an exemplary manner, but failing to recognize the true villain, each assumes
the other must be to blame for the destruction of personal
dreams, hopes, and ambitions.

There are, surely, few losses more devastating than the loss of one's means of livelihood. We work in order to eat, but also to create, to make a better life for ourselves and our loved ones. We work to "make a living" out of our work—not to make work out of our living. That's why the historic battles between labor and capital have been fought on the territory, first, of wages (the means of subsistence), then conditions, then the length of the workday and week, and finally, job security and security after retirement.

The advances working people have made on all these fronts, often at tremendous cost in life, limb and liberty, are now in jeopardy. It is natural for anyone who loses his or her job through no apparent fault of loyalty or hard work to blame someone else for the pain, and whoever is closest will do. Individually, it is as traumatic to the unemployed manager as it is to the worker. But there are more workers than managers and, contrary to the adage, misery does not love company. It's an agony that is pandemic in the United States today.

The agony of unemployed hands and minds, of idle factories and fields, is all the more tragic because it is self-inflicted, not by the workers and managers on each other, but by all of us, as a nation, attempting to do what our ancestors knew better than to do, what the tax history of the world has proven and our own over seventy-two-year experiment has now confirmed. There is only one transaction in the economic system that can be taxed without incurring side effects that are at least damaging, if not devastating to the entire system—consumption. Income and profits cannot be taxed.

As with the problems that are theoretically causing the failures of our industries, unemployment is not in itself a problem except insofar as it represents a tragic waste. It, too, is nothing more than a symptom of the real problem.

The vast majority of our work force files an IRS "short form" 1040A for their income-tax returns. Regardless of what their paycheck says, they are not now, and never have been, paid their stated $10, $15, or $25 per hour, as agreed in their employment contract. They are paid the net of their check, after deductions. The balance is the government's "wage" for the work it didn't do on the product; it will be paid out eventually through the maze of government expenditures to the producers of other goods and services, including holders of debt incurred to finance prior deficits that the hidden tax couldn't cover. This unpaid balance of the worker's paycheck (the tax) is an expense of production that adds nothing to the value of the product being produced—unless one can trace the costs and benefits of the government's transfer payments and assign some portion of the value of national defense, infrastructure (highways for transportation, dams for water supplies, and so forth) and other essential services to that product as a legitimate "social cost" of its production, an absolute exercise in stupidity.

Taxes extracted from one worker, company, or sector of the economy to pay suppliers of goods and services to another worker ("income support" programs for the poor, unemployed or disabled), to another company (subsidies or "bailouts") or sector are not necessary evils. They are unnecessary complications at best; at worst, they compound the fundamental problems created by the tax by adding to the bureaucratic overhead, draining resources from more productive activity and multiplying the number of transactions that are subject to the tax. They are evils made necessary to cushion the effects of a greater though less necessary evil—our system of hidden taxation.

With any change from our current system of taxation to a sensible sales tax or VAT, there should be a reduction of all salaries and wages to the current net amount, the net after withholding and FICA. The employee would not lose one cent in real income. He would have exactly the same amount of spendable wages he now enjoys. Employers would charge only 10-percent markup to enjoy the desired 10-percent profit. These events would cause the price in the marketplace to drop by 60 percent. The product that once cost $1.00 could be priced at $.40. The government, in order to maintain current expenditures, its own level of consumption, and the national standard of living, would have to add a 150-percent consumers tax, which would equal $.60. Together with the $.40 charged by the final seller, the citizen's purchase would cost the same $1.00 as before, an amount his current check, net after taxes, allows him to pay. Each consumer would, therefore, have exactly the same amount of money to make purchases, and the goods would cost exactly the same as they do now.

There would, therefore, be no change in anyone's financial position. But what a dramatic change there would be in the economy and the condition of the unemployed, the poor, and those currently on welfare. These symptoms of our problem would be relegated to the same status as the black plague, smallpox, and polio. They could be eradicated, except for the bad memory we would use to remind ourselves and our children of how far we had progressed.

The current nonsensical tax system has forced surviving industries in the U.S. to streamline, cut budgets, and economize as never before. Businesses are, currently, as lean and hard as any time in history. They are in fighting form; and no industry of any nation would be able to compete, if they were relieved of their absurd tax burden.

American cars, trucks and heavy equipment, selling in the tax-free export market at a 60-percent discount from current prices, would flood the planet. Orders would be backed up for years. Workers currently employed would have lifetime security. The recently unemployed would be hurriedly called back to fill the needs of plants that were previously operating at 40-percent capacity. Suddenly, they would possess orders requiring full operation. Plants that are currently closed, but are still operationally viable, would be reopened and their employees would be recalled.

The recall of all past employees would not, however, even begin to fill the void in the demand for labor. With industrial America freed from its shackles, there would be no limit to the demand for our products.

The poor and those on welfare, who have never been more than marginally employable, would have to be trained. They would not be trained by a government program to work in an obsolete trade, as is now occurring; rather, they would be instructed by the industries that would then require their work. For once, it could honestly be stated that no person truly desiring a job need be on welfare.

As a side benefit, such a revolution would probably resolve our current immigration problem as well. We could stop patrolling the Mexican border to prevent illegal immigration. We could welcome these people, instead, with open arms. Or we could build factories there to provide the jobs our hardworking neighbors so desperately need and want, at a wage that would not undercut U.S. workers like a "runaway shop" trying to escape the tax burden here. The only problem we would probably face would be the "gangs" sent down by industry to kidnap Mexicans who would no longer want to come to the proverbial "Great PX to the North."

The possibilities virtually defy the imagination. Our steel industry, which once dominated the world market, which is now in shambles as a result of being undersold by 20 percent to 30 percent even at home, could recapture its share. Our mills could discount from their current prices by 60 percent and be profitable and 30 percent to 40 percent under their competitors' prices. They and their employees could enjoy the same income as before the closings and layoffs. Our shoe-manufacturing workers—who were as recently as May 1985 recognized as a disaster—could stop begging for quotas to be placed on imports to protect their few remaining jobs. Our textile and clothing workers struggled for years—all but chained to machines by day and confined to ghettos by night—through bloody strikes and decades of discrimination against immigrants to have their children and grandchildren share in the dream of America. Today, these workers survive only in quality, name-brand, and designer lines that can demand the higher prices. Mills that moved from the northeast to the Carolinas are closing again. The garment industry has been highly profitable in Southern California, more dynamic even than electronics or aerospace, thanks to cheaper, nonunion, immigrant labor, much of it illegal. Now even these low-wage centers are threatened by foreign imports. With an honest, open tax, domestic sweatshop employers would be forced to compete for this skilled pool of workers, who would have a real chance to improve their wages and conditions. The boom would reverberate through all segments of the economy.

The recovery of steel, auto and coal; the rejuvenation of textiles and apparel; the regeneration of all our atrophied export industries would trigger demand in raw materials, minerals and their processing, in metal-fabricating, machinery and machine tools, in electrical equipment, electronics and computers. The economic multiplier would ripple through the economy, reviving cities left for dead and pumping new life into regions that now resemble corpses. And this stimulus would reduce the unemployment rolls and the welfare lists, thereby reducing the tax required for their support, reducing the costs of psychological trauma for families, school dropouts of demoralized youngsters, crime, and a host of social problems that now appear beyond solution.

We don't have unemployment because our people don't want to work. We are blessed with, if not possessed by, the strongest work ethic of any nation on earth. We are simply the victims of The Lie. We have no employment because there is no employer. There is no employer because he, too, is a victim of The Lie.

Hell, it's our lie. Let's stop telling it. Let's start telling ourselves the truth! Let's admit we need a tax in order to maintain a government and that we all need to contribute to its payment. Let's contribute to it, each according to his purchases, in the amount his income permits, and let's stop worrying about it.

Nothing will change on the consumer level! Exactly as the liberal politicians forewarn, a sales tax will cause a lower-paid person to pay a larger percentage of his income in taxes. A wealthier person, who can save part of his income and thus not have that part subjected to the tax, will pay a smaller percentage rate of his gross income. What's new about this? It's exactly what happens now. The fact that we lie to the poor, pretending the rich and middle class are paying it all in income taxes, does not refund one cent of the 150-percent hidden consumption tax that the poor are paying today on their every purchase.

But the inequity could be corrected. If we truly do not believe the poor should have to pay the tax, refund it. It's easy when we know how much it is, and that's the beauty of a consumer's tax. We will know. We will know exactly how much to refund when it's clearly printed on the sales receipts, instead of buried in an unfathomable labyrinth of taxes that neither the tax collector nor God himself can decipher. (Actually, I don't think God would even try. I believe our system of taxation is one of those creations of man that is a befuddlement to the Lord. He must wonder how man, his creation, blessed with such a marvelous brain, could possibly screw things up so completely. If God doesn't wonder, I do.)

We can start the tax at 150 percent, as it is now, but we don't need to. The 1985–86 budget is only $950 billion. We have a $4 trillion economy, of which 60 percent is tax-induced. The full amount is not paid in taxes because of refunds, incentives, and credits; but the burden we impose in taxes induces higher prices that inflate the gross national product as measured in dollars.

The employer neither knows nor cares whether or not

the employee or dividend recipient receives a refund. The only important fact to him is that the withholding and FICA checks are mailed. This costs him money, and he must add it to his sales price. Once it is added, he becomes less competitive at best and uncompetitive at worst. Once the burden of the lie is relieved, the results are startling.

A maximum 60-percent tax on the actual goods and services consumed could generate the entire $950 billion required in the 1985–86 budget. Not 60 percent *of* the gross sale as it now is, but a 60-percent tax *on* the sales price. This amounts to only 37.5 percent of the total purchase price.

This presumes our industries and workers can produce the amount they are currently producing. It presumes the cash black market remains intact and contributes nothing, and it presumes imports remain at the same level and are exempted from the tax. None of these assumptions are fact, of course; but if they were, the results would be the same. The cash black marketers would lose their competitive edge and be forced to return to the fold, as would the foreign importers. Their goods and services would no longer be competitive here in the states, and our industries would absorb their market. That is, production would be taxed. That which is now untaxed and remains competitive would produce additional tax revenues once it was included on the tax rolls. New unemployment and the pains thereof would be unnecessary. They would be self-inflicted, and they would be self-curable.

With rare exceptions, I do not believe even the most liberal antagonist of the consumption tax is evil. I believe that the results of his efforts to tax the rich and affluent corporations for the benefit of the poor are the result of a sincere desire to relieve the suffering of his constituents, not to further harm them. He is simply misinformed, not misanthropic. He, too, is a victim of the lie! When the truth is recognized, he will be the strongest of supporters. Conservatives are already, at least subconsciously, supporters. They understand that the first requirement of a worker is a workplace that can afford to pay the worker. The second requirement is a product of the workplace that is competitive in the market, will sell, and will produce revenues. The third step for the conservative is a short one. He needs to recognize that industry does not need relief from the current tax system, it needs the system to be abandoned. It needs it to be replaced with a system that taxes our industry's competitors on the same basis that our industry is taxed.

Politicians, liberal or conservative, will do what is necessary to be reelected. The unemployable, the unemployed, and the soon-to-be-unemployed need to make it abundantly clear to their politicians what is required to obtain their next vote: The Truth! The truth followed by a fair and open consumption tax to replace the zombie with which we are now afflicted.

The truth is, our industries are *today* producing for costs that would permit them to sell their every product for only $.40 of the dollar we now pay were it not for the hidden 60-percent tax which it is required to collect for the government. Business collects a dollar, but only $.40 remains with the business to pay for its labor, materials, capital, administration and all other costs. The remaining $.60 is mailed to the government.

Once that fact is recognized, the hidden 60 percent eliminated, and a fair open consumption tax imposed equally on our industries' products and their competition alike, the benefits to our poor and unemployed will be virtually immeasurable.

1. The employable unemployed will become unemployed.
2. The currently unemployable (or marginally employable) unemployed will be retrained to become employable and will in due course become employed.

Those two feats alone reduce the cost of government by the amounts previously allocated to their welfare. When the cost of government goes down, taxes should go down. When taxes go down, more money remains in the economy to buy more products, which require more producers to produce them. The purchases will contribute more funds to taxes, which should produce a surplus which would require tax reductions, which cause more . . . which causes . . . which causes . . .

The benefits are immeasurable because each benefit triggers an event which triggers another benefit which . . . which . . . which . . .

Even the poorest poor, the untrained and untrainable, those retired on less-than-sufficient fixed income and the disabled would receive immense immediate as well as long-term benefits. Without raising their stipend one cent, the simple issuance of a "Tax Exempt Card" assuring them a refund of the 60-percent tax would make them the equivalent of immediate beneficiaries of a 259-percent pay raise. They would instantly have available to them two and a half times the buying power the same income now affords them.

Eventually, as the marketplace demands become greater, even those with the most marginal capabilities would be needed and those desiring to do so could rejoin the gainfully employed.

These are not high hopes! These are not pie in the sky, wild-eyed projections of what could be if certain other things came to pass. These are the costs at which our surviving industries produce *today*. These are the costs at which our "dead" industries were producing at the time of their death. These are the costs at which every operating nut, bolt, cog and wheel of our industries are producing as you sit reading this chapter of this book *today*.

The only reason we are not *today* the beneficiaries of the Utopia such industry should produce is our absolute refusal to admit the truth! Our refusal to:

1. Stop taxing the wrong economic event—income.
2. Start taxing the only economic event that can be taxed—the correct one, consumption.
3. Stop penalizing our labor, management, industry, and capital with an unfair system of taxation on income.
4. Stop rewarding the labor management, industry and capital of our foreign competitors.

It is time for the truth. It is time for truth in taxation, and it is time that we the American people began to enjoy the just fruits of our production. When that occurs you will realize that the title of this chapter is a misnomer. There will be no "benefits to the poor" because there will be no "poor" to be benefited.

CHAPTER 7

Benefits to the People

WE, THE PEOPLE, HAVE never been so divided. Abraham Lincoln's warning that "a house divided against itself cannot stand" is as true today as it was then. This division is the direct result of the lie and the symptoms of the lie, which we call problems.

Virtually every element of our society is pitted against another. It's race against race; the poor, the middle class, and the rich against each other; liberal against conservative; labor against management; labor against capital; the people, in general, against the government.

How divided can we get? Each of these divisions can be traced directly to the fact that each element of our society is attempting to obtain its fair share of our ever diminishing economic pie. In many ways, 1985 was remarkable: real economic growth was 4.7 percent, an apparent vindication of claims that tax relief would help the economy recover. But the long-term trend, especially when the war-induced growth of the late 1960s and early 1970s is considered, is not so susceptible to the magic bullet of limited tax "relief." The pie is no longer growing fast enough to give everyone the slice he or she thinks they deserve, let alone the larger slice we expect as a reward for hard work as we grow older. In economic terms, what we have is

79

slower rate of growth in the gross national product—the total value of goods and services we produce—and an even slower rate of growth, sometimes a decline, in the GNP per capita, the share in the pie available for each person in our growing population.

As a result, even though 7 million new jobs were created in 1985, the unemployment rate dropped below 7 percent, and the number of people living below the official poverty line declined to its lowest point in years (14.4 percent of the population—9.7 percent when the estimated $113 billion value of noncash benefits like food stamps, Medicare and housing subsidies are counted), all this apparent progress is deceptive. Consider: The number of new jobs created by the economy each year has shrunk to the lowest annual level since the early 1970s. The great industrial belt that stretches from New England to the Great Lakes lost 1.5 million manufacturing jobs, or 13.7 percent of the national total, between 1979 and 1985. (Although the Bureau of Labor Statistics points out that the loss was nearly covered by gains in the service sector, the new service jobs usually pay less and, more important, do not produce a product for export; thus they do nothing for the balance of payments.) The decline in the poverty rate in 1985 must be viewed in light of the fact that the 33.7 million living in poverty outnumber the official figure for 1964. We exult in a decline in unemployment that leaves 8.5 million without jobs! Twenty years ago we would have been appalled at a rate above 4 percent.

Our problem is not a crisis of "rising expectations." Americans for the first time in their history are in fact being told to lower their sights, to tighten their belts and give up hope permanently, not simply as a temporary sacrifice to meet some national emergency. But since we don't recognize the cause, we fight each other and the world over the symptoms.

Each segment of society is certain that some part of what was previously its piece of the economic pie is gone. It never occurs to the affected group that the piece no longer exists. It is presumed that since the piece was here a short time ago, someone must have taken it, and the deprived group wants it back. Each segment is convinced it did the best job possible, and if blame exists, it must rest on another party to the effort. Hostile feelings are inevitable. Thus, labor against management, the rich versus the poor, the middle class against both, and so forth.

This social and political fragmentation is due almost completely to our system of taxation. The system is the correct target for the hate. Once that is recognized and our efforts properly directed, the people of this nation can reunite in a common effort. No symptom or problem can stand against a united America, just as none is resolvable with divided efforts.

We the people are largely in opposition to our government. That is a division no nation can stand. Every element of society can name a dozen reasons for its feelings, but almost without exception it is traceable to our tax system.

Almost every stated reason for the divisions is rooted in the belief that the government isn't doing enough for a pet area of interest or is taking too much from us in taxes. We discovered in chapter 3 that this system of taxation is incapable of collecting enough to do all the things we ask of government and that any amount it collects is too much. There's the problem. In effect, every segment of society is correct: The system takes too much and the total of the take is insufficient to pay for the services we need.

Since it's the one system we have, the government tries to collect more and each attempt results in its collecting less, while further alienating the people by the attempt to collect it. The alienation will grow as long as this system is used. The system cannot do its job, so government will be unable to do its job. Government will try to collect more, will receive less, and the fight will continue.

Of course, the initial reaction of the people is against

the man or the agency responsible for the collection of the tax. IRS agents are not inherently evil, any more than other employees or supporters of the system are. Like any other group of 88,000 people, there will be a few bad apples, but by and large they are good, honest, loyal Americans. For sixteen hours a day they would probably make excellent neighbors that you would be delighted to welcome to your community. For eight hours a day, however, they are employed in an impossible task. It is their job to take away from the average citizen that which the citizen believes is his and intends to keep. The IRS agent's employer, the government, disagrees with the citizen and, to make matters worse, the agent's employer is going broke. Like any other distressed employer, the government blames its clients and customers. It thinks its clients are demanding more and more but paying less and less. The government thinks its clients, you and I, are deadbeats and orders its agent to get tough and make clients pay up.

To the contrary, we, the clients, believe we are overcharged already and have no intention of paying more. The lines are drawn, and the battle is engaged. In that light it should be obvious to all that the only direction from here is straight down. There will be no winner, only losers. The people can't whip the government; they are the government. The government can't whip the people because it is of the people. We can, however, mutually destruct, and we are rapidly doing precisely that. We cannot even compromise. Any amount for which the government "settles" in taxes, especially after a dispute or audit, leaves the people angry over whatever amount was taken. Any amount the government leaves was needed by the government because the government cannot pay its bills. That forces the government to then go after another element of the people.

As long as both the government and the people are in contention over the same dollars, there will be a fight. As long as there is a fight, they will remain antagonists. Peace will occur only when each has his own turf and when the retention of that turf does no damage to the other, nor does the other need it.

As things stand, both are convinced that there is enough to go around. Both are convinced we are able to meet all our needs. And the fact is, both are right. The two true statements, however, lead us to the wrong conclusion: that someone else must not be paying his fair share. The correct conclusion has to be that it's the wrong system of taxation. Any tax which is collected by this system is too much. The fact that there is enough wealth to pay enough tax to pay for our needs if collected correctly doesn't matter. The tax isn't being collected that way.

So where are we? Divided. The people against the government, because they believe it takes too much from every one of them. The people against the people, because each element is convinced the other elements are cheating by not paying their fair share.

Of course, the poor think the government is withholding proper support because they aren't getting it. Or it must be the fault of the rich, who are not paying their fair share. So hate develops. It goes on and on. I defy anyone to trace a single animosity of any group in our country for another to its root source and find a cause other than the system of taxation. Exceptions may be pure bigotry or ideology, but even those who aim their wrath at scapegoats are not immune from the influence of tax economics and the dissimulations of our tax system that have masked the real villain.

The thinking behind these beliefs is invalid, but it destroys our unity as a nation just the same. Reality and logic based on the factual evidence prove all those beliefs to be false. The taxes are too well hidden, and we can't see the tax forest because of all those trees of purchases. All of this hate and divisiveness is created by a false system of taxation, and we refuse to address the truth.

A consumption tax would eliminate that. Every American would have receipts up to the amount of his purchasing power to prove his contribution. We could eliminate the hate stories about the poor and minorities escaping taxation, and the suggestions that the middle and upper classes are hiding in tax shelters. Each can prove and all will know they each paid their fair share at the cash register.

A consumption tax would lift the veil that hides the fact that the true payer of taxes is the consumer.

The direct and indirect benefits to the people are beyond count, but two of the most important would be comprehension and control. Those two accomplishments eliminate the roots of the divisive, self-destructive hate that is consuming us. Comprehension will force us to admit reality. The open tax on consumption eliminates the need for a collection procedure that foments divisiveness between the people and their government. Every citizen would know his exact contribution. He would have no defense against the payment, and he would not object to it. Abusive collection procedures currently in vogue at the IRS would have no benefit and no use. The people would owe no tax other than that collected on their purchases. With no personal tax to pay, there would be no need for government collectors to harass the people or invade their privacy. In fact, there would be no need for tax collectors!

With a direct open tax on consumption, the exact tax imposition would be obvious to all. It would be known and its effect comprehended by all the people. A sales tax of 20, 30, even 150 percent added to each purchase is not difficult to understand. It is clearly printed on the receipt.

Comprehension and understanding are the first results of a consumption tax. The next most important is control, control in the correct hands, the hands of the people. The power to tax, we now know all too well, is the power to destroy. That's why our forebears set up barriers to the income tax in particular and limits on the power to tax in general: The constitutional requirement that all bills for raising revenue must be initiated in the House of Representatives, by Congressmen elected from districts of equal population (rather than in the Senate, which until this century was an appointed body representing states of unequal size), was a clear expression of their idea of checks and balances, especially when it came to balancing the national checkbook. But now it's hard to tell who has hands on the pursestrings and whose hand is in our pockets. In the current system, which no one understands, there is no control by us. We are at the mercy of our employee, the government. Even the controllers, the IRS, do not understand it. If it is not understandable, if it is beyond comprehension, it is out of control.

The means of control by the voters is vested in their right to vote. However, if the voter cannot understand the system, if he is unaware of the effects, he will have no conception of the result of political promises and thus no basis on which to determine his vote. If he is unable to determine what the promise was, how can he decide whether or not it was fulfilled? The voter not only has no control over the tax, he has no control over his representative that sets it.

It is not surprising, therefore, that once a tax in this system is imposed, it is never removed. World War II is a perfect example. It cost a lot of money. No patriotic American would have dreamed of objecting to the tax increases it prompted. The problem is that we lost control. Those taxes remain today. The government and bureaucracy found new ways to spend them. Each subsequent "emergency" caused new taxes, and again the government found new ways to spend those dollars when those emergencies were over.

The government can do that because we have lost control. The tax and its use were not specified, nor were beginning and ending dates set. When these taxes remained on the books, the government and taxes were able to grow at ten times the rate of the economy for almost forty years.

A sales or consumption tax, on the other hand, is very

apparent, is in full view, and is controllable by the people. In Colorado the state imposed a gasoline sales tax to make "emergency" repairs caused by the 1965 flood. When the repairs were finished, so were the taxes. Virtually every city, county and state has had similar emergencies and similar emergency tax levies. Those levies that were added to taxes other than sales (consumption) invariably have remained on the books and continue to be collected today. One bureaucracy continues to collect them, and others find new ways to spend them. I have been unable to find one instance of an "emergency *sales* tax" anywhere in the U.S. that was not removed instantly when the emergency was over, or at least fully disclosed as continuing, with reasons given for the extension. To the contrary, I can find no hidden tax for the general fund that has ever been removed. They only go up.

There is an obvious reason. The people are in control of sales tax. The people are aware of the tax. The people know when the emergency is over and the problem is resolved. No politician and no bureaucrat in the world would dare attempt to retain so obvious a tax. The people know it has served its purpose and there is no continuing need for it.

It's called control—control by the people, control of their own taxes. Why not? We control every other dollar we spend. Why shouldn't we control our single largest expenditure, taxes?

The news gets better. Why should the requirement for precise budgeting prior to the imposition of a new tax be limited to emergencies? Every government program is supposedly a solution to a problem. With a sales tax, every new bill proposed in the Congress could have requirements:

1. That it define the problem to be addressed.
2. That it state the proposed solution.
3. That it state the exact cost (budget) of the solution.

4. That it state the percentage increase in sales taxes required for the solution.
5. That it state the dates of commencement and the target date for solution of the problem.
6. That it state a date for the termination of the tax.
7. That any extension of the tax require new legislation.

This mechanism may sound complicated, but compare it to the one we have, compare it to the volumes of the federal tax code, the stacks of regulations required to implement it, the learned tomes written by experts trying to make sense of it, the judicial opinions attempting to interpret it, and the piles of records, receipts and documents the citizenry must keep in order to pay it. A sales tax with these simple requirements permits control by the citizens. Today we have no control by us and we have no control *of* us.

Such a sales tax would prohibit the passing of legislation with no conception of how the program is to be paid for. The citizens would be made aware of the purported benefits and the exact costs. That cost would be printed on their grocery bill. If it is more than promised, we would know who the liars were and who to punish at the next election.

The IRS could be abolished. It would be unnecessary. Since a consumption tax is virtually self-regulating, there is no requirement for such a service. The importance of the abolition of the IRS cannot be overstated. It is now the closest thing America has ever had to a Gestapo or a KGB. It is already above the law, and it becomes more oppressive daily. It routinely violates rights of citizens, which would not be tolerated for a heartbeat if committed by the FBI, CIA or any other agency. Ask yourself, "Am I intimidated by the IRS?" This answer, for most Americans, is yes. Any government agency with the power to intimidate a law-abiding citizen is beyond redemption. It must be abolished, but that will be discussed more fully in Part Two.

A consumption tax will do that. The true tax will return control to the people. It will allow us to abolish the IRS and eliminate the cause of the divisive hate that is now destroying us. It will again make government, and government agencies, responsive to the people because the tax can be controlled by the people. We may not be able to determine exactly what percentage of income tax each level of income can afford, but we can damn well determine what percentage of sales tax we can afford to have added on to our purchases. Further, we will know that everyone else pays the same rate. We will know that people earning less buy less and thus pay less. People earning more will buy more and pay more. Each will be paying his fair share, and we will have no reason to hate or distrust.

All power in any nation either derives from or is expressed in the control of taxation. We cannot be a nation *of* the people, *by* the people or *for* the people without that control.

CHAPTER 8

Benefits to the Voters

INFORMATION AND KNOWLEDGE ARE required elements of an informed decision. A decision is required to cast a ballot. Eloquent speakers, taking convoluted positions on seemingly unfathomable problems, abound in our state and national legislatures. They are elected in large part by voters who possess not the foggiest notion of what the politicians are saying. Worse yet, politicians are elected to a larger and larger extent by default—in effect by nonvoters who have given up trying to understand. (The percentage of the voting-age population that participates in presidential elections has declined in every election but two since Calvin Coolidge.)

We all know of amendments, bills and political positions that are craftily worded to say the opposite of what they appear to mean. No better example can be given than a referendum in Colorado in 1972 to decide whether or not to host the Winter Olympics. The referendum was worded so that voters in favor of the Olympics had to vote NO. Those against the games voted YES. The result: a state whose opinion polls favored the Olympics by a large margin voted against the games by a margin nearly as large.

Our tax system today is worse. It is a system so huge

that few citizens understand it even slightly. Yet every citizen is required to file an annual tax return stating under "penalties of perjury" that his return is correct. IRS employees will refuse to sign that same statement even after their own audit. They will tell you that the laws are too complex and that they can't be sufficiently certain of the correctness of their audits to expose themselves to so drastic a consequence.

The budget, the debt, the wastes, and the expenditures are so vast that they escape the comprehension of our foremost economic prophets. No two agree in their forecasts on the consequences of any element of the budget or the tax law. The results normally prove both such forecasts to have been wrong.

Yet we continue to go to the polls and attempt to elect someone who promises to bring order to this chaos. We do that with virtually no comprehension of what we expect because we have no idea what is wrong, much less what has been promised. Thus, we are not terribly surprised to discover that the person we elected has failed to do what we weren't sure he even said.

There is an ultimate solution—a value-added or, preferably, a sales tax. It is easy to collect, to compute, and to comprehend. Voters would know instantly how much of their salary has gone where. The awareness would permit an informed vote. Since we would be fully informed as to what we expected, we would not only be shocked, we would be justifiably irate if the elected official performed contrary to his campaign promises.

Today we are informed that our spending is broken down into five general categories (1985–86 Budget—the operable budget at the time this book was written):

29%	Defense	$275.5 billion
13%	Interest	$123.5 billion
5%	Federal operations	$ 47.5 billion
11%	Grants (state and local) . .	$104.5 billion

42%	Benefits to individuals . . .	$399.0 billion
100%	TOTAL	$950.0 billion

"Benefits to individuals" can be broken down to spending as follows:

51%	Social security	$202.2 billion
17%	Medicare and aid	$ 67.2 billion
4%	Unemployment	$ 16.3 billion
28%	General welfare	$113.3 billion
100%	TOTAL	$399.0 billion

Those expenditures are paid for by collections from six sources:

20%	Borrowing/Income	$190.0 billion
36%	Personal income tax	$342.0 billion
8%	Corporate income tax	$ 76.0 billion
29%	Social security	$275.5 billion
4%	Excise tax	$ 38.0 billion
3%	Miscellaneous	$ 28.5 billion

The national debt reached $2,074 trillion in early 1986. At that time, interest alone reached $207 billion, $5 billion more than the total social security payouts. By 1987, the annual budget will be one half of the gross national product.

So now you know all there is to know about the budget and how it's paid. How do you vote? Democrat or Republican?

In reality you know only one thing: The system we have doesn't work and there is no cure for it. The only possible reform of the system would be to increase income taxes by $190 billion. Not for you, of course, but for all the other guys. Right?

Suppose the raise were level across the board, with no

deductions. That would require everyone to accept a 55.6-percent increase in taxes over and above what they paid last year. Can you afford it? Of course not, and neither can anyone else. Nor can the economy. Nor can the nation.

Try a new one. Let's pay off the national debt, too. Let's get a payment plan for ten years. That would require you and everyone else to pay for the next ten years two-and-one-half times what they paid for 1985, which would be a difficult task for all and an impossible one for those individuals and corporations already in the 50-percent bracket. That is assuming, of course, that raising tax rates by a factor of two and one half would raise tax revenues by the same factor—a mathematical trick that contradicts historical experience.

Remember: Raising income taxes hurts business and *lowers* net tax revenue income to the government.

Who do you want to vote for now? Right, there is no one to vote for who has a solution because there is no solution with this system of taxation. The system doesn't work.

Has any candidate for office ever told you that? Of course not! Anyone who did would receive between three and five votes, all from recently released inmates of the state mental institution forced on the streets by budget cuts. Even Walter Mondale barely scratched the surface of the real requirements to balance the budget, and we all know what happened to him at the 1984 polls.

At least now we know why we have regretted our votes for the last few years. Sure, the guy failed to do what he said he would, but it can't be done, not with this system, because the system doesn't work. But if we can't understand the system, which we can't, surely we can at least admit we can understand that *it doesn't work!*

There is a system we can understand. There is a system that will work. There is a system that will return control of our destiny to us, the voters. There is a system that will permit us to make our elected officials accountable to us. That system is a tax on consumption.

We know we had a $4-trillion-a-year economy in 1985–86. We know 60 percent of the dollar value of those goods and services was tax-induced (that is, expenses that are not real measures of goods and services produced). We therefore had a *real* $1.6 trillion economy. If all other taxes had been eliminated and replaced by a 60-percent consumer's tax, the government would have collected the entire $950 billion it supposedly needed, while the gross price paid for the products, tax included, would have been only $2.75 trillion—almost $1.5 trillion less than we are now paying for the same goods and services from the same *net* paycheck. That would be the equivalent of a $7,000-per-annum pay raise for every man, woman and child in the U.S.

Every merchant, every firm (except perhaps accounting and law firms), every worker would have exactly the same take-home pay as now, but his purchases would be priced 36 percent lower. Realistically, since the same spendable income would be available, most of it would probably be spent and taxed at the point of consumption. Thirty-seven-and-one-half percent of that spending would be additional revenue to the government and available for payment on the national debt. The debt would be paid off in three years and six months. All of which presumes no new jobs occur, no new production of lower-priced, better U.S.–built products replaces one item now being imported, no new exports are achieved (even though our products would be reduced 60 percent in price), and we don't collect the sales tax on imports. None of these assumptions would be true, but even if they were, we would accomplish the same thing.

In reality, we could probably balance the budget, pay off the debt, and reduce the consumption tax to 23 percent in 18 months.

Think of it. Everything produced in 1985–86 for $4

trillion would now be selling for $1.6 trillion plus a 23-percent sales tax. The gross costs of all U.S. citizens' purchases including taxes would thus be $1.97 trillion. Every American would suddenly find himself paying only $1.97 for what today costs him $4.00. He would have $2.03 left over and would spend or save it. If it's spent, more taxes are paid; if it's saved, someone will borrow it, spend it, create more production, and pay more taxes. All this presumes not one single government program is eliminated or reduced in services.

And having regained control of our finances, we would know exactly the amount of our tax; it would be printed on every receipt for every purchase. If it goes up one cent, we know it. If a political candidate makes a promise, we can ask how many percentage points in the tax it will cost. If the majority of us decide we're in favor, we will vote him in, knowing the exact consequence, and after he's elected we will know if he lied. We will see it on our next grocery bill, where it will show as a *tax*. It will not be buried in supposed inflation, to be blamed on an innocent citizen called a merchant.

If wastes occur, like those notorious $435 hammers or $4,000 coffeepots, we can ask how many such products we purchased and what percent of the budget that was. The same percent times the amount of tax we paid represents the exact cost of the waste to us individually in U.S. dollar bills.

If I earn and spend $20,000, I know 37.5 percent was spent on sales taxes. That amounts to $7,500. If the fraud or waste was one half of one percent of the gross budget, it cost me $37.50 and I can figure out exactly how mad I am about it. I can ask my Congressman what he is doing about it and decide whether or not his action is in my opinion sufficiently appropriate to warrant his retention.

We can look at entire programs the same way and make the same decision—a considered decision based on its exact effect on us. The program would require budgeting, the amount of its percent of the budget could be determined. If its cost will require a 1-percent increase in sales tax, we can decide, "Is this program important enough to warrant every American's commitment to reduce his consumption by 1 percent to pay for it?" If so, pass it. We voters will tell you at the polls whether or not we agree with your decision, Senator.

There is no way to do that now. We don't know the effect. A computation of the percentage on the income taxes we paid is no computation at all. First off, we didn't pay the tax, the consumer did. Second, the effect of the tax is so far-reaching that the 22-percent tax on our personal income resulted in a 150-percent increase in the cost of consumables; it resulted in the breaking of "X" number of businesses which encountered "X" number of imports which paid no tax. Maybe God could figure it out, but he wouldn't bother.

Perhaps even now you are not convinced of how important that knowledge and your informed vote truly are. If so, reserve final judgment of the importance until you finish Part Two, "A Threat to Freedom." If you remain unconvinced of your vote's importance, we don't live in the same universe, much less the same country. At minimum, we do not share the same values.

The consumption tax permits knowledge and understanding. Knowledge permits us voters to demand accountability from our representatives. I simply do not believe government need be so complex. I am certainly no longer prepared to accept the excuse that its complexity causes our problems. Any complexity it may possess is not inherent; it is the result of the passing of unfathomable laws.

The tax laws don't have to be complicated. No small part of any real complexity of government is the result of the attempt to use the tax system to accomplish a multitude of other purposes besides raising revenue. Having erected an inequitable and incomprehensible tax structure, our representatives attach new ornaments, prop up new additions, gussy up the facade, and truss up the eaves to keep it from collapsing, all in the name of fairness and simplicity. Hell, this system can't even collect enough taxes, so how is it supposed to do anything else? And, if it could, would we want to use it to realize those goals? If we want these other goals, get them out front and pass a law to do it, a separate law that *is* simple. Any complexity in any law is the result of a desire for complexity—not of legal requirement. We make the laws, and we can change them.

The old and trite excuse that sanity cannot prevail because "it's an oversimplified solution to a complex problem" just won't sell anymore. In fact, if the problem is so damn complex, "How in hell do you understand it, Senator? Maybe we'd better simplify it."

I have met and known quite a few Congressmen and Senators. The vast majority of them are solid, honest, loyal and bright men and women. They have the best of intentions. Card-carrying, certified, notarized geniuses they are not. If they were, we wouldn't be in this godawful mess we call an economy. But that's all right. We mostly aren't geniuses either, and that is why we need simplistic answers to simple problems.

However, if there is a genius residing among them perhaps he can dig through the complexities and find the excuse for what seems to me a simplistic question. Why don't we have a simple tax that simply collects enough taxes to do what we need to do and then gets the hell out of the way?

We citizens have been paying into social security for over fifty years to ensure our retirement. We realize many expenses have been added. We realize there are more retired persons living longer today than earlier. The fact remains that social security collects more today ($275.5 billion) than it pays out ($269.4 billion), even with all those additions and growth in numbers of retirees. It has done so for most of its history. How did it go broke? Forget the vast quantities of interest that the surpluses for forty years should have earned. Where is the cash? Where is the amount collected?

Any private citizen responsible for a private insurance company with a comparable record would have a return address of Federal Prison, Leavenworth, Kansas. David Stockman said as much shortly before his departure from the Office of the Management of the Budget: "If the SEC had jurisdiction over the executive and legislative branches in such matters, many of us would be in jail."

That's the problem with complexities. They create a myriad of excuses and curtains behind which to hide unconscionable acts. It's time for simplicity.

Let's start with simplicity in taxation. Let's start with a consumption tax. I think we will be amazed by the amount of simplicity there is to government financing once that curtain is raised on the treasury.

It will be so simplistic that we idiotic citizens may be able to cast a competent vote.

CHAPTER 9

Myths of the Income Tax

I NEVER CEASE TO BE amazed by the number of people who are thoroughly convinced that, while the income tax may have a few flaws, it is overall a wonderful tax. In fact, many of these people believe it is a perfect tax. And not only is it perfect, it is so established and institutionalized, any attempt to replace it would be a disaster. These people believe its loss, as our principal tax, would mean the destruction of many of the traditions we hold dear, of what makes America great.

Among the myriad of good reasons to retain the current tax system, the one mentioned most often is the support of charities. It is claimed that the charitable deduction is key to the financial survival of every charity we possess. It is presumed that our churches, our private school systems, our museums, our symphony orchestras, our medical research foundations, the Girl Scouts and Boy Scouts, the Red Cross, the United Way, and disaster relief funds such as Red Cross famine relief for Africa and CARE are absolutely dependent on the deductibility of public gifts. Without the deduction, it is assumed, each would surely fail.

Charity volunteers, college deans and presidents, medical doctors and museum directors engaged in fund drives, all assure me that the first questions asked by any potential donor are, "What is my deduction? Am I assured of my tax treatment?" I'm told that without the deduction, the contributions would be zilch.

Well, I say Garbage! Not that the volunteers' fears aren't real or that their statements aren't sincere. It is just that their anxieties and beliefs are unfounded. These questions are asked because of the system, not because it is a prerequisite to the contribution.

We had churches, and churches were supported for centuries before the abortive idea of an income tax was ever conceived. The Catholic Church became one of the richest institutions in the world before there was an income tax. It is only getting into financial difficulty now, *after* the imposition of the tax. The greatest cathedrals were erected in Europe, the U.S., and Latin America largely from donations whose donors never heard of an income tax, much less a deduction.

Harvard, Yale, Dartmouth, Cambridge, Oxford, and virtually every other major privately funded college in the world were endowed without one cent being deducted by any donor.

The Pasteurs managed to accomplish miracles without one tax-deductible gift, and symphony orchestras flourished simultaneously throughout the world. The funding of the greatest museums in the world originated from the people's desire to collect things of beauty, to preserve them for posterity, and to ensure that the pleasures and joys of such might be shared by all. There was not a second's equivocation concerning a tax deduction in the mind of any donor.

The Red Cross was founded fifty years before the Sixteenth Amendment was passed and a hundred years before it was eligible for any supportive gifts.

Other national religions—Hinduism, Islam, and Buddhism—continue to support their churches without such a tax or its effect. We have no monopoly on museums, symphonies, or Nobel foundations and awards. Since when did the rest of the world become more caring and charitable than we?

I'll tell you what the income tax has done. It has stripped donors of the joy, the pride and the respect which their actions deserve. It has hardened hearts that might otherwise have acted in love, and it has turned gracious or generous acts into acts accomplished or performed, or perceived to have been performed, for the wrong reason.

Americans, historically and today, are the most benevolent people on earth. Individually, and through our churches, we have always responded to the needs of our less-privileged neighbors. In the past, if a home burned, the neighbors rebuilt it in a spirit of joy and partying. They did it with a well-deserved happiness that poured from a wellspring within their souls. It's called "the act of giving." We do it today, but fewer people are permitted to personally participate and feel the "hands-on" thrills. The volunteer experiences this, as does the mother or child that walks door-to-door for the March of Dimes. But their opening remark, "It's deductible," strips the donor of any such joy. It's a subtle way of saying, "I know you don't care; but here, here is a receipt; take it off your income tax; it doesn't cost you anything!"

That's not why most people give. Ninety percent of all charitable collections come in $5, $10 and $20 donations, and 90 percent of the receipts are thrown away and the deductions are never taken because the vouchers are lost or the donors file the short form. The gifts aren't given for a deduction, so none is taken. They are given out of the desire to give, to share.

I'm certain I am not alone, that I am among other Americans in my often felt hurt as I give with the recipient expecting me to record the deduction. I want to ask and say, "Why do you do this to me? I give to you, and you steal from me. You steal one of life's greatest joys, the joy of giving. You negate my gift by implying it is nothing more than a business transaction, a profit by deduction."

A few years ago, for two years, I sponsored a basketball team of fourteen-year-old boys. We went all the way to the National Junior Olympics Championship to take second place the first year and third place the second year. Most of these fantastic kids were from the depths of the ghetto. I remember one who lived with his mother in a frame house. Flattened pasteboard boxes formed the interior walls, and rags were stuffed in between as insulation. Apparently, neither the deductibility nor the "safety net" had reached this family. The kids were prime candidates to become high school dropouts.

To the contrary, without exception, each of these twenty-four boys have not only remained in school, they have gone on to high school and college. Some are even attending special schools which require distinctive academic achievement for athletic qualification. (I should add, these kids were also blessed with a special coach, Dr. Bob Brewka. Bob had a talent not only for teaching basketball but for educating the boys that life continues after the game is over.)

The second year, after the national tournament, I gave a banquet for the boys. At that dinner, one of the six-foot, nine-inch "kids" took me aside, looked down at me and said, "I wish there were more businessmen like you. There are so many others they could help. If only you could show them it doesn't cost anything, that it's deductible." I wanted to cry. I probably would have, if I could have figured out what to cry about first: that I had touched the boy deeply enough, that he had cared to give me what he intended to be a great compliment, or the fact that it had happened again: with the warmest of feelings, he had robbed me.

I did not give that banquet or sponsor the team because it provided me with a deduction. In fact, I have taken no tax deduction for my support of the "Big Orange" through this date, not for the thousands of dollars spent. Neither my name nor my company's name was ever advertised on any jersey or letter jacket. I took no financial gain.

My thrill and my joy were vested in the gift, my contribution to some improvement in these kids' lives, not in the credit or the deduction.

I tell the story now only to make a point. I withdrew from further participation in the program after that occasion—not solely on account of it, for finances dictated a large part of the decision. But certainly the joy was gone. Perhaps others have taken my place. I hope so, and I hope they know the same pleasure I felt until the theft of my joy occurred.

I sincerely believe the deduction loses more contributions than it acquires. That's proven in many ways. As mentioned, the majority of gifts are not deducted anyway. The United Way's prime support comes from payroll deductions. Most of those so giving file the short form and take no deductions. Others simply forget. I ask, "Do you still have your receipt for Girl Scout cookies or for the March of Dimes?" Do you even ask for a receipt at church?

The deduction makes no financial sense anyway. Anyone who gives a gift in order to acquire a deduction is financially dumber than a fence post. It's cheaper to pay the tax. You have to give a dollar in order to save fifty cents on taxes. People stupid enough to give a dollar to obtain fifty-cent refunds would buy swampland in Siberia. Or maybe they could be induced to give to a worthy cause without the deduction by giving half as much as they normally might!

The majority of the work done in raising money is accomplished by volunteers who give their time. Time is not deductible from taxes, except in rare instances such as charity shows by entertainers. Even then, do you really believe Jerry Lewis would be any less dedicated to raising money to fight multiple sclerosis without the deduction? How much more time do you think Eleanor Roosevelt would have given the March of Dimes if time had been deductible? The deduction is not the prime consideration in the determination to give.

I've talked with hundreds of other businessmen who actually become irate, not over the request for the donation but over the abysmal stupidity of the manner in which they are solicited. Businessmen do not remain in business by making dollar investments to obtain fifty-cent returns. The time of the solicitors could be far better spent explaining the social benefits of the donation or the joy of giving rather than the availability of a deduction. The businessman can get the same deduction by purchasing a new piece of equipment, and he will receive a lot more than a fifty-cent return. (He can even get the same deduction for a three-martini lunch with his favorite hooker, provided he invites an associate. And the hooker doesn't destroy the occasion by reminding him, "I'm deductible.")

Businessmen know better. That is why more and more gifts are given anonymously and greater numbers are not taken as deductions. The donor, at least, has the personal satisfaction of knowing his gift is as pure as his intent.

The income-tax deduction is not a supporter of charities. It is their worst enemy. More gifts are withheld because of it than will ever be induced by it. It is persuasion to only the dumbest and least caring. The stupid have little ability and no propensity to give, and they are not giving now. The tax deduction is, at best, a nonentity. At worst, it is a barrier to be overcome by those with charity in their hearts and the ability to be charitable.

The effects of the current tax system permeate our entire economic structure, and the majority of these incursions are now by design. The most obvious are tax shelters and tax incentives, but there are many other commercial deductions.

Contrary to the articles in the liberal press and the protests of Congressmen who attempt to separate themselves from negative side effects, tax-beneficial positions are not created by evil men attempting to escape their just tax. They are created in Congress.

1. The deductions for interest on home mortgages were not deviously conceived by evil men with evil intentions. They were created in Congress to relieve some of the ill effects of the tax system and to encourage home ownership.
2. The deductions for research and development were created in Congress to encourage such effort because the system had eliminated the availability of surplus funds for scientific endeavors.
3. The drilling and depletion allowances were passed by Congress to create additional funds in the economy to ensure a consistent and long-range energy supply.
4. Energy tax credits were created by Congress to provide alternative energy when the world's political problems threatened our supply of oil.
5. Investment tax credits were created by Congress to encourage industrial acquisition of the newest and most efficient equipment.
6. Movie and entertainment production tax incentives were created by Congress to recapture the industry from Europe.
7. Charitable deductions were created by Congress to induce the public to do, for themselves, the things which they could do better.

The list could go on. Obviously, those elements of society that are not beneficiaries of the deductions oppose them. Up goes the cry of special interest groups. Immediately, the laws passed are blamed on lobbyists and political contributions. That is demagogic trash.

The law was passed because there was a problem. There was a problem of sufficient severity that something had to be done. Too many people were losing their jobs; too many production facilities were closing; too many industrial products were becoming unavailable or available only through imports. Certainly, the lobbyists pointed out the problems, and the Congressmen listened. It was their job. But the law was not passed because of greed; it was passed because of need. IBM would certainly like foreign imports cut off. It has lobbyists and the money to pay for them, but no protective tariffs or tax benefits have been passed for its protection because IBM remains profitable and has no need. The laws have been passed because of need, and the history of their success abounds.

The Movie Industry. At the end of World War II, over 90 percent of all movies, English-speaking and European, were produced in Hollywood, California. It was a growing, dynamic industry. By 1955, over 80 percent were produced in Monaco, Spain, Italy, Greece, Hong Kong, and everywhere else except Hollywood. The reasons were obvious. Those nations provided tax havens for movie production. Our government was taking up to 92 percent of the profits on successful movies. With nine out of ten movies being money losers, production here was a prescription for failure. Hence, Congress passed a law to relieve some of the burden. We now produce about 50 percent of the world's movies.

Real Estate/Home Ownership. After World War II, Congress recognized that the majority of our people were ill housed, and that the majority of these were renters. It was decided it would be socially beneficial for the majority to be home owners, with the pride and stability inherent thereto. Interest deductions, real-estate tax deductions, FHA loans, VA loans, and investment credits for builders came into being. We are now the best-housed nation in world history.

Drilling and Depletion Deductions. Energy was recognized as the key to world economic dominance, but our tax laws did not encourage further exploration. Congress recognized the problem, gave relief, and our oil industries scoured the world for new reserves. It found, and controlled, the Middle East, South and Central America, the Gulf of Mexico and, yes, the Alaskan fields.

The list continues. It is used by the supporters of income tax as proof of the tax's value to direct commerce into areas of need. Hell, it created the need. The need didn't exist until the tax destroyed the industry.

Our oil industries are, and have always been, the cutting edge of innovation and production. They stopped progressing because the tax made it economically unfeasible to go further. They recovered when the tax burden was relieved.

The endless examples of the benefits obtained by using the tax system to direct industry and commerce are, in reality, like the idiot beating himself with a hammer because it feels so good when he quits. He probably felt damn good before he started, too. The hammer is the problem. We should never have commenced beating ourselves. To now say, OK, no more beating on face, fingers or toes, is not a solution. To say, Maybe next year we will eliminate kneecaps, is not a solution. And to then praise the hammer because we discontinue its use and allow fingers, toes, face, and kneecaps to feel better is idiotic.

The proposed reforms in the spring of 1986 are admitted reflections of the problem. Industry, real estate, and commerce are paralyzed, awaiting the decision as to which part of the body receives the next clubbing and which receives relief. New construction starts await the decision. Industry dares not invest in new equipment until the effects of the reformed laws are determined. Businessmen wait to decide on expansion or contraction. None of this occurs because the tax system is good and gives direction, but because these vital business decisions must await the determination of the extent of the next beating.

Any tax law should collect taxes, and taxes only. To create a tax law to determine which business will prosper is ridiculous. To praise it for relieving the pain which it initiated is insane.

Congressmen, Senators, and well-meaning neophytes point to the innumerable and desirable social needs that have been addressed by income tax considerations.

1. The rich pay more because they are the greatest beneficiaries of this nation's largesse. The rich are able to pay more, and they should pay more.
2. The poor pay less because they have not yet reaped the rewards. They need help in acquiring the benefits. They have less with which to pay, and they should not be burdened.
3. The income tax is a great leveler. It's a Robin Hood, which equalizes our society by taking from the rich and giving to the poor.
4. Social and economic problems can be addressed by Congress giving special tax incentives to industry and individuals. The problems can, thus, be resolved by Congressional direction.

Suppose that all of these applications are true and absolutely worthwhile, that they are supported one hundred percent by every citizen, and that they are critical to our national economy, our social well-being, and our national defense.

So what! We are analyzing the method by which we raise the taxes to support our government and the services we require of it, nothing else. An excellent argument can be made that a large part of our problems have been created by this exact procedure of mixing social and economic programs with tax collection. It's like mixing apples with oranges, trying to blend in a few bananas on the side, and then wondering who's going to eat the mess.

The purpose of a tax is to collect a tax. We need a tax that will do this with absolutely zero consideration of other applications. The fact that we have attempted to justify a bad tax by incorporating other goals says nothing. Whether it is a good or bad tax should be determined by its effectiveness in collecting the required revenues, not by its ability to level society. If we need income averaging for the rich to pay more and the poor to pay less, for the government to direct the economy in some manner or to control social justice, so be it.

Pass another law. Let the tax law stand on its own merit; let the new social law stand on its own feet. Let the results of each be evaluated individually, and don't mix the two. The Senate and the House are fully capable of writing two laws. We have 535 men and women earning an average of $75,000 per annum. They are provided staffs and budgets costing over $1 million per annum each. They have free postage and a world of other perks. If any one of them is incompetent to write a second law, be assured there are numerous others standing in the wings, lusting for the opportunity to try.

I do not believe the majority of Americans have any interest whatsoever in leveling income. I do not believe they feel it is just to tax the achievers not only more but also at a higher rate. I certainly do not believe the majority want Congress to orchestrate and direct a national social system and economy straight from Washington.[1]

That is what I believe, but my belief doesn't matter, not to the tax law. If we are convinced, as a nation, that it is desirable for everyone to be entitled to exactly the same income, regardless of contribution in effort, time, risk, intelligence, or value, pass a law. It's easy to write, I can write it here in four paragraphs.

As of this date, every American will have a net worth of not more and not less than $50,000 and an annual income of not more nor less than $25,000.

All assets of all privileged parties in excess of that amount are hereby the property of the state for safe-

---

[1] Nationally planned economies and social systems, historically, do not work. Five hundred and thirty-five men and women sitting in Washington are ill equipped to determine the gross needs and desires of a 230-million-person marketplace. The majority of Congressmen have never run even a small business or faced the awesome task of meeting a minimal payroll. They are, certainly, not qualified to commence operating what would be the largest business in the world, the economy of the United States.

keeping, until they can be redistributed to those with less, to level everyone's net worth to $50,000. Any income over $25,000 earned in any year will be turned over to the Council of Redistribution of the U.S. All excess assets and income in excess of the maximum will be transferred not later than December 31 of each calendar year, commencing December 31, 1986.

Those less privileged will prepare an annual statement of income and assets, also to be submitted to the council annually, commencing not later than December 31, 1986. Supplementary distribution for leveling to $25,000 income and $50,000 net worth will occur no later than February twenty-eight of the subsequent year.

Failure to submit either filing is punishable by not more than expropriation of all assets and all income, and by incarceration for not more than 100 years.

There, it's done. Perhaps it's good, perhaps it's bad. Make your own decision, but make the decision based on facts and anticipated results. Decide, then vote. Vote for the political candidate who promises to get the new law passed. Only please, for God's sake, don't bury it in a tax law! Don't hide it and say that's not what we really mean. Because that's exactly what leveling and equalization mean. Through the tax law, we are expropriating a portion of the assets of the wealthy and middle class for the benefit of those less fortunate. The desire to help them is an admirable intent, but it does not justify the theft of the assets of others in the disguise of a divesting, counterproductive tax. Ask any taxpayer next April 15 whether or not an element of his wealth has been expropriated. The answer is obvious.

Leveling, too, has a problem. It, too, doesn't work. The concept of leveling incorrectly presumes that wealth is finite and that the number of people to possess wealth is finite. It presumes that in order for the poor to have more

(1) the rich must be given less or (2) there must be fewer poor among whom to divide that which is available to them.

Neither is correct. Wealth is not limited; it is not even a substance. It is a reaction. It is the result of an action.

Example: I mow a lawn and am paid $1. I buy $1 worth of food from the grocer, who pays for $1 worth of his accountant's time, who pays his office supply store $1, whose owner's lawn I will mow again next week. By the growing season's end not one new $1 bill has been printed but four people have benefited twenty-three times from the value of $4 for an "oversimplified" creation of $92 worth of new wealth. This new wealth is the result of an action that created an increase not in money but in that money's velocity.

Income leveling takes out a vital step. It takes from the grocer, the accountant, and the home owner 33⅓ cents each, thus decreasing each party's wealth, but leaves the lawn unmowed. Each time the step is repeated the value of the neighborhood goes down another notch and the ability to repair it is decreased by $1.

Leveling is tantamount to saying the tidal wave that struck Bangladesh was good because it resolved the famine. Sure, it resolved the famine for about 50,000 souls. They're not hungry anymore. They're dead. Now, however, the land is laid waste; there is less food than before; and what's left is contaminated and not edible. Everyone remaining is hungry. It sure eliminated the problem for the 50,000, but it created bigger problems for 3 million others. To make the wealthy and middle class poor does not alleviate the pain of the poor. It simply eliminates potential solutions by making everyone poor.

Taking from the rich and giving to the impoverished by any means does this. It punishes success and rewards failure. It's like the flood. It destroys the base from which jobs, income, food, clothing, and shelter are derived. Eliminating 50,000 hungry accomplishes nothing if it creates millions more.

Very few people obtain their wealth by digging gold from the ground. They obtain it by producing more and better goods and services for less cost than their competitors. To take away the ability to continue production, to create more jobs, to provide an opportunity for others to climb the same ladder is like praising the "flood which cures famine."

Nothing herein is meant to imply a lack of concern for the poor. If their plight is our real concern, *pass the law*. It can be written in less space, with less effort, than the one for expropriation.

But, first, pass a *tax law*. Pass a *tax law* that will raise the revenues to pay for itself. The income tax, with all its supposed flexibility, has not done this—not unless the Welfare Department's recent reports, stating the number so afflicted, are false.

The income tax is a lie. It has never taxed what it professes to tax. It has never collected enough funds to pay for our needs or desires. It has failed to equalize or level, to direct our economy correctly. It has failed by every definable measure in its every endeavor and application.

It accomplishes nothing and damages everything in its attempt. It has had its chance. It has had over seventy-two years, seven more than God promised man to accomplish all he could. If it's enough time for man, it's enough time for a law.

CHAPTER **10**

Time Has Run Out

In January 1985, we received the news. Financially, as
a nation and an economic society, we had exhausted all
the alternatives and remedies to patch up our irreparably
flawed tax system.

President Reagan, a man who is personally and publicly
committed to sweeping cuts in government spending and
tax reduction, announced his budget for 1985–86. He
called for expenditures of $950 billion, $178 billion more
than would be collected from an already overtaxed economy, $178 billion to add to a $1.8 trillion–plus then existing debt that already can't be paid in the foreseeable
future.

Under our present system, this is as good as it is going
to get. President Reagan's entire political career has been
devoted to balanced budgets. We have not had in the past,
nor are we likely to acquire in the future, a President of
equal, much less greater, commitment. Yet, this is the best
budget he could present under the current system. It is a
budget that a dedicated cost cutter could not reduce and
that still exceeded, by almost $200 billion, the amount this
system is capable of collecting. And this is the good news!

The bad news is that we did not even achieve the goals
of this, an unacceptable budget. To have met even that

112

objective required a $50-billion cut in popular social programs like student loans, school lunches, farm support, transit aid, public housing, Small Business Administration, and aid to states, counties and cities. There was no way the special interest groups and their various elected Senators and Congressmen could, or did, allow this. Therefore, even this budget, with its admittedly unacceptable and unpayable deficit, could not be achieved. The budget was exceeded, just as all the others have been for years. The additional drain on the economy, incurred by the increased debts, will have its effect. The Treasury will collect less, and the symptoms of our real problem will expand.

It's ridiculous. This is the richest nation in the history of the world. It is fully capable of meeting its every need. It cannot, however, bear the burden of the unconscionable-waste pandemic in the bureaucracy. It cannot withstand the support of real or imagined programs that are unsupportable, the proposed solutions that attempt to cure the symptoms rather than the problems themselves, or a system of taxation that cannot collect the money needed.

An employee of any commercial business who operates in the same manner as our government would likely be fired the first day. Any private business, so acting, would be liable to discover all lines of credit closed, and the corporate officers indicted for malfeasance. A head of a household would lose his or her household.

But, as a nation, 230 million Americans continue to accept the absolutely unacceptable from their government, a government over which they supposedly have unequivocal control. Of course, we don't have that control; the truth is that the government and the bureaucracy are out of control.

Why? Because we don't understand the political institution; and we have no way of comprehending it because of the way the budgets, debts, deficits, and taxes are presented to us.

Peter Grace and 2,000 other loyal, dedicated Americans gave two years of their lives to study the problem.[1] They proved, beyond a shadow of a doubt, the unconscionable wastes and losses in government operations. They proved abuses and inefficiencies in hundreds of billions of dollars. They also proved that the present system doesn't work. The economy cannot tolerate the tax burden, and the system cannot collect enough to pay the costs without destroying the tax base.

The commission did not address itself to the system of taxation. It was concerned only with "costs" of government as well as the discrepancies between revenues collected versus revenues spent. Since it is a generally accepted fact that there are no more dollars available to be collected without destroying the last vestige of our tax base, the commission principally addressed itself to tax saving—that is, the efficiency of the application of the available dollars. Its findings were astounding, and demonstrated billions of dollars in savings potential.

To what avail? To no avail. The report is being scoffed at by the abusers and ignored by the citizens. Why? They don't understand it. One million is difficult to understand. One thousand times a million is a billion, and less understandable. A trillion is a "forget it." And we now owe more than two "forget its."

Economists and concerned citizens have tried to explain the economy in hundreds, if not thousands, of ways. They've explained it as a debt per family, a debt per individual, and a debt in dollar bills that would encircle the earth so many times if laid end to end. None of these have

---

[1] Peter Grace—an acknowledged management expert, Chairman of the President's Private Sector Survey of Cost Controls, better known as the Grace Commission. Grace and the others gave of their own time at no cost to government. He took the time from his own career and company (Peter Grace Company, of which he was chief executive officer and largest shareholder) to make the study.

explained the problem in understandable, much less meaningful, language.

To the average American, $975 billion is read as 975 somethings, somethings that are uncontrollable, beyond concern, and don't relate to me. Everett Dirksen expressed it best on the floor of the Senate with his statement ". . . a billion here, a billion there, a billion somewhere else, soon adds up to *real* money!"

To the average American, real money is computed in much lower figures than billions or trillions. The common American will drive across town and spend two hours' time to save $2.00 or $3.00 on a sale. He will drive to the next county to save 1 or 2 percent on a $100 purchase. This he understands, and this is the only way to bring comprehension to the entire tax system and the needs of our economy.

More important, it is how we must pay our national debts and our national expenses. Regardless of where the government obtains the money, it is ultimately paid by us at the point of consumption, a few dollars at a time. If it were admitted and printed on our sales receipts, it would be understandable. A 10-percent increase in sales taxes would be recognized immediately. We might not like it, but at least we would be aware of our dislike. We would become more aware with each additional purchase. No amount of fine print in the tax law could hide the 10-percent increase at the cash register. No amount of political rhetoric—that someone else is paying or that your burden is so great only because someone else is not paying his fair share—would negate the obvious 10-percent increase in our every purchase. We would be aware.

The hiding of the consumption tax creates the entire problem. All we are left with is gross figures that are beyond comprehension. The dollar amounts are so vast, they cannot seemingly relate to us, and so we ignore them. None of it seems to have any relevance to us, as individuals. It's too well hidden.

Regardless of whether the cover-up is by design or by accident, time has run out. With the best efforts of the most cost-conscious, tax-opposing President for the past fifty years, blessed with a Congress showing more concern than any in recent history, we remain cursed with a budget that is incompatible with our tax system's ability to pay.

We no longer have the luxury of thinking about it and planning for the future. We don't have a future. Time has run out. In fiscal 1985–86, the national debt has already exceeded $2 trillion. This is one half of the gross production of the nation.

The President has come out with a supposedly wide-sweeping reform. It is even being hailed by many of his most fervent opponents. For what? We cannot reform the nonreformable.

What does his plan do? What does it intend?

It's an admitted neutral reform. It doesn't even propose to either raise or lower the net revenue to the government. Therefore, it cannot possibly reduce the national debt or the annual deficit. It simply shifts the burden. It will theoretically give some relief to the very poor and the very rich by placing more of the burden on the middle class and the affluent corporations.

It relieves no one and shifts no burdens. I'm certain the poor will be delighted to learn that the income tax they are not paying will somehow be reduced. I'm equally certain the very rich will be happy to learn that if they sell their business and retire they will save $25,000 in taxes out of each $1 million they receive. Of course, the middle class, which constitutes about 60 percent of our population, will be furious. The rich corporations (the ones that remain in business, having been made that much less competitive by whatever the increased tax amounts to) will have only a few problems. Problems like how much more will they have to charge the rich, the poor, and the middle class for their consumables in order to pay the tax being collected; how can they charge it while remaining competitive; and how many employees will have to be laid off.

Foreign trade remains the same. If it is truly neutral in revenue collections, all should remain the same. So, where does this leave us?

1. Our industries will remain noncompetitive in foreign trade.
2. Our industries will remain noncompetitive domestically.
3. Our industries will close.
4. More workers in our industries will become unemployed.
5. Our relief and welfare rolls will increase.
6. Our annual deficit will increase in relation to the difference between the newly increased budget for welfare and the newly decreased collections resulting from now closed but supposedly rich corporations.
7. The national debt will now require less than three years to reach $3 trillion.
8. There will be more strife, more pain, more broken lives, more shattered dreams, more freedoms lost, and less money with which to pay for any relief.

This isn't a reform, it's an extension of the existing disaster. It's a rain dance in the midst of a flood.

Every single problem (symptom) that has been initiated by this failed system is being exaggerated in the name of reform. All of them, save one. Complexity. The new system is being simplified. Fantastic! The means of our destruction is being simplified to make the destruction easier to pay and easier to collect.

We are out of time. We need a sensible tax, and we need it now. We need a tax that does not favor imports and punish domestic production. We need a tax that we can understand. We need a tax that will accomplish its purpose. In short, we need a consumption tax and the abolition of the curse of the income tax with which we are now afflicted.

PART TWO

A THREAT TO FREEDOM

CHAPTER 11

You Have to Know Freedom and It Is Scary

IN THE SUMMER OF 1985 my then fourteen-year-old son Ty spent four weeks in Europe. In the manner to be expected of youth, he deigned to take from his vacation sufficient time to mail us but one picture postcard. Amazingly, that one card showed a wealth of insight.

The picture, vintage 1961, was of an East German soldier. He was separating the concertina wire dividing the East from the West to permit a three- or four-year-old child to cross the border. The expression on the soldier's face, as he furtively looked to his right, aware he was about to be caught by the camera, said it all. I thought so at least until I read my son's short comments on the back. "West Berlin is nice and friendly with action, but East Berlin sucks. You are constantly being watched. *You have to know freedom and it is scary*." (My emphasis.)

I started thinking, again, about just how precious and fragile freedom really is. Relative to the history of man, it has been known to but a few, and then for only fleeting seconds. We in the United States have been blessed with it for over 200 years; that's a quantity of people over a length of time unparalleled in history.

We fought for this freedom, and it has remained secure to us by virtue of one astounding document, the Constitution of the United States. One of the thirty-nine men who conceived this amazingly farsighted and all-encompassing document reportedly said upon his departure from Constitution Hall, "We just gave you a Republic. Keep it, if you can!" That remains our challenge.

Freedom is fragile. Inherently, and by definition, freedom requires that its largesse be distributed to all, its friend and its foe alike. Its enemies may freely exploit it to their advantage, this very freedom they would like to take from us. For us, who cherish freedom, to deny these enemies that right would be self-denial of that which we profess to hold sacred. Therein lies the fragility of freedom. It is its own worst enemy. It is similar to the relationship between good parents and a wayward child. The child's acts may hurt and even betray the parents, but the parents will continue to love and bestow their gifts with unremitting patience.

Which is not to say that freedom is doomed. Many a wayward child returns to the fold. An occasional freedom is sometimes temporarily sacrificed for the expediency of the moment; yet, it is recovered when it is recognized that the gain is not worth the loss. This is to say, freedom must be jealously guarded by those who cherish it, or those who covet its strengths will take it away.

I do not believe we are currently possessed by an evil conspiracy of covetous men. I believe we are afflicted by our own benign neglect of that which demands jealous stewardship. Too often, when afflicted with what we perceive to be a problem, we have permitted an agent or agency to say, "The problem can be resolved, and all that is required is this small infringement on one little freedom." Too often, we have accepted the cavalier explanation that what we are losing is not that important to our overall situation.

I do not claim that we are an oppressed people. Nor am

I as concerned with the results of the current deprivations as I am with the ensuing potential for mischief. What I am most concerned about is our lack of interest regarding these intrusions upon those rights which should be held so dear. This is the source of my greatest fright.

I speak from experience, and I want to give you some of that experience now as one man's example of government intrusion on our constitutional rights, the subject of this part of the book.

I was born in 1933 in Wichita Falls, Texas. My parents moved to Lubbock in 1938, where I was raised and educated. I graduated from Lubbock Senior High in 1952 and Texas Technological University in 1956 with a degree in finance and accounting.

Having lived through and been old enough to understand the implications of World War II, I grew up with unquestioned faith in and love for God and country.

On graduation, I entered the United States Army as an infantry lieutenant. I applied and was accepted for flight training. I was assigned to Mountain Search and Rescue at Ft. Carson, Colorado, where I ultimately became a test and instructor pilot.

I resigned from the service in 1960 and joined the Denver office of the company for which I had worked my senior year in college. In seven months, I rose from salesman to senior supervisor for the Western U.S. I resigned to establish an electrical appliance franchise in a twenty-two-department-store chain. Seven months later, I was recalled to the army. I sold my business and willingly returned in November 1961.

I came back to Denver in August 1962 and established Barita Helicopters, Inc. I developed the first helicopter traffic report for the city, and in five years Barita grew to become the largest helicopter company in a seventeen-state area. I split up and sold off the company in 1967 to establish Guardian Transmissions, Incorporated. After working in that business for about a year, I developed a franchise operation. It grew in the next seven months to be the second largest chain in the U.S., with seventy-two stores open and operating. I merged the company in 1969 with a large conglomerate and remained for five months in an executive and directorial capacity, before resigning in a dispute over corporate policy. I could not prove my way was right, but I could prove their way was wrong. Seven months later, I bought back the corporation for ten cents on the dollar. I attempted to save the company, but arrived too late. The company filed for bankruptcy in late 1970.

In September 1970, I accepted a position as a salesman with Horizon Land Company and started over. In six months, I rose from salesman to sales manager to branch manager to district manager. Four months later, I was recognized as "King of the Conference," as the number-one district manager of the eighty-five districts worldwide.

In September 1971, I was "pirated" by Great Western United to establish a "legal" land-sales division. Great Western's prior sales procedures had been declared illegal. In six months, the company regained its previous position in sales volume, and I resigned to establish my own land development corporation, William A. Kilpatrick, Incorporated.

From 1972 to 1977, I developed properties in Colorado, Arizona, New Mexico, Belize, Costa Rica, Bolivia, and Nicaragua. The largest property was located in Costa Rica, where I was in partnership with Anastasio Somoza, the President of Nicaragua.

When Scotland Yard informed us that the supposed European bank cartel that was financing this $44 million development had no money and the principals had been arrested as the largest frauds on the continent, we took our losses and abandoned the project. The fact that the perpetrators were convicted and served time did not revive the development. Of course, Somoza's problems with the Sandinistas didn't help either.

I recite the successes and failures of my life to demonstrate a point. My father died when I was sixteen, after an extended illness. I inherited all the poverty I could use the following morning. My mother worked for $116 per month, and I worked part-time through high school and college. We accepted no aid and no welfare at any time. The only government check we ever received was the standard $27 per month salary I realized for ROTC participation. We never requested, nor received, any other government payment. It never occurred to either of us that things would not get better.

To the contrary, I was thoroughly convinced, despite the abject poverty in which we lived, that I had the greatest inheritance imaginable. I lived in a land blessed by God as the greatest nation on earth. I could grow, achieve, work, and acquire anything I had the intelligence and sufficient determination to accomplish. What else could I ask? My questions today are, Can I leave the same legacy to my children? Can you leave it to yours?

Even in 1977, when I was required to start all over again, no doubt existed in my mind that I could do it. After the failure of the Costa Rican project, I began my new employment as national sales manager for Cal-Am Corporation with an enthusiasm that bordered on exultation. At forty-three, I thought I had it made.

The next eight years of my life became a nightmare, a nightmare of government run amok, violating every principle upon which it had been founded.

In the first three and one-half months, I built a sales force of more than 400 persons. The company was grossing an annual $50 million doing what my government had passed laws to encourage us to do. On December 8, 1977, the bureaucracy of that same government closed Cal-Am down and bankrupted it.

Even so, since I worked for Cal-Am by contract, as president of William A. Kilpatrick, Incorporated (subsequently United Financial Operations, Incorporated), I was unaffected. I took the sales organization, established a new company to provide the inventory, and still made $9 million in sales in the last twenty-three days of the year. I completed 1977 still believing that Cal-Am must have done something wrong. Otherwise, the government of this, the world's greatest and freest nation, would never have taken the action it had.

I was wrong. Without one complaint from one investor, without even any alleged wrongdoing on my part, four months later, in May 1978, the bureaucracy decided to investigate to see if it couldn't find something wrong with me too.

By the end of 1980, two years and seven months later, I had survived two investigations by the FBI, four by the SEC, one known CIA intervention, and hundreds of others by the IRS. Not one investigation disclosed a single inappropriate act, much less a crime. You would think the obvious bureaucratic conclusion would have been that I owned and operated a legal, legitimate organization, did business in a legal and legitimate manner, and that I should be left alone to pursue my legitimate objectives.

You would have been wrong. Not to be discouraged, the IRS sent a sixteen-page request for a grand jury investigation of my company to the Tax Division, Department of Justice. This amazing document disclosed and admitted that all prior investigations had revealed no indiscretions. It went so far as to state, in essence, that it would therefore be difficult, if not impossible, to *make a case* by civil or administrative procedures. (Civil procedures were the only legal procedures available to collect taxes which were *civil* in nature.) This amazing document then proceeded to request that the Justice Department impanel an illegal and unconstitutional *criminal* grand jury for the *civil* purpose of helping the IRS collect taxes from my investors, taxes that the same document had just admitted they did not owe.

It went further. It identified me as a "unique threat to

the Treasury of the United States," and it stated that if a case could be made against me—that is, not an illegal act found, but a case *made up*—it would be of great value as a deterrent for other Americans to claim their *legal tax deductions*. The Department of Justice, the very Department of Justice charged with enforcing the law, of securing justice for all citizens of this nation, promptly agreed to perform this illegal and unconstitutional act.

The first grand jury lasted six months. After it could find no charges to make, it was dismissed, and a second grand jury was impaneled. This jury lasted fifteen months. During the course of that time, the IRS and the Tax Division, Department of Justice, broke every law and violated virtually every right guaranteed a citizen by the Constitution (see Appendix C). When these bureaucrats were unable to locate any wrongful act, which their own initiating document admitted didn't exist, they attempted to create some. It is my belief, based upon my personal observation of these individuals, that they perjured themselves and created nonexistent facts to acquire an indictment, any indictment, to justify their five years of wasted effort, as well as their own existence. Each of their initial lies and crimes required two crimes to be committed to cover the first, and then four to cover the two.

With anonymous phone calls and illegal letters identifying me as a probable criminal, letters written on letterhead stationary stolen from the office of the U.S. Attorney to lend credibility, the IRS agents attempted to destroy my reputation with my investors, my credit with banks, and the confidence of my business associates.

All for the purpose of collecting a tax from my investors that was not owed. All with the prosecutors' stated goal, according to the testimony of the witnesses at the trial, that, "We may not be able to convict Kilpatrick, but we can break him, and we intend to!" Only that would have collected the tax!

I won! I won because I was blessed with $6 million to

pay the legal fees. I won because I was blessed with a family of sufficient courage, as well as friends and business associates willing to stand by me in the face of this awesome power. I won because I was willing and able to close my business for five years and devote my life to bringing sanity to this chaos. I won because I was blessed with federal court judges, District of Colorado, who were possessed with the same determination as our Founding Fathers, who decided that this land of laws and the Constitution would not be subverted by a power-crazed bureaucracy attempting to collect an uncollectible tax. If you do not possess any of these blessings, I suggest you, too, become concerned about how this could occur in the land of freedom.

My victory will be hollow as long as we permit the system of taxation that initiated these incredible acts to remain on the books. By its nature, the system requires these acts for its collection. The same acts are, today, being perpetrated on vast numbers of other citizens. The Department of Justice and the IRS as much as admitted it in their appeal of my case to the 10th Circuit Court. They actually demanded that one judge's opinion be barred from publication because it disagreed with them and that the other be "recused" from the case for the same reason. They stated: "We do these things all the time, we do them in every circuit court, we do them to all citizens, and we don't see anything wrong in doing them."

Well, I do. We are casually giving away rights and freedoms to our government that, had any foreign interloper attempted to usurp them, would have been fought for with our dying breath. No giant leaps, just small steps. Not the entire freedom, just one piece, one element at a time. It is never a large enough piece to cause alarm, just a sufficient amount, one small bite at a time, ultimately to consume the whole body without the body knowing it is under attack.

Perhaps a case can be made that such an insidious process requires direction, that someone or some agency is conspiring to accomplish it. Many such arguments have been convincingly made. I contend that our laziness, bordering on contempt for the protection of our rights, in concert with the very nature of a growing bureaucracy, accomplishes the same result as would an underground conspiracy. I further contend it is of no importance which theory is correct. Once my home is burned to the ground, it is of no consequence to me whether the flames were initiated by an arsonist's match or by a faulty pilot light on the stove. The fact remains, my house is in ashes.

Either way, what must be recognized today is that our house is in flames and that far too many of us have not yet even smelled the smoke, much less felt the heat. We have the fire hose, better known as our vote, and we have a Constitution to which we can demand adherence by our public servants. We can squelch the embers now or hope to overcome an inferno later. I say, Let's recognize the problem and resolve it while it is still of manageable proportions.

Incursions have been made into the First, Fourth, Fifth, Sixth and Seventh amendments of the Constitution. These comprise five of the ten provisions of the original Bill of Rights, 50 percent of our guaranteed freedoms. And the intrusions are not small. In one manner or another, each amendment has been laid waste for one deserving purpose or another. Not to belittle a deserving purpose, but there is simply *no* purpose deserving of such consequences.

The majority of the atrocities committed thus far against our freedoms have been committed in the name of attempting to collect an uncollectible tax on nontaxable economic events. In this part of the book, I shall concentrate on how each of these rights, and a multitude of others, have been corrupted by the IRS in this attempt at collection. I think you will, at least, smell the smoke.

You are right, Ty. Thank you for reminding me. *You have to know freedom and it is scary!*

CHAPTER 12

The Constitution
and the IRS

To APPRECIATE THE BENEFITS to our treasured freedoms of an honest tax, a tax on consumption, requires first an analysis of what is at stake. The stake is those freedoms we have historically presumed to be foregone conclusions. Whether you have yet become aware or not, they are disappearing at an alarming rate.

That most Americans have not yet become frightened is attributable to the subtlety with which our rights have been taken.

Our freedoms have been seized by the IRS and used to collect taxes. If the FBI, CIA, army, or any local law enforcement agency committed even one of the numerous violations routinely committed by the IRS, we would already be in armed rebellion. The fact that certain freedoms have been usurped by the tax collector, rather than by the branches of government historically used in other nations, makes their loss no less onerous. These freedoms are precious and require defending regardless of the identity and intentions of the usurper, or the seemingly good purposes for which they are supposedly suspended or ignored.

Yet the vast majority of us have blithely submitted to the loss, justified it as a means to the end of tax collection, and we have done it largely in the name of patriotism. Our patriotism and national loyalty are deserved by this country, but they should not be misplaced. The country is not synonymous with its government, nor its system of taxation. We enjoy a great nation that has served us well, and by and large our Constitution has assured us that the government, too, is required to serve the public well. Taking exception to a governmental act, or to an act of a governmental employee, is in no manner at cross-purposes with love of or loyalty to one's country. Such a mentality would have required that all Germans approve the gassing of Jews or be traitors to their country. To the contrary, the dedication of loyal Americans to the principle of assuring the continuity of the government's adherence to the laws and the Constitution is the highest form of patriotism and national loyalty.

While the payment of any tax is never a joy, we assume it to be a necessity, and for the most part, we pay it willingly. Most Americans assume that all tax objectors are simply tax-evading criminals or some sort of constitutional nuts. That assumption is not an accident. As patriotic Americans blessed with a free press, we presume that our government and its agents tell the truth. Press releases from the directors of governmental public relations offices carry great weight and credibility. When they originate from the IRS and identify the tax objectors as criminals and nuts, this identification is accepted by us as factual. We assume that they are criminals or nuts because our government, in the form of the IRS, tells us they are. The free press confirms it. When we are informed that none of the tax objector's excuses make any sense, we accept that. After all, we need only to look at the excuses as described by the IRS and the validity of our acceptance is confirmed.

The nuts claim:

1. Income taxes are voluntary, and I don't volunteer. (That's crazy.)
2. The IRS has usurped the judicial and legislative branches of the government, and I won't cooperate. (That's a constitutional nut who's gone crazy.)
3. Being forced to sign my tax return violates my Fifth Amendment right. (That's a nut who must think we are as crazy as he is.)
4. The IRS routinely violates the Sixth Amendment. (That's the same nut again.)
5. The filing of a tax return is a violation of my Fourth Amendment rights, my right against unwarranted search and seizure and my right to privacy in my affairs. (Good Lord, where do these guys come from?)
6. The IRS deprives me of my right to trial by jury as guaranteed by the Seventh Amendment. (Go get 'em IRS, this is absurd.)

Obviously, these claims are all absurd. They are erratic allegations employed by the nuts to avoid their just taxes. None of these things have ever happened to me or my acquaintances, we tell ourselves. The IRS wouldn't dare try it. These are just crazy excuses utilized by the nuts to justify their insane acts. We believe the IRS.

Hold it! There is nothing crazy about the importance of these rights. Regardless of the reason for the objections of the nuts, if there is any credence to their claim, we had better know it. We had better look into it. Our rights and principles are not to be trifled with. They were provided and guaranteed to us by men who had lost them and recognized their importance.

There is nothing crazy about checking the constitutionality of a law. We certainly don't want one that violates the Constitution, the foundation of all our freedoms and of what makes this country deserving of our love, loyalty, and patriotism.

If income taxes are voluntary for some reason, we had

better ask, "What is all this IRS zeal to enforce a voluntary law?"

The separation of powers, the balance of powers, and the checks and balances they provide are critical to the protection of all our freedoms from any would-be detractor. We need to ask, "How has the separation been negated?"

The Fifth Amendment is a cornerstone of our freedom. Certainly it has been used by guilty people to escape punishment, but so what? The authors of the Constitution knew it would be, and they intended that it should be. It was presumed, by our founders, that it was better for ten guilty men to go free than for one innocent man to be convicted. It was intended that every American be presumed innocent of any crime until proven beyond a reasonable doubt to be guilty. There was to be no requirement that he, in any manner, be forced to aid the prosecutor in accomplishing the fact.

The Sixth Amendment ensures a defendant's right to an attorney. If charged with an offense, the defendant can be absolutely candid with that attorney and have no fear of that confidentiality being used against him. The right of the attorney/client privilege is as essential as the very right to an attorney, and it is critical to any free man and his society as a whole.

The Fourth Amendment is very specific. It ensures Americans their right to privacy in their affairs and their lives. It guarantees that your home, your concerns, and your person are sacrosanct; they cannot be subject to an unwarranted search or prying at the mere whim of a bureaucratic official. It stipulates that your assets and property cannot be seized for any cause without the due process of law.

The right to a trial by a petit jury of peers, only after a finding of probable cause by an unprejudiced grand jury also of peers, is a precious freedom. The English civil war that led to the signing of the Magna Charta was fought

largely to gain this right. It has unequivocally been a key
to the maintenance of all our freedoms for our entire
history.

If the freedoms or rights of any American have, in fact,
even been infringed upon, much less usurped, and even if
that American is a nut, we are in serious trouble. The
Constitution does not secure these rights to all except tax
protesters or objectors—that is, nuts. The Constitution se-
cures them for *all*. If any American even alleges such a
violation, it warrants close investigation of the claim.

While we ignore the claims of the nuts, each and every
one of the aforementioned rights are being usurped by
the IRS, not just in isolated instances relating to the nuts,
but as a routine course of business on a daily basis from
ultimately every American. This is accomplished with subtlety and with great positive publicity, as a claimed necessity of IRS releases. If we happen to notice these releases,
we assume that any usurpation of rights is a rare requisite
of an occasional tax collection from a nut. We assume
these constitutional violations to be applied only to tax
protesters and never to legal, patriotic Americans like the
rest of us. Consciously or subconsciously, we decide these
crazy individuals aren't really worthy of the same rights
we possess. We permit it to happen in the name of collecting a tax we presume to be legal. We permit it to happen
to "others."

We are wrong! We forget the lessons of history. Other
than in war, freedoms are never lost suddenly. They are
lost gradually, one at a time. Usually they are taken from
one group at a time, starting with small groups with little
public support, groups like the tax nuts, under the guise
of accomplishing a greater public good. Once precedence
has established governmental authority over the rights of
the small unpopular groups, the power is then extended
to ever larger segments of the populace. Ultimately, it extends to all. Nazi Germany was the epic example. The
Gestapo and the SS were founded to control the Commu-

nists. Then the Catholics were included, then the Jews, and by war's end it was the general population. Such is the evolution that turns freedom into slavery.

We are experiencing that evolution here. Rights are now systematically being lost by the nation as a whole. By allowing ourselves to swallow the myth that the violation of a right is a limited tool to be used only against "tax evaders," a group that doesn't deserve the constitutional protections allowed the rest of us, we will someday have to pay the consequences as surely as did the German Jews for their support of Communist suppression by the Gestapo.

The IRS is now imposing, with equal vigor, its new-found powers against law-abiding, income-earning, tax-paying citizens.

If you doubt it, explain away the list of clear violations that are systematically and routinely imposed on *all* Americans, the same violations the nuts have been screaming about for years.

Let's go back to the claims of these nuts, as cited earlier, and see how crazy they really are.

1. *Income taxes are voluntary, and I don't volunteer.*

You have to begin by understanding one thing. The income tax is, in fact, a voluntary tax. The only question is, how is it voluntary? Is it voluntary as to whether or not you must pay it, or is it voluntary to the extent that its collection is dependent on the honest straightforward manner by which the citizens voluntarily submit the information necessary to make the assessment?

There is a world of difference between the two. In the first instance, the total decision as to whether or not to file and/or pay the tax is completely at the discretion of the taxpayer. The second interpretation presumes that the tax is mandatory, it must be paid, and your failure to do so subjects you to whatever penalties are necessary for its enforcement. In this instance, "voluntary" simply alludes to the fact that, since it is impossible to have every citizen

shadowed every moment of every day, the collection of
the tax is largely dependent on the citizen's willingness to
volunteer the truth, to submit the necessary information
voluntarily and pay his just tax without stringent enforcement. It presumes the majority will do so voluntarily; and
those who do not will be harshly dealt with when caught,
an example to others who may be similarly inclined.

A close reading of the law permits either interpretation,
though common sense dictates that the latter interpretation is the intent of the authors. It would be absurd to pass
an altogether voluntary (in the sense that you could decide
not to pay) tax law. Even God had to put some teeth in the
tithe by specifying that it would be paid. God did not suggest, "Send me whatever amount you wish, whenever or if
ever you decide to do so." I think we are safe in assuming
that the authors of the tax laws were no more benevolent
than God.

The courts have interpreted the voluntary clause in the
second way for forty years, and the majority of the people
have accepted it for the same period of time. We are a
nation of common law, and under such decree the established precedent of forty years' acceptance of the second
interpretation is more than sufficient to establish the fact
that it is commonly accepted as the law.

So even if the authors intended it to be the first type of
voluntary tax, it no longer matters. The subject is moot.
Number two is now the law by virtue of its common acceptance.

Still, we must recognize a danger in that acceptance, and
it is this: Any controversy against other IRS violations can
be colored by arguing the first interpretation, obviously a
losing argument, and the IRS uses this losing argument
against its opponents to destroy the credibility of its otherwise sound contentions on many other subjects and violations of rights that are not open to debate. Thus I do
hereby state that I am not and have never been a proponent of the theory that it is my right to voluntarily pay or
not pay my taxes.

2. *Income taxes are unconstitutional because the Sixteenth Amendment was never constitutionally adopted.*

I do not hold with those who claim income taxes to be unconstitutional because the Sixteenth Amendment was never constitutionally adopted. Like the second interpretation of the voluntary tax, it too has become a matter of commonly accepted law. However, there is nothing in the Sixteenth Amendment, no clause stating that the Fourth, Fifth, Sixth and Seventh amendments are thereby repealed. It does not say that the required separation of powers of the three branches is suspended in the interest of collecting this income tax. It does not, in any manner, even imply that the power to levy and collect this tax infringes on such immutable rights. To my regret, it also does not say that such rights may not, for the benefit of laying and collecting this tax, be infringed upon for a sufficient amount of time so as to negate the rights by precedent. This omission has paved the way for a new tyranny in government, a tyranny in the service of this lie of a tax law.

The clock is ticking. Our Fourth, Fifth, Sixth and Seventh Amendment rights, the balance of powers that have sustained our democratic republic for so long and so well, are falling victim to IRS authority. The checks and balances of the Executive Branch by the Judiciary and the Congress have been usurped by the IRS. Some judges are beginning to accept the establishment of precedent. Others are not, so some time remains. But whatever time remains is fleeting.

By intimidation, the IRS is virtually immune from Congressional check, as the few Congressmen who have tried to maintain it can testify. Not one has survived the vote of subsequent elections. They are now ex-Congressmen and ex-Senators.

Immediately after questioning or requiring an accounting of an IRS activity that seems unusual or oppressive, the Congressman is quickly identified as an enemy of the Service. He is then called for an audit, at which time serious discrepancies are discovered in his tax return. Immediately, the IRS's press releases become headlines in the Congressman's local news media. He is identified as a tax violator. The legitimacy of the motives in his previous questioning of the IRS therefore instantly become highly suspect as personal problems. His charges against the IRS then become specious, and the question becomes what did "he" do, not what has the IRS done. The IRS press releases grow in intensity right up to Election Day. The allegations become more serious, and the possibility of criminal charges being filed against the Congressman becomes a strong possibility. All is reported in IRS press releases, which are picked up by the local press. On election day he is defeated.

Shortly thereafter, there is normally another IRS press release, a short one. This one notifies the world that the final audit has revealed no discrepancies in the ex-Congressman's tax returns and the case has been closed. The IRS graciously allows as how no hard feelings should exist. After all, it was just a routine audit like all Americans periodically suffer. Surely, the ex-Senator understands there is no animosity, it is just routine. The allegation that the Service has cost him the election is absurd. Surely all Americans, including the ex-Congressman's electors, understand it was just an audit; no real guilt should have been attached until after a trial. The ex-Congressman should thank the Service. The Service has completed a full audit and proven him to be an excellent American, one who pays his taxes and assumes the full responsibility to pay his fair share of the tax burden. His defeat was simply incidental.

This scenario is not a figment of the imagination or an isolated event. The list is long and well documented. Ask ex-Senator Montoya of New Mexico. Ask ex-Senator Long of Missouri. Ask ex-Congressman Hansen of Idaho. Ask any one of the innumerable ex's to whom this has happened.

What these tactics have accomplished is to lay the groundwork for the absolute usurpation of the legislative function. They establish fear in the best of Congressmen, the very elected representatives who are supposed to maintain checks on the IRS. The lesson of the few is not lost on those remaining. Sure, they know they are innocent. So were Montoya, Long, and Hansen, but it didn't save their jobs, their families, or their reputations. Congressional investigations by their oversight committees become fewer and further between.

This fear extends further. Most tax laws are passed only after Congress has been besieged by lobbyists, lobbyists of the people and lobbyists of special interests (still people). The most powerful, and certainly the most influential, of these lobbyists is the IRS. Therefore, only the IRS among lobbyists actually takes part in the writing of the law. It makes its desires well known; it helps write the law; and Congress considers it in light of the results to prior legislators. I am not suggesting that 535 members of Congress sit whining and sniveling in their offices in mortal fear of the IRS. It's more subtle than that. It's just a matter of each knowing he can be singled out, and each knowing if he were, the other 534 would stand idle because of the same gnawing fear he feels. Therefore, none speak up, and the IRS generally gets exactly what it wants.

George Hansen was an exception. George Hansen spoke up through seven terms in Congress. For a long time, the IRS could find nothing with which even to begin to make an allegation against him. But eventually it found what it wanted: a Disclosure Statement to Congress. In that statement George Hansen failed to disclose some of his *wife's* financial affairs under the assumption that since (1) she was not serving in Congress, (2) he and his wife had acquired a court-ordered separation of finances, and (3) the Congressional Ethics Committee had been so notified and (4) had approved the separation for the disclosure statement, (5) *her affairs were not the business of*

Congress. Over 150 other Congressmen were to admit the same failure, including Geraldine Ferraro, our first female vice-presidential candidate. None of the others had filed any separation forms nor had any even attempted to establish a separation status, yet nothing happened to any of them. Not one was even censured by Congress. Bear in mind that the requirement to disclose is an *internal disciplinary* procedure of Congress, not a criminal law, and there is no prescribed criminal penalty for any failure to observe it. The only punishment is that which may be administered by members of the House (such as failure to seat, loss of committeeship, or a civil fine of up to $5,000). And not even that was imposed on any one of the other 150 who failed to disclose, not even Ferraro.

But then, none of these others had challenged the IRS. George Hansen had. The IRS first "leaked" his tax returns to his opponent in an earlier election, hoping to defeat him at the polls. When that failed, he was indicted at the request of the IRS by the Department of Justice for a disclosure crime that doesn't exist, then tried in court for that crime that doesn't exist. At the IRS's behest George Hansen was tried criminally, in court, for a *civil* House of Representatives Rule. He was convicted, and he was sentenced to fifteen months in prison and a $40,000 fine. George Hansen was defeated at the next election in 1984, and George Hansen was thereafter no longer a Congressional thorn in the side of the IRS.

Any control required by the IRS that is not achieved by intimidation is simply usurped. It is usurped by the IRS's reinterpretation of the law. The law is changed to meet the service's desires by their reinterpretation of the meaning of the law.

Immediately after the passing of any bill by Congress and its signing into law by the President, it is reviewed by the IRS to decide the intent and effect of the law. Isn't that astounding? Five hundred and thirty-five legislators whose primary stock-in-trade is communication, the ability to express themselves, require the IRS to interpret their intent. Representatives and Senators may do splendidly on radio and television, in newsprint and public addresses, but their ability to say what they mean in tax law requires reinterpretation by the IRS. Of course, the IRS doesn't hold itself to its original "interpretation." If its original definitions of meaning don't accomplish its goals, the IRS just reinterprets, reinterprets, and reinterprets. It's terrifying! No man can possibly know the law if it can be changed at any second at the mere whim of the "sheriff," not Congress, not the judge, but the sheriff in IRS clothing.

The examples of the IRS reversing by reinterpretation the purpose and goals of legislation, and thereby becoming legislators themselves, are legion. No better example exists than the reinterpretation of Code Section 435.

Congress passed laws eliminating the deductibility of most expenses incurred by nonrecourse financing, the potential expense for which liability is limited to the pledged security. Simultaneously, Congress recognized the energy crisis and the need for the development of coal as an alternative energy source. It knew that the historic risks inherent in coal investments were so great that most investors would refuse to invest if such investment carried liability beyond their agreed commitment. It decided, and the President concurred, that coal investors required the inducement of the deductibility of nonrecourse financing. We needed coal and, therefore, Congress specifically stated in the law that coal was exempted from this law. This was not by implication or hazy legalese. The law specifically stated that coal was exempted. Numerous promoters and investors accepted Congress's invitation and did, indeed, take steps to resolve the energy problem by investing in coal, with limits on their liability. And like any prudent business person, they availed themselves of the most favorable terms permitted by the tax law. Millions of dollars in cash were invested, and millions more were borrowed, nonrecourse, exactly as Congress had foreseen and permitted. Each such investment allowed deductions from current taxes, which was exactly as Congress had intended.

This was not a new procedure, nor was it a scheme devised by shifty, greedy businessmen in back rooms and cellars. It was a law designed by Congress, passed in open session into clearly worded law, and signed by the President of the U.S. This same procedure had served us well in the past. Tax deductions for interest on homes had made us the best-housed nation on earth. Special tax deductions for troubled industries saved some and delayed the demise of others.

But those deductions for coal were not appreciated by the IRS, which perceived its job to be the collection of taxes. Those deductions reduced collections. And so the IRS just reinterpreted the law. It simply took the position that Congress didn't really mean coal, and excluded coal for deductions. The IRS offered no explanation as to what it was that looked like coal, burned like coal, acted like coal, or was spelled like coal that Congress did mean. It simply took the position that Congress didn't mean coal, and the deductions were disallowed.

Of course, the American citizens who were being so clearly defrauded took exception to such a ruling. They took their case to court, the only court available, the tax court.

The judges of the tax court have unanimously and invariably found the IRS to be correct. Congress simply didn't mean what it said. The IRS knew best.

Of course, not one of the 535 Congressmen or Senators who passed the law uttered one word of protest over this complete usurpation of their legislative authority. Coal and George Hansen fit the same mold.

Such legislation by reinterpretation is rampant in the tax law, and cases like Code Section 435 abound.

Another example of equal conspicuousness and perhaps greater importance is the IRS's interpretation of the principle of form versus substance. The IRS, as we have seen, takes whatever interpretation is necessary to collect the tax. The fact that its interpretation on one collection procedure is a non sequitur to its position on another is totally immaterial to the mentality of the Service. If a procedure collects the tax, it *is* the law, and so it will be interpreted by the IRS in a particular instance.

In the case of form versus substance, the theory of the law is that the substance controls. In any transaction between two or more parties, regardless of how much documentation may be put together and signed to demonstrate a transfer of property (the form), the key IRS question is, Did title to the real and valuable property transfer (the substance)? The method, the terms, the coin of payment, or the statements in the documents—that is, the form—are not material. The theory is that if the payment to the seller is sufficient to cause the seller to release title, the payment must constitute ample payment; and the sufficiency is proven by the release of the title. If title transfer fails, there is no substance and the form is irrelevant.

In a tax prosecution case in the 9th Circuit Court in California, the IRS took that position. In *U.S.* vs. *Carruthers* (a cattle-feeding program), the government seemingly proved no cattle existed to which the taxpayers had title. No title to cows had passed, and thus no transaction had occurred. The form was irrelevant, and therefore no deductions were permitted. The prosecutor even pleaded to this effect in open court. Substantially, the prosecutor pleaded, "The payment is not relevant. Even though the method of payment (the form) may be objectionable to the Service, the government concedes that if there were substance to the transaction, i.e., had title to the cattle transferred, *it would be legal and the deduction would stand despite our objections to the form.*"

In *U.S.* vs. *Kilpatrick* in the 10th Circuit Court of Colorado, the same prosecutor, Jerrod Scharf, pleaded the opposite. He pleaded in essence, "The fact that the coal exists and the fact that the taxpayers have title is not relevant. It is not necessary for the government to prove lack of substance. The government's objection to the method of payment (the form) is sufficient to not only deny the deduction, in fact it is sufficient to file felony charges against the parties for attempting to take the deduction."

It is further interesting to note the method of payment to which the IRS objected. The payment was alleged to be a "money circle." It was charged that the money was simply passed around to make supposed payments, but that it wound up in the same bank where it started. Therefore, there was no real payment. It was like a check kite, he pleaded. Nothing really happened, no real payment was made, the money was just circled around.

When the transaction is described in that manner, anyone might take objection to the reality of it. However, the fact remains, the law says if title is transferred, the payment is sufficient and the form is irrelevant. Even if the payments are as scurrilously performed as described, it is still a legal transaction and a legitimate deduction.

Try a different description of the same method of payment, a more conventional description. *The money is borrowed and it is paid back.* Of course the money circles. The bank loans the money, and we pay it back to the bank that loaned it. Of course the money winds up at the same bank. Return of the money to another bank, a bank other than the lending bank, does not satisfy the debt. Banks are funny that way, they expect personal repayment. They want the money they loan to circle back to them.

The IRS's next contention was, "But they paid it the same day they borrowed it, or at the latest, two or three days later. That's not a real loan. It's a money circle." Fact: The buyer had presold a portion of his purchase and some rights to the balance of a third party. The proceeds of that sale were sufficient to pay off the loan; he paid it to avoid more interest.

Not good enough for the IRS. Why? Because the original seller guaranteed the third party's loan at the third party's bank. So it was a money circle. Fact: The seller did the same thing the Chevrolet dealer does when you buy a car and finance through the General Motors Acceptance Corporation. The seller (the Chevrolet dealer) guarantees the loan to help the buyer get the loan in order to make the sale. It's a standard method of doing business. The IRS was attempting to write new laws by reinterpreting old laws.

This assuming of the powers of the legislature, the reinterpretation of law, can also be described as the usurping of a judicial function. I include it here under legislative because of the manner in which the meaning of the law and the intent of Congress are changed. The IRS rewrites by interpretation. And in its function as an executive branch enforcer, rewriting the law by interpretation, I allege it assumes a legislative authority. It is legislatively creating laws. As long as Congress fails to deny this, it is abdicating its responsibility, and the IRS is taking over the legislature.

Appendix C of this book contains a "Listing of Violations." A perusal of the contents will reveal many more instances of changes and/or interpretations of law that also constitute legislation by the IRS.

IRS usurpation of the Judiciary was and is far less subtle than its usurpation of Congress. The IRS simply doesn't use the Judiciary. It bypasses the U.S. District Court, the trial level of the Federal Judiciary.

Until 1984, tax disputes were tried in a very interesting tax court. It was presided over by a judge who did not even pretend to be an employee of the judiciary, the branch of government that supposedly provides the checks and balances on a part of the Federal Executive branch, the IRS.

To the contrary, this judge was an employee of and his wages were paid by the IRS. The large majority of the judges were appointed from the ranks of IRS prosecutors —nine out of twelve, in fact. Uniquely, these judges were empowered to appoint assistant tax court judges with the full authority of the appointing judge. Needless to say, an even larger percentage of these assistant judges were appointed from the ranks of IRS prosecutors. None were appointed by the President, as required by the Constitution, and none required the approval of the Senate, as is also required by the Constitution.

Even the courtroom did not belong to the Judiciary. It was rented by the IRS, which provided it for its employees, the judges and assistant judges.

The possibility that these magistrates—so appointed, so serving, and so paid—would be less than unbiased or perhaps influenced by their employer was lost among all the other potential abuses inherent to this court. The procedure was so rife with possibilities for abuse, so clearly adverse to constitutional intent, so alien to the required checks and balances, and so foreign to the principle requiring a judge's disqualification to preside over any dispute in which there was even the remote possibility of personal interest, that such minor discrepancies were not worthy of consideration.

Congress did change this procedure in 1984. It made the judges Article III judges and placed them under the authority of the Judicial Branch. They are now appointed for terms of fifteen years, and they receive their pay from the Judicial appropriation.

Obviously the new law relieves some of the immediate concerns. However, it leads to others. Since the judges are no longer on the Executive Branch's payroll and are assured of fifteen-year terms, they are less beholden to the IRS, but *they are still the same judges as before.* Since nine of the twelve were tax prosecutors before becoming judges, we are left with the same predisposed biases as before the transfer to new bosses.

I am informed, and it is general knowledge, that prior

to the appointment of new or replacement Tax Court judges, the majority of the investigation of a person's fitness for the judicial job is performed by the IRS. I am further informed that the fitness report by the IRS is the primary report relied upon for appointment and confirmation.

To some extent, even this small recapture of freedom is encouraging. It proves that the power to reclaim rights still exists. But it also vividly demonstrates how difficult a lost freedom is to reclaim. The IRS yields a little; but in light of its control of fitness reports, this is damn little.

Of course, the most troublesome questions remain, regardless of how well this reform works out. How in blazes did any such procedure ever come into effect in the first place? More important, why did it take sixty years, from 1924 until 1984, for the reform to occur? And most important of all, why is the reform being watered down by permitting the IRS, a proponent in any procedure the court ever hears, even to comment on the appointment, much less prepare the primary fitness report?

Thus, checks and balances are void. The IRS now legislates the tax laws through intimidation and interpretation. It enforces the laws it creates through its constitutional authority as an agent of the Executive Branch, and if anyone disagrees the IRS decides the debate in its own court. Guess who loses.

3. *Being forced to file my tax return violates my Fifth Amendment right.*

The Fifth Amendment states:

> No person shall be held to answer for a capital, or other infamous crime, unless on a presentment or indictment of a Grand Jury, except in cases arising in the land or naval forces, or in the militia, when in actual service in time of war or public danger; nor shall any person be subject for the same offense to be twice put in jeopardy of life or limb; nor shall be compelled in any criminal

case to be a witness against himself, nor be deprived of
life, liberty or property, without due process of law;
nor shall private property be taken for public use with-
'out just compensation.

The Fifth Amendment is the cornerstone of our freedom. It requires the burden of proof to be borne solely by
the government in any criminal prosecution. The presumption of innocence, until disproven beyond a reasonable doubt, inherently permits the accused to say nothing.
The accused certainly is not required to perform an act or
make a statement which, of itself, creates a crime that does
not otherwise exist if the act or statement is not performed. Any exception is obvious entrapment, and it
makes a shambles of the Fifth Amendment.

The IRS requires just such an act annually, not of criminals or nuts but of every taxpayer. Each year, every taxpayer must sign his tax return under the terms of this
statement: "Under penalties of perjury, I declare that I
have examined this return and accompanying schedules
and statements, and to the best of my knowledge and belief, they are true, correct, and complete."[1]

"Under penalties of perjury . . ."

To be required to make this statement is a direct violation of the Fifth Amendment, but if you fail to sign your
1040, it will be returned for your signature. You have the
right to say nothing, but by signing your return you waive
that right. The IRS *forces* you to sign, and it thereby
coerces you into waiving *your right,* an act the Constitution
forbids of any branch of government. It forces you to do
that which the Constitution says you cannot be forced to
do.

Tick . . . Tock . . . Tick . . . Tock . . .

---

[1] Department of the Treasury, Internal Revenue Service, *1040 Federal
Income Tax Forms and Instructions* (Cincinnati, Ohio: Internal Revenue
Service, 1984).

Hear the clock?

Tick . . . Tock . . .

Read the Fifth Amendment again. Where does it state ". . . witness against oneself, *except in the instance of tax collections*"?

Tick . . . Tock . . . Tick . . . Tock . . .

Read the Sixteenth Amendment again. Where does it say the Fifth Amendment is suspended for the necessities of this tax?

Precedence isn't gaining on us, it has caught us. To our eternal shame, no more ticks . . . and no more tocks . . . are required. The clock has struck midnight. With the exception of "source," you have no Fifth Amendment right in relation to this abominable tax.

The courts now hold that this right against self-incrimination extends only to the source of income and not to any other elements of the tax return. In other words, if the source of your income is an illegal source—that is, prostitution, drugs, and so forth—you are not forced to disclose the source. The courts hold that all other information *must* be disclosed and that no Fifth Amendment right exists.

Isn't this great?

Try filing a return stating: "Income: $100,000; Source: I refuse to answer based on my right." See how long it takes for the FBI to show up on your doorstep.

And so this one small element of the right that has been preserved by the courts accomplishes exactly the opposite of the intent of the Fifth Amendment. It does not protect against self-incrimination; it becomes self-incriminating because the IRS routinely shares its information with other agencies and has done so for years. It brags, when all else failed, the IRS "got" Al Capone. Isn't that great? Let's see, first we get the unpopular groups, the Commies, then the gangsters, then the Catholics, then the Jews . . .

This unconscionable intrusion into a sacred right is not inadvertent. In every other instance, where any possible denial of this right is presented, the right is preserved to the extreme. The same judge who rules that the Fifth Amendment right extends only to the source in relation to a tax return will invariably rule that not even a deposition in a civil matter may be required of a party as long as a collateral criminal action is pending. It is a fact recognized by every court that any waiver of the Fifth, without a court-ordered stipulation to the contrary, may be construed as a total waiver of the right. The defendant is not permitted to testify only to the extent that the testimony is beneficial to him and then rely on the Fifth to avoid rendering that testimony to the contrary. Therefore, any waiver is a total waiver.

Conversely, it is a legal principle of long standing, and it is still recognized as such, that the "taking of the Fifth" is extremely prejudicial. This fact is so firmly established that federal prosecutors are *forbidden* to call a witness who they know will take the Fifth, if their purpose is to force him to take the Fifth. For a prosecutor to do so before a grand jury is grounds for dismissal of any indictment presented by a jury that has been so prejudiced. To do so before a petit jury is grounds for an immediate mistrial. Yet, virtually every judge in every district rules exactly opposite in relation to income tax returns.

The first response of most people to this intrusion is, "So what? If a taxpayer makes $100,000 selling dope, running numbers, or as a hit man, he should go to jail." Wrong. Criminals should certainly be punished if caught and found guilty, but not because they are forced to waive a right or stand prosecution for an alternative process. Who do we think the Fifth Amendment is intended to protect? People who are not charged with a crime? A person does not need protection against self-incrimination for a crime he is not charged with committing. Only the person so charged, or the person contingently so chargeable, has any need for such a right, and the Fifth Amendment was adopted solely for such a person's benefit. To deny this right to that person denies it to all of us, and for all of us this privilege is now being refuted by the IRS. The precedence has been established by the courts.

I'm not talking about habitual criminals, I'm talking about you and me. I'm talking about how an ordinary citizen can be routinely entrapped into committing an act that becomes a crime which would not be illegal if the Fifth Amendment hadn't been laid waste for the benefit of supporting an abominable system of taxation. I'm talking about the routine perpetuation of precisely that procedure against hundreds of honest, taxpaying, loyal Americans.

The payment of taxes is *a civil act*. The failure to pay the correct amount is punishable under civil law only by fines and payment of damages, interest, and the correct tax.

The signing of the tax return under the penalties of perjury converts any such failure to pay the correct tax to *a criminal offense*. Perjury is criminal and is punishable by imprisonment. Your signature converts the government's rights for collection from a civil to a criminal procedure, or to any combination most favorable to the IRS.

It gets worse.

As an ordinary taxpayer, not a protester, the burden of proof for deductions rests solely on you. You and your accountant read and rely on the tax law as written by Congress. The IRS has now declared that Congress doesn't mean coal when it says coal, and the tax courts have sustained this. Suppose you have, in good faith, taken a coal deduction and declared the deduction to be correct under the penalties of perjury. You have perjured yourself, committed a criminal act. You are now subject to incarceration under the penalties of the criminal act of perjury.

You have been entrapped. Without the government's violation of your Fifth Amendment right, taxes are civil. If you are wrong in your interpretation of the law, your liability under the civil law should be only the payment of the correct tax and, possibly, interest and penalties. It should not be a crime. No crime was intended by you, the entire act on your part was in the spirit of being a good, honest, law-abiding, taxpaying, burden-sharing American. But the fact is, you are now a criminal.

Dozens of Americans are currently in jail for this exact sequence of events. The IRS puts out press releases bragging that hundreds of additional such cases are on the docket. The names are available on request.

Yet with all the above, the IRS is still not through with your Fifth Amendment rights.

The Fifth Amendment guarantees that before any citizen can be tried for a crime he must first be indicted by a grand jury. The government must initially present its evidence to a grand jury of the accused's peers for the establishment of probable cause. The government, having completed its investigation, presents its case, and the grand jury decides whether it agrees that a crime has been committed. If so, it must also determine if the accused is the likely perpetrator of the crime and if there is enough evidence to warrant a trial—not a conviction, just a trial of the accused. This is to ensure that an individual's reputation is not ruined by the publicity and defamation attendant to a citizen being accused of a crime in the event there is no indication that the party is guilty. That is also the reason the grand jury and its proceedings are secret, secret for the protection of the same rights the procedure itself is designed to protect.

The grand jury has great powers. If it decides the government is being vindictive, oppressive, or abusive, it may turn on and indict the accusers—the sheriff, the prosecutor, even the judge who impaneled the jury. It may commence its own investigation of the government and the other parties involved, wielding vastly greater powers than those possessed by the agency that brought the original charges. The grand jury has historically been the greatest single protector of our freedoms; it has been the greatest barrier to any transgressor of our rights. The grand jury does not convict, it simply protects against wrongful or vindictive charges being brought. It determines probable cause. It decides if the government has sufficient evidence to warrant a trial or is simply "fishing," trifling with lives to maybe "make a case."

If indictment does occur—that is, if probable cause is found—the accused is tried before the more commonly known petit jury, also consisting of his peers. This is where proof of his guilt is required to be not only probable, but to be proven beyond a reasonable doubt to every one of the jurors. This is the jury responsible for conviction, and if it fails to so find, the accused is forever free of *ever* again being charged for the same crime in reference to the same event.

Apparently, the IRS doesn't like these odds and procedures. It now routinely supplies IRS agents to work as agents of the grand jury in the grand jury. On April 3, 1983, before the Honorable Judge Fred Winner, in U.S. District Court, District of Colorado, such an agent, Paul Raybun, admitted such action on the witness stand. He also identified another IRS agent, Richard Mendrop, as another agent of the same grand jury. Raybun then proceeded actually to engage in an argument with the judge over the legality of such an act. In subsequent testimony in the same trial/hearing, high-ranking officials of the Tax Division, Department of Justice, and the IRS admitted that it was a routine procedure, accomplished in all circuits of the U.S. The representatives of both agencies argued with the judge that there was nothing improper with the procedure. However, the record indicated that in order to obtain the indictment in that case, these same agents may have committed perjury, obstruction of justice, and contempt of court. The record also indicates that they threatened some witnesses, gave improper immunity to others, tricked defense witnesses into not appearing, used and signed letters on stationery stolen from the U.S. attorney to lend greater credibility to their acts, destroyed evidence potentially favorable to the defendant, and violated the grand jury secrecy rules for the apparent purpose of destroying the defendant's reputation. The IRS and its agents apparently believed they could get away with all this because it was accomplished under the veil of the secrecy of the grand jury.

Secrecy was established to protect the reputation of the citizens, not to secure a safe harbor for the crimes of the prosecutor. The grand jury's extraordinary powers were usurped by the IRS to prosecute the very citizen those powers were created to protect.

The case in which all this occurred was *U.S.* vs. *Kilpatrick*. I was the target. I possess all the records of the hearings that discovered the acts, as well as the court orders damning those acts and dismissing all the charges against me. I possess, in fact, the series of orders, signed not only by Judge Winner but also by the Honorable Judge John Kane, who continued the hearings after Judge Winner's retirement. The records show that not only were the charges dismissed for the violations of the IRS and the Department of Justice, but also that my actions did not constitute a crime. It is my belief that the *only* crimes committed were committed by the prosecutors, the IRS, and their agents.

If you believe this to be an isolated case, think again. Granted that *U.S.* vs. *Kilpatrick* was initially hailed by the IRS as its flagship case against tax shelters, but it is not an isolated case. These abuses are not isolated abuses. Despite the fact that the events I've described are *admitted* by the IRS, the Service is currently appealing the decision in my favor, not by denying the acts but by maintaining that its acts are acceptable. High-ranking officials have testified that they do it all the time, in every circuit. They now plead in their brief for the appeal that there is *nothing wrong* with committing such acts, *as is proven by the fact they do them all the time.* Suddenly such points of law as precedence, estoppel, laches, mitigation of damages, and ratification by subsequent acts take on more ominous meanings, don't they? The loss of these rights we hold dear is an imminent possibility, folks. The attempt is being made to seize our privileges, as you sit reading these words. The beginning is now.

Tick, tock . . . Tick, tock . . .

I agree that the Sixteenth Amendment was passed, and I concede that filing a tax return is mandatory. But I also contend that passage of the Sixteenth Amendment did not repeal the Fifth Amendment. Nothing in the Sixteenth even refers to the Fifth. The Fifth Amendment is a retained right, regardless of the status of the Sixteenth Amendment.

Now, hold that thought. The insidiousness of the invasion of the Fifth Amendment becomes more pervasive. Suppose it is applied not just to tax law, but to all transactions and events. Why not? The application of a principle of law in one type of commercial transaction is routinely and traditionally applied to other commercial transactions. If the Fifth Amendment right is not valid in tax law, why should it have stature in cases of rape, robbery, murder, or fraud? For that matter, why should it apply to a traffic ticket?

Tick, tock . . . Tick, tock . . .

Today, while we average citizens sit idle, 50 percent of our original Bill of Rights is being corrupted. Its only defenders are labeled as nuts. Thank God for the nuts! But the nuts are not winning because all the rest of us are cavalierly allowing the principle of "ratification by subsequent acts" to be established. If we don't wake up, it will be too late. We will be foreclosed from protest by estoppel. And since we failed to mitigate our damages as they occurred, we may be prohibited from recovering them.

Don't forget, even laches is not a defense against a precedent with the government. (To give an example of laches: If a party permits a motel to be built in violation of the homeowners' covenant, he may not complain after the fact. His complaint and action must occur prior to the expense of the construction being incurred.) The government is not subject to such prohibition; it may complain and receive recovery at any time. Granted, it takes some stretching and twisting of the principle of the law for laches to apply, but as we have seen, this is not a problem for the IRS. Stretching and twisting of the law are perfectly all right if they accomplish the IRS's purpose—to collect money.

If you can stand more, how about ex post facto? Article I, Section 9, Item 3 of the Constitution says, "No bill of attainder or ex post facto law shall be passed." No American can, therefore, be held accountable for a crime that was not a crime when it was committed. The government cannot decide that it doesn't like what you have already done legally, pass a new law, and then charge you with violating it. But this is exactly what happens with the IRS. Congress passes a law which says one thing; it is the current law. You file a tax return depending on your attorney's, your accountant's, and your own reading of that law. The IRS subsequently legislates a new law by reinterpreting what it says Congress means. Congress says coal counts, and American taxpayers take Congress's word for it and take the deduction. IRS writes a new law, by reinterpretation, that says coal doesn't count. An intimidated Congress exercises the Fifth and says nothing. The tax court upholds the IRS. Honest American citizens go to jail for misinterpreting the *civil* tax law, subjecting themselves to *criminal* perjury by being forced to waive their Fifth Amendment rights. The law changed. That it was changed after the act, changed by reinterpretation, makes it an ex-post-facto law. Americans are in jail for crimes that were not crimes when the acts were committed—for crimes which would still not be crimes had not their Fifth Amendment right been usurped.

Tick, tock . . . Tick, tock . . .

4. *The IRS routinely violates the Sixth Amendment.*
The Sixth Amendment states:

> In all criminal prosecutions, the accused shall enjoy the
> right to a speedy and public trial, by an impartial jury
> of the State and district wherein the crime shall have
> been committed, which districts shall have been previ-
> ously ascertained by law, and to be informed of the
> nature and cause of the accusation; to be confronted
> with the witnesses against him; to have compulsory
> process for obtaining witnesses in his favor, and to have
> the assistance of counsel for his defense.

That's fairly clear. You get:

1. *A speedy trial*—most districts have held this to mean
   no more than 90–120 days from the date of charging to the date of trial.
2. *A public trial*—your family and friends, the public
   and press can attend the trial; you can't be convicted
   in a secret "star chamber," far removed from the
   time and place where you were accused.
3. *A trial by jury*—an impartial jury of your peers.
4. *A statement of the nature and cause of the accusation*—
   that is, the right to be informed of *exactly* what you
   are accused of doing. The charge must state clearly
   and precisely how you supposedly violated the law.
5. *Confrontation by the witnesses against you*—the right to
   face your accuser. An accusing witness must come
   forward in open court before his fellow citizens, not
   hide behind his anonymous accusations.
6. *Compulsory process*—that's the ability to force witnesses for your innocence to testify, regardless of
   their reluctance or fear to testify.
7. *The right to an attorney*—this right has been held to
   extend as well to the right of privilege and confidentiality in communications with your attorney. Even
   if you confess your guilt to him, he may not testify
   against you, nor disclose the knowledge. And if you

> cannot afford to hire and pay an attorney, the court
> must appoint one to represent you at public ex-
> pense.

Actually, the Sixth Amendment should have no application to any dealings with the IRS. Notice that it
begins with, "In all criminal prosecutions. . . ." Since
taxes are a civil matter, criminal proceedings should not
be pertinent. The Sixth Amendment, together with the
Fifth Amendment, sets up the foundation for criminal
procedures. The Fourth and the Seventh contain the
foundations of civil procedures. (Elements of the Fourth
also pertain to criminal proceedings.) The two procedures are vastly different, with vastly different citizen
protections contained in each. The IRS invasion of the
Fifth Amendment permits it to pick and choose the procedure most advantageous. In fact, it permits the IRS to
flip from one to the other and, if necessary, back again.

It can commence its actions under civil procedures,
where the citizen has no Fifth Amendment protection
against self-incrimination and no Fourth Amendment
rights against unwarranted search of his papers and effects.

Once the IRS obtains all it needs by procedures not
permitted in criminal prosecutions, but available in civil
ones, it can and does switch to criminal prosecution. It
then avails itself of the awesome powers of the criminal
grand jury, under the guise of prosecuting that which was
coincidentally discovered in the civil procedures. Once it
has everything available on the criminal side, regardless of
whether an indictment is achieved or a conviction attained,
it then flips back and uses the criminal information to
collect the civil tax.

This is not my own contrived allegation. It is the subject
of two cases heard by and ruled on by the U.S. Supreme
Court as recently as the summer of 1983. The cases are
U.S. vs. *Sells* and *U.S.* vs. *Baggott.* Fortunately, the Court

still holds such tactics to be unconstitutional whenever the IRS is caught. However, the secrecy requirements of the grand jury prevent its being caught most of the time. Any question as to the frequency of the application of the procedure was resolved in *U.S.* vs. *Kilpatrick* by the testimony of the Service's own agents, as well as by the assistant U.S. attorneys from the Tax Division, Department of Justice. They testified they do it all the time, in every District. And this was *after* both the *Baggott* and the *Sells* decisions that reaffirmed the unconstitutionality of the tactic. The IRS is appealing the *Kilpatrick* decision. Its basis for appeal, signed by an assistant attorney general, seems to be: "The judge must be crazy; we do it all the time and get away with it; it is, therefore, legal for us to do it."

Specific violations of Sixth Amendment rights by the IRS are legion. The right to a speedy trial is a joke. For years, the IRS has made this right a farce by dragging out the cases until the legal fees exceed the value of having an attorney even should the defendant win. The delays make it cheaper to yield to what the citizen knows is an incorrect assessment, rather than to hire an attorney. An attorney lost, or unavailable by virtue of being too expensive, is as certain a loss of the right to counsel as of the right to have one in the first place.

We lose the right to an attorney in other ways. For years the IRS has intimidated attorneys by charging them with the same crime as the taxpayer if the attorney has advised his client that the client's tax position is legal. If the IRS wins, they both go to jail. Such a risk to an attorney requires a higher fee, and this in turn often makes advance legal opinions too expensive to obtain. That's why tax lawyers are the highest paid members of the bar. All of which, in effect, deprives most citizens of their right to counsel.

The situation also eliminates the best defense available in the potential commission of any crime, a defense of intent. If a law has been violated but the violator had no intent to do so, there is no crime. For example, if a criminal is caught in a cross fire between police officers and a ricochet from one officer's gun kills another officer, there is no intent by the first officer and no crime on his part.

For years, judicious citizens and businessmen availed themselves of tax opinions from the officers of the court, their attorneys, to certify the *legality,* in advance, of their tax position. This did not assure the deduction, but assured the proof of no intent to violate the law. At least it negated some of the effects of the Fifth Amendment violation. The taxpayer had availed himself of the best advice available. Now, such opinions are either not available or they are prohibitively expensive. The risk is too great for the attorney, which makes the cost too high for the average citizen.

Since 1984, the IRS has gone farther yet. It uses the RICO (Racketeering Influenced and Corrupt Organization Act) to totally deprive the accused of any legal counsel. No clearer example exists of how the deprivation of rights of an unpopular individual or small group can be and inevitably is expanded to the deprivation of those same rights of the public at large.

The very title of the RICO Act tells the whole world who the target of the act is—organized crime, dope peddlers, and so forth. Understandably, the accused has little public sympathy. In the interest of bringing real criminals to justice, we, the people, not only permitted, we cheered as Congress passed the law to stop such people from using the fruits of their crime. The law permits all of the party's assets to be seized and impounded by the government for ultimate expropriation, if convicted. It even allows this property to be seized when a person is charged, *before* he is convicted. That increases the chances that the party will be convicted simply because he has no funds with which to acquire an attorney to provide a defense. *Any* attorney becomes too expensive when you have no funds. But apparently we think this is OK for such criminals. They're just filthy dope peddlers who are turning our children into addicts, prostitutes, and pimps. They don't deserve the same rights we law-abiding citizens enjoy. Right?

Wrong! Freedom demands that its largesse be extended to all—the guilty and the innocent, the good and the bad, the hero and the villain. Denial to anyone of his rights will quickly be followed by the same denial to all. And that is precisely what has happened.

The IRS now applies the RICO Act not only to organizers of criminal enterprises, but to the organizers of capital formation companies if they have availed themselves of the tax benefits provided by Congress in tax-preferenced investments. It's happening all over the country.

To my knowledge, the first such case was in Denver, *U.S.* vs. *Rogers,* before the Honorable Judge John Kane in early 1985, barely six months after the act was passed.

I know very little of Jerry Rogers. I've met him only once, after his indictment under application of the RICO Act. This was at the request and in the presence of his attorney, shortly after a dismissal was handed down in *U.S.* vs. *Kilpatrick.*

I am not in a position to know, and I have made no effort to learn, anything about the substance of the investment programs Rogers sold. Other than that the investments concerned gold mining, which is certainly not in the category of dope, prostitution, numbers, illegal gambling or any other racket, I know nothing of his operations. I do know that legal opinions as to the legality of his programs were provided each investor by qualified attorneys. I do know that the partnership's annual tax returns (K-1's) for the investor's tax returns were prepared by a major accounting firm. And I also know that neither the attorneys nor the accountants in question would have staked their reputations by so acting without due diligent investigations of the substance. Further, I am informed that no unsatisfied complaints exist from Rogers' investors. And most important, I understand that the indictment does not even allege his participation in, nor his association with, any parties who participate in the activities of organized crime or racketeering.

It seems that the IRS now takes the position that the only requirement for RICO to apply is for the "event" (tax event, that is), to which it takes exception and has labeled a crime, to have occurred more than once with more than one person. The occurrence of the second event is suddenly proof that the crime is "organized."

How is that for reinterpretation, folks? It not only changes Congress's intent, it redefines the meaning of "organized" from an organization participating in crime to a crime that is organized.

That is deserving of a literary award for creative writing. The ability to convert the *legal* acts, of two or more citizens of *legally* investing in a *legal* program to obtain a *legal* deduction from their legal civil tax obligation, into an *organized crime* requires great imagination and should not go unrewarded. It's far more imaginative than *The Wizard of Oz, Alice in Wonderland* or George Orwell's *1984*.

Clearly, the application of the RICO Act in *U.S.* vs. *Rogers* is the application of an unconscionable and unconstitutional law against a party for whom RICO was not created. We good citizens permitted RICO to be passed for the good reason of getting some bad guys. Now it is being turned on the good citizens that permitted its passing.

Freedom does not permit discrimination. It is indivisible and universal, or it is meaningless. Let's convict the criminal, let's get him off the streets, but not at the expense of denying him his rights before he is proven guilty.

If Jerry Rogers is denied his Sixth Amendment right to qualified counsel by the impounding of his money (the asset in question is Monarch Ski Basin, a facility enjoyed by thousands of men, women and children who have nothing to do with organized crime), he will be convicted or forced to plea-bargain for a lesser charge. His investors, hundreds of law-abiding Americans, will then be denied their legal deductions. They, too, will have lost their Sixth Amendment rights.

The difficulties of obtaining legal counsel under RICO have been mentioned. Now consider another fact. No attorney can afford to wait five years to receive payment for the work he does now, and even if he should win, his family and business expenses are just like yours and mine, payable currently. He simply will refuse your case because he cannot meet current expenses if he accepts it. Even if he has been prepaid, the funds are escrowed and unavailable to him. Therefore, you have been totally deprived of your right to counsel. No one will work for you.

And still the IRS is not finished with the Sixth Amendment. Should you be so fortunate as to find an attorney dumb enough or rich enough to take your case, in most instances you won't want him, not with the IRS's position on all that silliness about attorney/client privilege. If an attorney is involved with the preparation of your tax return, he must flag the account for the IRS. He must insert a special note with your filing, to alert the IRS to audit this return. And he must call to the attention of the IRS whatever he believes could be of interest to the IRS—that is, any element of your return which he believes the IRS could best use to deny your deductions. He is, thereby, required to violate the confidentiality of attorney/client privilege, which the Sixth Amendment guarantees may not be violated. Supposedly, this is to ease the work load of the IRS and reduce government spending. Bull! The Constitution makes no provision for the right to counsel "providing it doesn't cost the government money!" The Sixth Amendment guarantees you the right to counsel and confidentiality, period! If you hire an attorney to be certain your actions are legal, his first obligation is to you, not the IRS. Tick, tock . . . Tick, tock . . .

Your Sixth Amendment rights no longer exist in this situation.

5. *The filing of a tax return is a Fourth Amendment violation*

against unwarranted search, seizure, invasion of privacy and deprivation of assets without due process.

The Fourth Amendment states:

> The right of the people to be secure in their persons, houses, paper, and effects, against unreasonable searches and seizures, shall not be violated, and no warrants shall issue but upon probable cause, supported by oath or affirmation, and particularly describing the place to be searched, and the persons or things to be seized.

Read the eighth word again: secure. It's a wonderful word with far-reaching implications in this use, yet . . . ? The IRS violations of this right are so numerous and rampant, they could easily fill a book. In fact, they have filled many. The mere filing of the return, which requires complete disclosure of your entire financial affairs, is an obvious invasion of the privacy the Fourth Amendment guarantees.

The requirement to file is not accompanied by a warrant. It is, therefore, an unwarranted search of your documents and affairs. The fact that the search is not personally conducted by the sheriff in no way lessens the invasion. But that's only the beginning. If the return is questioned, the IRS demands that you bring all your records to their office. Failure to do so will result in an agent's appearance at your office and/or home, where he will forcefully avail himself of your registers, totally without warrant, simply by his own presumed authority. Or, even worse, the agent can declare your failure to appear with such documents as grounds for denial of the deduction, declare the tax payable, and seize your assets for payment. Either way, your Fourth Amendment right against unwarranted search has been violated.

The seizure violation is legend. As with the search, I doubt there is alive today an adult American without personal knowledge—if not in his own experience, then in others'—of seizures without due process. The horror stories of padlocked businesses, confiscated bank accounts, forced sales of farms, homes, cars and other assets are legendary. All are accomplished without warrant and without the constitutionally required due process of law. When caught in a particularly heinous act, such as the dragging of a woman from her car in Alaska a few years ago, the IRS immediately repents. A higher authority of the IRS supposedly reprimands the offender and issues volumes of self-serving press releases stating that the procedure was not an IRS–approved act and that memos are being issued to prevent any such future violations. The IRS then commences the same procedures all over again, though more quietly for a while. (Less than six months after the Alaska incident, the same thing occurred in Craig, Colorado; which again resulted in protests that it would not recur.)

As recently as this current spring, a neighbor of mine, a schoolteacher with two school-age children, in the process of a difficult divorce, was treated to such a procedure. The IRS had disallowed a deduction to which another court in a collateral case had given tacit approval. The teacher's individual case had not been heard, but the IRS decided it wanted to hold the money while awaiting the hearing. It garnisheed her salary. Suddenly her net after "taxes" was $65 a month less than the amount of her house mortgage payment, with no provision for food, clothing or transportation. She pleaded for some relief and was granted such, in return for her agreement to sell her house and pay all the money. This was to be accomplished as soon as the children completed the school year in their neighborhood school, in three months.

Two months later, one month before school was out, she was notified that the IRS had changed its mind. It wanted all the money now. She was ordered to be home the following day in order to receive a seizure notice, preliminary to her eviction. She had no place to go, and the children would be required to change schools. The fact that the appraised value of the house reflected her equity to be three times the value of the *not-yet-adjudicated* tax judgment, and was not likely to depreciate below that price in the next thirty days, failed to impress the IRS.

What did finally impress them was the results of a call I made to the local CBS station, Channel 7, inviting their cameras to the festivities. As in the Alaska case, the IRS's press statement pronounced that such action was not the policy of the IRS, that reprimands were being made and memos were being issued.

It's all a lie! It's all policy! Reprimands are tongue-in-cheek, and the only point of the memos is to do it quietly! The intention is to maintain fear in the hearts of the citizens as the only means by which to collect this abominable tax. Don't take my word for it, take the commissioner of the IRS's word for it. Roscoe Egger has so testified before Congress, while requesting *more powers yet*.

Tick, tock . . . Tick, tock . . . Tick, tock . . .

Of course, as was pointed out earlier, every wage earner is also a victim of seizure, without due process, on the receipt of every paycheck. There is no warrant or court decision involved in withholding taxes by employers. The IRS simply takes it. It will close and seize any business that fails to collect for it. If the business can't pay, the Service will seize the homes and private assets of the corporate officers, directors, and owners. All of this occurs without any court decision, all without any due process, all in violation of the Fourth Amendment.

These seizures are the very governmental acts from which the Constitution sought to protect us. Neighbors and fellow citizens don't seize, that's called theft. Only the government can seize, and that is exactly the party and the act the Constitution is talking about.

And now for the bad news.

It's getting worse. Any remaining semblance of privacy

in your affairs is no longer merely being planned to be taken, it *has* been taken.

Numerous stories appeared in the press in the summer of 1985 from Pennsylvania to Texas to California, concerning IRS office procedures. The offices were getting so far behind, tax returns were just being shredded (16,000, 6,000, and 63,000 tax returns in those respective states). In other instances, interim payments of withholding taxes by business were not being recorded, threats of seizure were being issued, and actual seizures were being made, in some cases from businesses that had already paid.

Why all this chaos? Because you and all other Americans were being computerized! You, your neighbors, your friends, and your business associates were being computerized and cross-referenced. This took time, time that would normally have been spent processing tax returns or withholding payments. But don't worry, while this may have been an imposition on you and the Service then, the future benefits to the IRS are expected to be worth it.

This computerization was completed in October 1985. The Service now has total and immediate access to your entire life-style, how you presumably live. That life-style can now be cross-referenced with your tax return to determine if your reported income is commensurate with your way of life.

Your data will contain a total listing of your assets to make sure they match your reported income. The push of a button will pull up the cross-referenced county appraiser's valuation of your home, what cars you own, and how much you paid. Your credit file will show what department stores, furriers, jewelers and clothiers you patronize, and how much you spend. The push of another button will pull up your credit card expenditures to trace your every movement, where you eat lunch, where you buy clothes, who is on the plane with you, and who else is in the hotel. Cross-references with business associates will disclose how much you receive from or pay to each. Future inputs will, probably, disclose how many times you flush your toilet. They will disclose the existence, if any, of a mistress.

Can you imagine how jealous Mikhail Gorbachev must be? Why, it's enough to turn the most dedicated Communist into a free-enterprise capitalist. Who needs a KGB if you can get an IRS?

Tick, tock . . . Tick, tock . . . Tick, tock. . . .

Don't ever think you can escape by using cash, either. TEFRA took care of that in 1984. Until that year, if the IRS attempted to invade your bank account, all you had to do was say no. If the IRS still wanted access, it had to go to court and obtain a warrant, a warrant based on all that silly Fourth Amendment garbage about probable cause, supported by an oath or affirmation. That's all changed now. Now *you* have to go to court, *you* have to *prove* your rights.

Tick, tock . . . Tick . . . tock. . . .

You must hear the clock. It's *thundering* tick, tock . . .

All this to collect a tax? All this to catch a few cheats? Every one of us is being denied every element of privacy to enforce a tax law that doesn't collect enough revenue to pay for the government's expenses.

Tick, tock . . .

Forget it, the Fourth Amendment is gone!

6. *The IRS denies me the right of trial by jury, as guaranteed by the Seventh Amendment.*

The Seventh Amendment states:

> In suits at common law, where the value in controversy shall exceed twenty dollars, the right of trial by jury shall be preserved, and no fact tried by a jury shall be otherwise re-examined in any court of the United States, than according to the rules of the common law.

All civil suits in the U.S. are supposedly tried by common law. I can find no provision for any other type in the Constitution. Therefore, if the amount exceeds twenty dollars, the Seventh Amendment says that the case must go before a jury. You are denied this right by the IRS.

Unless you are able and willing to pay in full the amount in controversy with the IRS, you are tried in a Tax Court. (I sincerely doubt a Tax Court has ever heard any case of *less* than twenty dollars.) There is no jury in this court. There is not even a procedure by which to obtain a jury in this court, which is historically fraught with all the problems described for the judiciary earlier in this chapter.

If a taxpayer desires a jury in a tax case, he must first pay any and all taxes the IRS alleges he may owe, together with all interest and penalties alleged by the IRS. He may then file a countersuit in U.S. District Court for a refund. This is the only way to obtain the jury which the Seventh Amendment guarantees will not be denied. In other words, as soon as he acts guilty and pays up as if he had been convicted, he is permitted to attempt to prove his innocence.

The Seventh Amendment doesn't say your right is preserved provided the litigant pays up first. It says it *is* preserved. The Tax Court regularly tries cases involving millions of dollars. It has been known to try cases where hundreds of millions are at stake, all without jury. It's an absolute violation of the Seventh Amendment.

The act correcting the appointment procedure doesn't address this violation of a very clearly defined right. What we are talking about is far more serious than a judge's bias. A jury can override a judge's bias; but absent a jury, and the judge can run rampant.

The bias or fairness of Tax Court judges is not the issue, however. The issue is simply this: The juryless Tax Court is a forbidden procedure. It is forbidden for the same reason other specific acts are forbidden by the Bill of Rights, not because such powers, if granted to the government, would automatically and instantly be abused by every employee of the government, but because the power to perform such acts inherently carries the potential for abuse. The adage that power corrupts and that total power corrupts totally is as valid today as when it was written. This is the importance of the balance of powers provided for in the Constitution. It assures us that total power can never accrue to a single branch of government, much less to an individual. The Bill of Rights denies certain powers to all three branches of government, and it vests those powers rightly with the people, as a further check (balance).

Even if the current Tax Court judges were the twelve most unbiased and honest men in legal history, it would be beside the point. The provisions of the Bill of Rights were created to ensure justice, even in the face of individual human weakness and frailty. Only a jury of one's peers is guaranteed to ascertain balance against any inequities of individual judgment that may occur. It ensures this in advance, not in retrospect.

By current law, you have no Seventh Amendment right to a trial by jury, not in Tax Court. The excuse used is that a jury trial is more expensive. So what! The Seventh Amendment doesn't say "unless it is less expensive." It says the right *will be preserved.*

That just about does it. We have accounted for 40 percent of your Bill of Rights. The Fourth, Fifth, Sixth and Seventh amendments are gone in relation to taxes. They are gone along with the balance of powers and money backed by gold.

I hate to break the news, but the IRS is still not through. It also wants your First Amendment right. Remember that one, the one that guarantees your right to a free press, "the fourth estate" which rides herd on the executive, judicial, and legislative branches, sort of a free oversight committee?

The IRS and the Tax Division, Department of Justice, don't believe in that right, either. When Judge Winner issued his Memorandum Opinion on the occasion of his retirement and turned over *U.S.* vs. *Kilpatrick* to Judge Kane, these agencies attempted to gag the order and prohibit its publication. It seems that Judge Winner's blasting of the Service and its employees for perpetrating over one hundred admitted crimes, violations of federal rules of criminal justice, and constitutional violations against me shouldn't be released to the public. It seems it could damage the reputations of the individuals involved before they had their day in court. It seems these individuals didn't believe information about their *admitted* crimes should be made public until after the trial (should any occur).

These individuals include the same IRS employees who put out a twelve-page press release on me, the bank, three attorneys, my secretary, and a business associate on *the day* of the indictment, five months before we went to trial. The document was published in every paper in the land, identifying us in detail as the biggest tax fraud in history. We "enjoyed" that notoriety not for *admitted* crimes, but for alleged crimes, crimes that were all dismissed after four hours of court with the judge's decision that, even if we were guilty of every act of which we were accused, no crime would have been committed.

These individuals include the same agents working for the same IRS that orders every employee to obtain maximum publicity for every indictment before any citizen ever has his day in court.

Apparently, the system has been reversed. Now the government has the rights, and we citizens have the responsibilities.

As stated at the beginning of this chapter, if any agent of any office of any other branch of government were to commit even one of the constitutional violations this chapter has described, he would be sent to jail. Yet in the entire history of the IRS, not one of its agents or employees has ever been charged with any crime resulting from any act occurring in the course of collecting taxes. This statement includes the parties committing the acts just noted, who admit the commissions.

It is interesting to note, however, that when IRS agents conspire to help anyone avoid paying taxes, they are quickly and severely punished. The cardinal sin in the IRS is to fail to collect a tax; and they, not Congress, decide whether you owe. Any deviation from this course is not tolerated. They firmly believe the end justifies the means; fairness or dedication to strict obedience of the law is not allowed to stand in the way. If the IRS worked as hard to adhere to the law as it does to collect the tax, I probably would never have seriously considered any challenge to its being. But that time has passed. It is no longer a servant of the people; it is a law to itself.

Indeed, the IRS possesses, by law, its own enforcement rights and authority as an agency of the Executive Branch. It writes the law it enforces by interpretation; it operates its own courts to enforce its judgments; it has sufficiently intimidated all other executive agencies to prevent their interference; and it has usurped half of the constitutional rights of the citizens while subduing them into fearful compliance. The takeover is complete.

CHAPTER 13

The Schism
and the Solution

FEAR OF THE IRS extends to all elements of our society, even other government employees whose job it is to bring charges for lesser crimes against employees of other agencies, for they also are taxpayers. That such fear of the IRS has permeated them, as well as the Congress, has foundation from the highest to the lowest offices and is demonstrated by the circumstances of the William French Smith/ IRS confrontation.

As a highly respected attorney and confidant of President Reagan, Smith was appointed Attorney General of the U.S. in 1981. As head of the Department of Justice, he was the supervisor of all criminal and most civil prosecutions for the United States. He was also the director of the FBI; and he was the head of the Tax Division, Department of Justice. For domestic affairs, there is no more powerful position other than the Presidency itself. But even William French Smith, the attorney general, was not immune to IRS intimidation.

Shortly after taking office, he was confronted by the IRS concerning his personal taxes. It was quite suddenly noticed by vast numbers of newspapers and other media that

Smith had invested in what the IRS terms an "abusive tax shelter." There was considerable question as to the fitness of such a person to serve as the chief law enforcement officer and chief prosecutor of the U.S. The howls and screams from the press closely resembled the well-orchestrated press release activities frequently utilized by the IRS on dissenting Congressmen.

Smith remained attorney general after he appeared on national television and demonstrated himself to be properly humbled. He stated to the world that he had entered the investment in good faith, that it was an absolutely legal deduction, it was in absolute compliance with the intent of Congress, and was benefiting the economy and the nation by achieving Congress's desired goals. He was, therefore, entitled to the deduction; nevertheless he was withdrawing his legitimate request for his lawful refund only because it was *not politically expedient* to demand it.

Smith's investment was legal. It was lauded in law, and it was needed by the country. Indeed, it was an investment his government had induced him to make by offering the deduction. Yet he rescinded his request for the deduction, apparently because he feared he would be hounded from office, in exactly the same manner as Congressmen before him, if he did not withdraw. He called it political expediency, but the results were the same, regardless of how carefully the excusing words were couched.

Thereafter, Mr. Smith's employees in the Tax Division of the Department of Justice routinely continued to prosecute other American investors involved in exactly the same type tax shelters as his. The IRS thus deprived other Americans of the same deductions of which Mr. Smith was deprived. The tax shelters that were the subject of *U.S.* vs. *Kilpatrick* could have been Smith's shelter. If the word oil had been substituted for coal, the procedures would have been virtually the same, the very procedures which Smith had declared legal in his withdrawal of his request for a refund. He had been educated well by the IRS.

Perhaps this is overstating it. Perhaps one event did not spring from the other. Perhaps each decision was independently made. The truth is known only to Smith.

What we know is: He was attacked; the attack was strikingly similar to other IRS attacks on Congressmen; as chief attorney for the U.S., he stated his acts were legal, but he surrendered, for political expediency; he kept his job; and finally, he permitted the prosecution of others for making the same investments and requesting the same deductions he had declared legal.

If you can reach another conclusion than intimidation, do it—I can't! And consider, if there is a lesson to be learned from this conclusion, it is not lost on other government employees. For if the attorney general himself can't stand up to the IRS, who can? What other bureaucrats could conceivably find the courage even to try?

Nor is the lesson lost on the average taxpayer. The same fear permeates every element of our society. No other branch of government even approaches the IRS for its ability to strike terror in the heart of the average citizen. Try it. Take this one-question test.

QUESTION: If you received a phone call commencing with one of the following statements, which statement would concern you the most?

    A. This is the FBI calling. May I speak to . . .
    B. This is the CIA calling. May I speak to . . .
    C. This is the Sheriff calling. May I speak to . . .
    D. This is the City Police calling. May I speak to . . .
    E. This is the U.S. Army calling. May I speak to . . .
    F. This is the IRS calling. May I speak to . . .

The few Americans who would be concerned about statements A–E would probably have cause for concern, and each would know what that cause was. Only statement

F does not require cause or guilt or knowledge of guilt to strike terror. This is true terrorism in its worst form—it is fear, raw fear, of being caught doing what you are unaware of doing and probably haven't done.

IRS terrorism has produced an ever-widening schism between the American people and their government. This is not an allegation in support of my position against the current system of taxation, it is a fact confirmed by no one less than the IRS's own commissioner, Roscoe Egger. On June 5, 1985, before the House Ways and Means Committee, Egger admitted: "IRS employees are increasingly becoming the object of taxpayer frustration with the system." There it is, from the IRS's own mouth. Surely somewhere, sometime, somehow, the message has got to fall on other-than-deaf ears. The system doesn't work!

Egger continued: "It is tragic that some of this frustration is resulting in violence." Of course it's tragic. It's tragic individually to the parties involved, and it's tragic nationally for a people to be so at odds with the government that serves them. It is also inevitable—not excusable, just inevitable.

When an identifiably united 88,000 IRS employees armed with awesome powers accrued over years of growth try to take from 231 million citizens the assets the citizens believe are theirs, there are going to be disputes. Some of these disputes will become more heated than others, and a few will become vehement, even to the point of violence that results in death. That is exactly what occurred in September 1983 when James M. Bradley of Buffalo, N.Y., left his kitchen table, the scene of his dispute with an IRS agent, supposedly to obtain more records. He returned with a rifle and said, "Mike, say your prayers." He then shot and killed Mike Dillon, IRS collection officer.

I knew neither man, so I assume both were honorable Americans. Dillon may well have been the cause of the least of Bradley's frustrations. But obviously he became the focus of those frustrations, and he paid the price of it all when Bradley cracked, when he became temporarily insane and killed him. (Bradley pled temporary insanity and was convicted of manslaughter.)

I am not defending Bradley, whose act was inexcusable. I am simply saying that it was inevitable. And I am surprised that it has not occurred more frequently. With 96 million tax returns filed annually and 5 million resulting in audits (arguments), and another estimated 5 million Americans not filing at all (guaranteed arguments), it is astounding that we are aware of only one that has resulted in the death of an IRS agent.

At least 5–10 million Americans are stressed annually by a tax system that doesn't work and, simultaneously, inflicts suffering in virtually every other element of societal relations. Some will be less able to resist breaking than others, and inevitably some will break.

Commissioner Egger told the House Ways and Means Committee that 789 incidents of harassment of IRS agents were recorded in 1984, an increase of 49 percent over 1983. Of the 789 cases, over one hundred were violent physical assaults. David Hurd, team leader of the IRS Internal Security Division, added that 944 had been filed as of June 5, 1985. If that rate continued, over 2,000 would have been filed in 1985, an increase of over 250 percent. (Exact figures were refused in spite of my request as of the final date before this book's publishing deadline, so exact figures are unknown.)

Representative Ed Henkins, D-Georgia, told Egger that the situation should not be interpreted as one-sided. He informed him that he and other Congressmen received hundreds of complaints annually from their constituents of IRS agents being rude and abusive to taxpayers under audit.

Egger's reply? "Rudeness is against all precepts of training for IRS agents!" This from the same man who admitted to Morley Safer on *60 Minutes* on November 15, 1981, his belief that fear was a necessity to the collection of this abominable tax (abominable is my word). So how do you initiate fear—with calmness, courtesy, and understanding, or with rudeness and abuse?

The National Treasury Employees Union (NTEM) is now demanding that the Justice Department get tough. My God, how much tougher can government get? The First, Fourth, Fifth, Sixth and Seventh amendments are gone; the legislative authority of Congress is gone; our judicial system is gone; any executive authoritative restraints on IRS actions, normally imposed by other executive agencies, are gone. If the IRS is to confront a party on its "Enemies List," and over 1 million U.S. citizens are so listed,[1] an agent is now permitted to carry a gun. The purpose of the hearing of July 5, 1985 (and the expected result), was to induce the House Ways and Means Committee to increase the IRS's authority to deal more harshly with taxpayers.

Still and all, IRS harassment of citizens is not the problem. And taxpayer harassment of IRS agents is not the problem. Both are symptoms of the problem: We are cursed with a *system* that even the IRS commissioner admits is frustrating. It's a system that doesn't work, that creates more problems than it resolves (which are none).

Egger finished his testimony before the committee by saying, "While I recognize that tax reform will not solve all the problems that result from the job of tax collection, a system that is fairer and simpler for taxpayers is likely to be simpler, fairer and safer for our employees."

Thank you, Roscoe Egger. You just said it all. You are absolutely right. Reform of this system will not solve all of the problems. In fact, it won't solve any of the problems because the system is fatally flawed in its conception. It

---

[1] George Hansen, *To Harass Our People (The IRS and Government Abuse of Power)*. Washington, D.C.: Positive Publications, 1985, p. 130. This book also states, ". . . give the IRS an excuse to institute armed searches, send out SWAT teams and provoke dangerous confrontations . . ."

taxes the wrong thing, it expropriates from the rightful owner and conveys to the party with no claim, and it creates chaos.

The net result of these flaws is that two parties argue over the same dollar. More abuse and more force by one party does not make the other more amiable. It solidifies his will, and it aggravates his anger. Reform that lessens the abuse and force may momentarily relieve some of the acrimony of the dispute, but the dispute remains. Thus any reform, be it for lessening or increasing the tension, only sets the tone for the current level of the dispute.

Egger is not an evil man. He is simply a participant in a dispute. His job is in opposition to our interest, but it's a job we gave him. He is trying to do his work in the only way it can be done, by fighting us for the money. But time is running out, and the schism between our citizens and their government is growing wider. It will continue to widen, and our freedoms will continue to be eroded, as long as the present tax system lasts. It's designed that way.

This system is not blessed with a single saving grace. It is hated by every man, woman, and child on whom it has ever been afflicted. It has destroyed a two-hundred-year-old love affair between the citizens and their nation. The mention of its name panics an otherwise free people. It has demolished the most dynamic industrial complex in the history of the world. It has disenfranchised a working class possessed of the greatest work ethic on earth, turning them from producers to welfare recipients. It has turned class against class. It has caused millions of our people to drop out of the system and become common tax-evading criminals. And all this for what? *To collect a tax that fails to collect sufficient taxes to support the government services for which it is collected to pay.*

The system must be abolished.

So that is the solution, and it is the *only* solution because our present tax system *is* the problem. Everything else, all the inequities and usurpations of the IRS, are symptoms of that problem. And that's a wonderful dividend of the solution: With abolition of the system, we can also abolish the IRS.

As history has proven, any attempt to reduce the IRS's powers, amend its charter, or in any manner force its compliance with the Constitution has met with the IRS's resistance. And all have ultimately failed. Only the dissolution of its function, the need for its existence, will resolve the situation.

A consumption tax will do this, and it will do it immediately. Once all taxes are passed to and paid by the ultimate consumer, there will be no need for an IRS. There will be no need for any relationship, much less an oppressive one, between the citizens and the tax collectors. The citizen will pay his taxes at the grocery and the department store, simultaneously with his purchases. If he doesn't make the purchase, he won't owe the tax. If the purchase is made, the tax is paid. So don't call on us citizens, collect it from the grocer.

There will be no need for enforcement procedures against the citizen, for he will have no obligation to the tax collector. And the tax collector for such a system would have no need to:

1. *Usurp our Fourth Amendment rights* in order to collect a tax that we do not owe. There would be no need to invade our homes, our papers, our persons, or our affairs, *because it would be impossible for us to owe the government anything.*
2. *Usurp our Fifth Amendment rights* to destroy the purpose of the grand jury, deny us our rights to life, liberty, and property, or deny us the right to refuse to testify against ourselves, *because it would be impossible for us to owe the government anything.*
3. *Usurp our Sixth Amendment rights* to deny our right to counsel and our privilege in that right. There would

be no trials, *because it would be impossible for us to owe the government anything.*

4. *Usurp our Seventh Amendment right* to a trial by jury for any amount over $20. There would be no trial, *because it would be impossible for us to owe the government anything.*

5. *Usurp the powers of the Congress, the judiciary, and the balance of the executive branch.* The tax collector would not need these powers over the people, *because it would be impossible for the people to owe the government anything.*

6. *Make the American people fearful of their government.* The tax collector would not need SWAT teams, tanks, or planes to collect, *because it would be impossible for the people to owe the government anything.*

7. *Usurp the First Amendment rights.* There would be no atrocities being committed by the tax collector that the collector would not want published, *because it would be impossible for the people to owe the government anything.*

Cities, counties, and states collecting sales taxes don't need such weaponry as the IRS employs. There has never, to my knowledge, been a single allegation of even one of the atrocities listed above being committed by a sales-tax agent against a citizen. The powers are not needed. The tax funds collected by the merchant are identified as taxes, belonging to the government, at the time of collection. They are never the merchant's funds. Nothing of the merchant is taken from the merchant, so there is no resistance to the payment or the conveyance. In very rare instances, a business in severe financial straits occasionally uses the funds of the sales tax in violation of its trust. That's theft. We have laws hundreds of years old which make theft a crime. But there is no need to usurp the First, Fourth, Fifth, Sixth and Seventh Amendment rights to prosecute theft, and hence there is no need to subvert constitutional checks and balances. Theft is easily prosecuted without

bastardizing our courts and our rights to trial by an unbiased judge or jury.

There is no need for tax prosecutors, tax judges, tax
courts, tax liens, tax judgments, or tax audits against the
citizens. Gross receipts are easily tracked and do not require refining. Again, failure to pay the funds held in trust
is a theft. Prosecute the criminal merchant, but leave the
people alone.

The arguments in taxation today occur over the definition of the net. What is deductible and what isn't? What
should the IRS allow and what should it deny? This is
where the problem lies. The IRS wants the maximum, the
taxpayer wants to pay the minimum, and the fight begins.
Each party wants to win, each grabs for every weapon
available. Inevitably, the IRS grabs for our rights. Our
rights are not needed by an agency that has no fight to
fight, much less a need to win.

There is no argument over a level, equal sales tax imposed nationwide. You look at the gross total of the sale
and compute the tax. The only way to avoid paying the
tax is to fail to make the purchase. There is no argument.

Our freedoms can be reclaimed. The IRS won't need
them because there will be no IRS. The succeeding agency
will never have had them; and it won't attempt to acquire
them, as it will have no need for them.

This reason alone is more than sufficient cause to demand a sales tax to the exclusion of all other taxes. None
of the other benefits of a consumption tax even approaches its urgency. As a free nation, we can resolve any
other problems of government that the sales tax fails to
resolve. But any such solution is to no avail if freedom is
the sacrifice.

Today, the IRS is a headless monster. It did not make
its gains nor deprive us of our freedoms with the intent
and planning of a conspiracy for the specific goal of sub-
jugating the people. The events simply occurred as the
IRS grew—as it grew with the same mindless thrusts in-

herent to all bureaucracies. The IRS has no more direction for the goal of total subjugation today than it did when it acquired those powers. The majority of the employees of the IRS would be appalled even to contemplate that their actions have led to the abhorrent situation we now face. They have simply been doing their job, as they see it. The 88,000 IRS employees, for the most part, are good and honest Americans just doing their job with the tools they possess. When their tools are insufficient, they reach for another tool because, as honest men, they want to do the work they have been hired to accomplish. The fact that it is yet another of our basic rights is incidental.

Of course, this void in direction, in the control of these by-now awesome powers, will not last. Sooner or later, the IRS's vast authority will be recognized by an unscrupulous individual or group for its unlimited potential to enslave the freest nation the world has ever known. And once the void is recognized and filled, it will then, finally, be too late.

An initial tentative thrust was made in that direction with the now infamous "Enemies List" of the Nixon administration. The potential of directing the powers of the IRS to neutralize individuals whom that administration deemed to be its enemies was recognized. The attempt failed, but had it succeeded, the procedure would have been repeated to resolve every new problem, to neutralize any new opposition, and to solidify supreme power.

So the greatest IRS threat today is not the actual use of its powers, though Lord knows that use is insufferable, but rather the potential for those powers to be further exploited and abused by unscrupulous parties.

The reason most Americans are unaware they have lost their rights is due to the singularity of the application of those powers, only to the tax. This use is not sufficiently noticeable to have aroused sufficient outrage. The powers are applied annually on only about one out of twenty Americans. The unaffected nineteen ignore the situation, and the abused one forgets it until his turn comes up again.

If events continue on this course, most of us will remain unaware of or oblivious to the danger until the void is filled. Then, we will have only two choices, revolution or slavery.

Americans will not accept slavery, and if we act now we won't need a revolution. All we need to do now is return to the basic rights guaranteed by our Constitution, supported by a sensible system of taxation based on the truth.

Unlike our ancestors who fled here from other nations to escape these very abuses, we don't have another America to which we can flee. We can, and we had better, keep the Republic we have.

Even if every other economic and social reason presented here for the consumption tax system is false, and even if the consumption tax fails to accomplish every one of the other goals it is capable of accomplishing, the recapture of our lost freedoms is more than sufficient reason to do away with the system we have.

Any law, tax or otherwise, that requires the violation of the basic rights of free men for its enforcement is fatally flawed. It is an abomination on the face of the earth and before God! It cannot be repaired, it cannot be reformed, it cannot be salvaged. It is an abomination and it must be destroyed. It must be destroyed in the manner the emperor of Rome is reputed to have ordered the destruction of Carthage: "Let no stone, no pebble, no grain of sand remain tending to reflect its prior existence. Let history record its passing, not its perpetuation."

PART THREE

TRUTH IN TAXATION

CHAPTER 14

The Necessity

TRUTH IN ECONOMICS AND social relationships is merito-
rious. Its requirement by governmental statute is a concept neither unique nor original, but in fact quite
common. Lack of truth will destroy almost any transaction, be it casually social, passionately romantic, or legally
commercial. For this reason society has seen fit to require
it in virtually every relationship in which its members engage.

Historically, American society has enforced its requirements for truth in a variety of ways, under numerous
names, with a wide range of punishments for infractions.

Originally, it was fairly well limited to severe truth requirements in judicial proceedings. As philosophical ide-
ologies changed business relationships, the requirements
for truth were expanded by statutes of fraud, which required greater and more candid disclosure in contractual
transactions.

In recent years, federal and state legislatures have for-
malized the requirement and vastly extended its terms and
implications into virtually every element of business and
every profession. It has, apparently, been decided by governmental bodies that the *absolute* truth is of such importance that the requirements of truth provided by Common

Law for hundreds of years are no longer sufficient. The new "Truth-in . . ." laws, as they are generally described, reach far beyond any requirements previously enforced under standards of common law or statutes of fraud.

For example, the "Truth in Lending" law requires the lender to disclose the effective annual percentage rate (APR), regardless of the method of interest computation utilized. Simple disclosure of add-on interest as the method of computation is now insufficient. It may be the truth, but the law requires greater clarification. It requires the additional computation to reflect the higher APR that would have to be charged for the lender to earn the same amount of money he earns using the apparently lower add-on rate.

The same law requires additional disclosures to specify the effect that virtually every possible variable could have on a borrower's financial position during the term of a loan. In many instances, the law also requires the borrower to think about these disclosures for three days before returning for final signature, thereby confirming his comprehension and continuing desire to accept the loan.

"Truth in Advertising" requires comparable absolute truths. Advertisers are required to make many disclosures on every ad. Not only must the ad tell the truth, it must also state what it doesn't mean. It must relate how many of the units are available, if credit must be approved, and anything else that any reader might think should be included. And all this before any negotiations, much less any purchase, contract, or the incurring of an obligation. It is merely an advertisement, an offer to sell, but *truth* is imperative.

The same types of "absolute truths," to the exclusion of any possible misunderstandings, are included in every other "Truth-in . . ." law. They're included in truth in warranty, safety, insurance, medicine, content, durability, wearability. In fact, it is generally presumed in these laws, and so enforced in the courts, that any disclaimer *not* specifically required by the law should be included as well. Should its omission occasion a problem, that problem should have been recognized by the merchant. The merchant is therefore both responsible and liable.

To none of these requirements do I as a merchant object. It is presumed the merchant has more information available to him than does the prospective purchaser, and he should therefore make truth available. In effect, we are abandoning the philosophy of "let the buyer beware," but the merchant has been forewarned, and any failure to adhere is at his own peril.

The one thing I find strange in all this concern by our public servants over the welfare of the citizen is the conspicuous absence in the listing of "Truth-in" protections of the one event which contains the greatest potential for damage. It is certainly the most frequent event, occurring as it does at least annually and in some instances daily. The financial magnitude of its effect is infinitely greater than any other expense to the family budget. Consider the federal budget alone. Nine hundred seventy-five billion dollars is almost one fourth of the gross national product, and when imports are deleted it is well over one fourth. The national debt has reached one half of the GNP. With state and local taxes included, governmental expenditures reach over one third of the value of the total work product of the nation. As demonstrated in chapter 5, taxation amounts to over 60 percent of the cost of every purchase we make. Though I am a strong opponent of conspiracy theories, even I have difficulty attributing the omission of "Truth in Taxation" to oversight. Yet I do so attribute it.

It is not, however, an oversight I will continue to tolerate. Neither should any other concerned American. There is simply no excuse for it. If it is important for citizens to be made fully aware of every aspect of the interest they pay on borrowed money, which virtually never amounts to more than 15–20 percent of annual income, how can taxes continue to be overlooked? If "Truth in Advertising" and

"Truth in Contracts" are desirable even in the purchase of a home, which normally costs less than four times annual income (thirty years to pay—that is, 13 percent of an annual salary), surely "Truth in Taxation," the largest expense of every citizen, is *imperative*. Currently we are deprived of any knowledge of the actual effects of taxation on our economic life, other than exotic or "average" per person effects.

No one is average. To say the average taxpayer's (assuming 100 million taxpayers) average share of the national debt (assuming $2 trillion) is $20,000 means nothing. To say his general share of this year's budget is $9,750 means nothing. Individually, we are not average; and we don't have an average obligation to pay.

The only information we receive is noninformation. It is the equivalent of a banker telling you that the average borrower at his bank pays $600 a month at an interest rate of 13 percent. Such data discloses nothing to you about your position or your exposure. The "Truth in Lending" law would close that bank and send the banker who renders only that information to jail. The banker's attempt to make that disclosure sufficient to satisfy the requirements of "Truth in Lending" would be a crime. But that is exactly the type of disclosure we receive about our taxes.

Granted, we know the amount deducted from our paycheck, but remember, we aren't paying that. The purchasers of our production pay it; we are simply middlemen, tax collectors. We pay our taxes at the supermarket, drugstore, and auto dealership, where they are hidden in our purchases, and we know nothing about their effect or their amount.

Supposing we concede, for just a moment, that the present system of taxation is an acceptable system. Suppose we are willing to give it another try. We can't deny the costs of those taxes that must be re-collected by the merchants, but suppose the effects are not as devastating as I've represented, that they do not constitute as large a percentage of our net income. There is still no excuse for a failure to disclose. There is still no reason not to have "Truth in Taxation." Unless, of course, our public servants have decided it is better for us not to know. And if that is the case, not only is there good reason to know, it is imperative that we know.

The interest rate itself is not relevant. The only relevant point is that it must be disclosed and its full effects explained. Even if the present system is a perfect tax, it should be disclosed in the same manner as other "Truth-in" laws. For if it isn't, if we don't know what it is through "Truth in Taxation," how can we ensure that it remains a perfect tax?

Whether this omission in our lawmakers' quest for truth was or wasn't intentional is not now important. Any continuance of the omission is unforgivable. "Truth in Taxation" is the only way for us to reacquire any semblance of control over our lives and finances, much less over our supposed employees, the government bureaucracy, which more and more seem hell-bent on controlling us.

National debts, annual budgets and deficits, welfare reform plans, and balance-of-payments figures, none of these is useful. None tells us anything. None even vaguely meets the preliminary requirements of any "Truth-in" law. They contain no information that would permit even an approximation of the direct effects on us as individual taxpayers.

This is how "Truth in Taxation" must be structured. It must fully disclose its actual effect on each citizen at the time of its collection. Regardless of what percentage of the purchase price it may be, regardless of the dollar cost, it should be exactly disclosed on the sales receipt or demand for payment. Only then will we know its effect on us.

Whether a $5,000 purchase of an auto reflects hidden taxes of $10, $100, $1,000, or $4,500 is unimportant. What is important is that we *know* what it is. With this knowledge, we can make decisions. Once we know the cost, we can determine our willingness to pay (that is, to support and vote for the politicians). And we can establish priorities based on our ability to pay. If what is perceived to be an urgent need develops and the current tax is, in truth, 60 percent of dollars spent, we can determine if we are willing to pay 61 percent to resolve it. If a problem of minimal impact occurs and seems desirable to resolve, we can decide if the resolution is commensurate with the cost.

Scrutiny of government acts today does not even draw near such control. To the contrary, every problem is addressed by our public servants as if it stood alone, its resolution alien to any secondary effects. In the traditional manner of spendthrifts, any perceived problem simply has money thrown in its general direction. Little, if any, check is made to determine the effectiveness of the effort. How could it be? Absolutely no attention is given to the source of funds required for such effort, and since the fund source is ignored, it is impossible to determine the effect of the then required tax.

This is precisely why "Truth in Taxation" is not only a necessity, it is an imperative. We could presume every public servant to be saintly in his goals and it wouldn't matter. He, too, is operating in a void. He, too, has no information. He may be trying to do good, but there is no conceivable way he can make a qualitative or quantitative analysis of the effects of his attempt.

CHAPTER 15

The Truth

LET'S SUMMARIZE *THE TRUTH*. The truth is that every tax with which we are afflicted is, in fact, a consumption tax. The name is not important, only the fact that it is collected in every instance from the consumer. If any doubt remains, name the contrary, explain the source from which the tax can be collected. There is no other source. Whatever the tax, the consumer pays it.

Inventory Tax—Inventory has no money. The most zealous tax collector in the world can beat on, yell, and scream at the best refrigerator known, but no tax dollar will flow from it. Its manufacturer may "advance" pay the tax, but he actually collects it from the consumer. The tax is added to the price of the refrigerator, and the consumer pays it.

Luxury Taxes—We may sniff one million bottles of perfume, but there is no odor of one cent of tax money until the merchant sells a bottle to a consumer.

Income Taxes—Income does not exist, other than as an advance on wages, until the product of the labor is sold to the consumer. Any tax paid by any employee is another advance by the merchant/manufacturer on an anticipated sale to a consumer.

Corporate Profit Tax—Profit on what? The corporation's sale of its products to the consumers, that's what. The

193

customer, the ultimate consumer, pays every one of the taxes. They are buried in his cost of purchase. The consumer pays that cost, that expense to production, the same as he pays the costs of labor, raw materials, amortization of equipment, and real property. The seller adds in the taxes of his employees and his profit, plus whatever tax on profits he is expected to pay. The seller has no choice. Failure to collect each of these costs from his only source of revenue, the consumer, leads to bankruptcy. If he misses a payment to the IRS, the Service padlocks his doors and he produces no more products.

Burying the tax costs in fictitious names does not reduce the cost to the consumer one cent. To the contrary, it increases the tax cost to the consumer drastically. The merchant must add, to the price of the product, the maximum tax cost that might potentially be paid. He must build the reserve in order to cover the maximum tax exposure. The merchant may, subsequently, receive non-scheduled tax credits or deductions. And his employees may receive refunds. But such windfalls do not cause the purchaser of the previously sold product, encumbered with the maximum projected tax cost, to receive a refund. Its price is inflated by the projected tax expenses that are never paid. It remains inflated. *That is the Truth.*

Hiding the tax costs in the product causes the sales price of the product to be artificially inflated by an amount no less than the tax cost. If the product must compete with a like product that is not encumbered by the same hidden tax, at some percentage of taxation, the taxed product, regardless of the efficiency of its manufacturer, becomes non-price-competitive with the untaxed product. *That is the Truth.*

The tax on the production of commerce and industry in the United States keeps us from competing in basic industries, either here or abroad. The inability of our industries to produce products in quantities and at a price competitive with foreign manufacturers results in imports being sold here and our exports being sold nowhere. As a nation, we are now buying more than we are selling. In the vernacular of the government economist, this results in a negative balance of payments. As a nation, we must borrow in order to pay the difference. That makes us a debtor nation; and at the current rate, we will have the largest debt of any nation on earth in less than two years. *That is the Truth.*

Since our industries cannot compete, either here or abroad, there is no market for our products. Since it is silly to produce a product which no one will buy, the factories close. When factories close, the employees become unemployed. Today, we have an intolerable level of unemployment. As a merciful and benevolent society, we permit the government to relieve some of the inherent pain and suffering by paying benefits to those unemployed. The government has only one source of revenue, taxes. In order to pay the benefits, it must raise the hidden taxes on those workers and industries still operating, thus increasing their prices and making their product noncompetitive. The raising of prices puts more workers out of work and creates more unemployed. *That is the Truth.*

All of which returns us to the original problem. Profits, labor, wages, income, and inventory cannot be taxed. To do so creates a cost on the product. When the cost of a product reaches a certain level, the product becomes noncompetitive with similar, but untaxed, products in the marketplace. All the other problems become more exaggerated. *That is the Truth.*

A sales or consumption tax that is open and admitted does none of these things. A sales tax is not preferential. It taxes every product sold at the same rate. If the product is sold, it is taxed. Whether the product is foreign or domestic, it is taxed at the same rate. Neither product escapes the tax. If our only tax were a consumption tax, domestic products for foreign sales would not be taxed here in the U.S. prior to shipment. Our products could, therefore, compete on an equal basis with other exporting nations' products. *That is the Truth.*

These are all truths. They are all self-evident, they are all unimpeachable. No amount of rhetoric can deny them. Once these truths are recognized, we will be well on our way to the solution of all our economic woes.

The admission that all taxes are consumption taxes does not come easy. Two hundred years of denial cannot be dispelled immediately. The forty-year-old myth that somehow certain groups can escape taxes and that someone else can be made to pay the taxes dies hard. Unscrupulous politicians will never stop using the usual excuses as scapegoats for their own failed system of taxation.

Any suggestion of replacing any of their other taxes with a consumption tax will be instantly attacked as a scurrilous ploy of the rich to tax the poor. It will be labeled as a trick to impose even more taxes on the middle class. There will be political tears galore, all supposedly wept for the very people who would benefit the most from this true reform.

It is true that those with less income will pay a higher percentage of tax than those able to avoid taxes on a portion of their income by not spending it all. Those at lower income levels who are required by their limited funds to spend all they make for survival will, as a result, pay a tax levy equal to the exact rate of the consumption tax. But what's new about that? It is exactly what is happening now. The hidden tax bears down just as hard on the lower-wage earner. Moreover, it allows the unscrupulous politician a cosmetic deception important to the lie that impresses his constituents and keeps him in office.

The truly compassionate liberal will vote for a sales tax because it offers simpler and truer provisions for refunds to anyone below the poverty level. It is easy, and a gigantic bureaucracy is not needed to run it. Sales receipts, showing the tax, can be compared with earnings to satisfy the refund requirements.

The simplicity of the tax would not only effectively enable refunds to the poor, it would also benefit consumers not eligible for such relief though themselves less than affluent. For our entire history, every tax has supposedly been designed to relieve those less able to pay some of the burden. This has been particularly true regarding food, shelter, clothing, and medicine. Each attempt has failed completely, for it is impossible to relieve the poor of their burden as long as the taxes are hidden in the cost of their purchases as income, real estate, whatever, and as long as all the other taxes (paid by the suppliers of the services) are simply added back to the price of the poor's necessities. Obviously, elimination of a sales tax on those items would simultaneously cut taxes for the users who are not eligible for relief. Again, the solution is simple and, for the first time, effective.

Much like the proposed "negative income tax," simply have those below certain levels of income file a report. The federal government would then refund a percentage of the sales taxes paid by those below certain levels of income.

Numerous other spurious objections to a sales tax will undoubtedly be raised. The procrastinators will cry that charities will fail without income tax deductions. Why? As pointed out in chapter 9, all the needed charities were well supported prior to 1913, before there was an income tax. In fact, the majority of today's charities did not exist precisely because there was no need for them until the imposition of a 150-percent hidden tax on necessities, as well as on luxuries. Moreover, when 100-percent refunds go to the poor, lesser refunds can go to the first dollars earned by those with higher incomes. Such refunds can be designated for favorite charities, the way they are now.

Some might say that corporations can sidestep all taxation to the detriment of the poor. Again, what's new about that? It's true today. The only tax a corporation ever has, or can pay, is that which it collects from the consumers of their products. No business has ever paid a tax, and no business ever will. It has no money with which to pay one, other than what it adds to the price of its products and collects from the customers. This is an economic fact. Corporations are tax collectors, not taxpayers.

We can certainly anticipate the complaint that VAT procedures (if used) are cumbersome and unwieldy. Well, they may not be perfect, but they're better than anything we have. Most countries with VATs require less than twenty pages of revenue documentation. A simple retail sales tax would be even less complicated.

Ultimately, if all reason and logic itself fails to convince the nation, the economy requires it. We simply can no longer ignore the effects of the gobbledygook that passes as our current system of taxation. The economy simply cannot support it, as our $2 trillion debt, our $200 billion annual budget deficit, and our multibillion-dollar trade deficit all demonstrate.

Of all suggested modifications and reforms, only a consumption tax offers a solution to this economic mess. All of the proposed spending cuts, system reforms, import levies, and domestic content laws are nothing but more patchwork on a system built on a sandy foundation of lies. They all address only the symptoms of the real problem, and all are rife with special interest amendments.

None of the patchwork solutions can help. Job training for nonexistent positions in defunct or atrophied industries does nothing. Increased taxation aggravates the problem and reduces exports. Greater national debt reduces the investment dollars available for recovery and aggravates the costs of our production. More welfare relief increases both government and debt. Encouraging new industries that are saddled with the same hidden tax costs dooms them to failure.

Consider the potential benefit to our industries, which even with the gigantic hidden tax burden are still within 20 or 30 percent of being competitive in the world market. What if we simply obeyed Article I, Section 9, of the U.S. Constitution by identifying and eliminating the tax on any export goods? Imagine the market for U.S. computers, heavy equipment, technology, food and fiber, machinery (tooling), and medical supplies at a 60-percent discount! What nation could compete? Our products would flood the earth. Sure, we would pay the 60-percent tax here, but we wouldn't burden our foreign consumers with it, and we would collect the same tax on their exports to us, just as they collect on ours overseas.

Ten million unemployed could return to work, now able to afford a consumption tax equal to the current 60-percent hidden burden. This would generate at least another $120 billion in tax revenues, figuring on their earning only $9.61 per hour, which is considerably less than any union scale I know of. Simultaneously, welfare costs would decline $100 billion. These two events alone would eliminate both the current annual deficit and the negative balance of payments. The $2 trillion national debt could be zeroed out in due course solely on the taxes collected on imports that now escape U.S. taxation. Even better, most current imports couldn't compete if burdened by the same taxes our manufacturers endure. The imports would stop and the products would be supplied by U.S. labor, manufacturing, and production.

It's true: Any and all direct or indirect symptoms of the problems incurred by taxing the untaxable would disappear.

We face a momentous opportunity. We have elected a House, Senate, and President on their promises to resolve the current chaos. We are in a position to demand sanity in financial policies, to demand "Truth in Taxation." The challenge is ours.

CHAPTER 16

The First Step

NEITHER DROPPING THE OLD tax system nor starting a clear, fair consumption tax will come easily. As foreseen in the previous chapter, sincere liberals will fear for their poor constituents. And an even more difficult challenge will be contending with the professed liberals who know better but remain dependent upon exploiting the present system.

The two groups will make a formidable coalition, and we consumption-tax proponents can expect their bitter opposition, loudly joined by the liberal press. Already, just the initials VAT are fighting words.

Historical patterns suggest that, at least initially, the poor and the unemployed will rally to these expected liberal reactions. Unaware of the true cause of their dilemma, they will presume the new tax program to be another plot to exploit them. This may be paranoid, but it's a paranoia not unfounded. Lord knows, the system under which they've lived all their lives does exactly what they will fear of the new one.

What they need is a dramatic demonstration. They need proof that the current tax system is not relieving them of the tax burden it professes to be relieving; that it is, in fact, destructive and damaging to them. Concurrently, they need proof that the consumption tax is not the demon it has been portrayed to be. What they need is the Truth, unhampered by diversionary tactics and groundless clichés. They need the truth in a language any citizen can understand.

There is such a demonstration. There is an easily implemented, risk-proof program that can prove both the ravages of the current system and the benefits of a consumption tax.

Why cannot we, the American people, demand and receive "Truth in Taxation"? As if by magic, it can confront and demolish every economic problem we have. The magic is in simplicity. For the fact is, all our problems are a complexity of lies, and all of these lies are based on one lie that can be silenced only by the truth. As citizens we are subject to "Truth in Taxation." We are punished under the penalties of perjury for any untruths on our 1040s. Why should our elected officials, our employees in the bureaucracy, be accountable to any lesser standard than the one to which they hold us?

We should know exactly how much tax we are paying, what its effect is on our finances, for what it is being used, and how and where it is collected from us. If the information is available, it's only the truth, so why shouldn't we know what that is? It's our government, it's our money, it's our economy. And most importantly, it's our vote. If the Senate, the Congress, and the President want our vote, they must listen to our demands, especially if those demands are based on knowledge of the truth.

We can demand "Truth in Taxation." It's easy! Pass a law. Pass the same type of law that established "Truth in Lending." Make it mandatory that the receipt for every purchase we make carry two numbers. We can require that both the total bill and the total of the hidden taxes buried in the purchase price be clearly printed on the receipt in two separate numbers.

Why not? My grocer passes my cigarettes over a funny

shaped slit in the counter, and the cash register springs to life. It prints on my bill everything but the sex life of the butterfly that pollinated the tobacco plant. Why can't it also tell me the amount of hidden taxes on my nice dollar-and-a-quarter pack of smokes? It already tells me, "Benson and Hedges, Menthol, 100's, Deluxe, Ultra Lite, Home Office, Park Avenue, N.Y."

The technology exists to print two columns of figures along with all this other information. One column could be for the actual costs, the other for the costs of hidden taxes. They don't have to be broken down into types of taxes, just totals. They can state the sum of all the taxes hidden in the product, including the taxes for the farmer, truckers, manufacturers, distributors, and grocer. They can also contain the income, social security, and real estate taxes on all the people and entities that participate in the production. That goes for the road tax, tobacco tax, excise tax, and any special tax. We're paying all of these, and more, in the price of the product. Tell us about them, tell us the amount.

We have the right to "Truth in Taxation," to tell the politicians that we want our cigarette tally to state $.10 for tobacco, $1.15 for taxes, if that's the way it is. For bread: flour, $.44; taxes, $.66.

Every business person, farmer, and service operator already knows, and computes daily, all the figures and costs necessary to give us the information. How else could he write his checks to the IRS, and to other tax collectors? How else can the price of a product be figured? Anyone who doesn't know couldn't stay in business ninety days.

All that is required is for each supplier to furnish each buyer with his known cost breakdowns. His predecessors have managed to compute cost breakdowns for centuries with far less sophisticated equipment than he has. He would do this in two figures: the total price of the product and the amount of taxes hidden in the cost exactly like with the VAT.

For all the complaints predictable on this task of tracking costs, none will come from small business operators. After being falsely blamed for inflating prices for years, they'll be only too glad to hand out a substantiated bill that puts the blame for the high costs on the right shoulders.

Of course some politicians, those who work the present system for all it's worth, can be expected to feel differently. Nevertheless, the truly honest ones will not only join, they will want to lead the crusade. And all the rest, the myth workers of the current system, will become known for what they are.

How can anyone object? All we're asking for is the Truth. We are not asking for a change in the tax law, at least not yet, we are only asking for the truth about the effects of the taxes we have.

The bill is already written. Just copy this one:

Truth in Taxation

Purpose: To recognize the fact that all taxes of any form must be, ultimately, imposed on the consumer of the goods and/or services produced by the collector/payer of the tax. To better inform the public of the effect of these taxes on their personal finances and the national economy, as a whole.

Taxes to Be Included: Any tax imposed by any governmental body on equipment, raw materials, real estate, services, and wages paid to employees, as well as any profit taxes paid by the supplier and the producer of the product, as well as the projected taxes paid by the recipients of equity dividends paid by the producer.

Applicability: Every producer of a product and/or provider of a service to any party for a fee or payment.

Procedure: Concurrent with the submission of any statement, bill, or invoice for payment, the vendor will provide a breakdown in separate columns of the total dollar amounts of the actual costs of the item(s) sold and the total, in dollars, taxes paid in its production. Such detailing will not require the separate itemization of the taxes by type, but rather, simply, the sum total of all the taxes and the sum total of production costs. The sum of the two will be the sum total of the document rendered for payment.

Regulatory: All the percentages used in computations herein will be based on the end result of the average for the past four quarters, or the most current quarter, whichever *in the sole opinion* of the vendor most accurately projects the most realistic result. While the summary documents for the most recent four quarters of the computations by the vendor will be maintained on file for presentation to buyers, on request, such documents will not be subject to audit or validation by any third party or agency. The computation will be presumed as a good-faith, best-effort disclosure and, thus, permit each citizen a better understanding of the share of the tax burden he bears.

Quarterly Percentage Computations: All percentage computations will be based on the producer's quarterly gross sales, divided into the total of the gross taxes paid by the producer, his employees, his suppliers and his equity owners (pro rata to dividends).

Withholding (State and Federal): The total amount will be added to:

FICA (Employer and Employee Contribution): The total gross sum will be added to:

All Other Employee Taxes (and government insurance): Regardless of whether the tax is supposedly paid by the employer or employee, the total will be added to:

Real Estate Tax: The pro-rata per-quarter share of taxes (fourth), paid on any real estate used in any manner in the production of the vendor's product, will be added to:

Profits Tax: The computed gross net of the vendor before taxes times the percentage of the tax applicable to the vendor, if no deductions other than direct operating expenses are available, and the total will be added to:

Dividends Tax: One eighth of the gross dividends paid by the vendor for the year and the total will be added to:

Personal Property Tax of Vendor: One fourth of the most recent annual tax paid by the vendor and the total will be added to:

Inventory Tax: One fourth of the most recent annual such tax paid by the vendor and the total will be added to:

Supplier's Taxes: The gross amount of all taxes paid and submitted on receipts by such suppliers, including appropriate taxes of utilities, transportation, raw materials, and insurance, submitted by their suppliers on the appropriate documents during the quarter and the total will be added to:

Hidden Employees Tax: Two and one-half percent of the gross payroll of the vendor to cover miscellaneous employee taxes (home real estate, auto license, and so forth) and the total will be added to:

Import Tax: One fourth of the gross such tax, paid in the past four quarters, and the total will be added to:

Miscellaneous Tax: The sum total of any taxes paid on any product or service, acquired from any source or paid by the vendor, not otherwise covered herein and computed pro rata to the subject quarter, and the total will be added to all of the above.

The total of the hidden taxes aforementioned will be divided by the quarterly gross sales. The resultant percentage factor will be the percentage applied to the vendor's gross list prices for the subject quarter. There will be no requirement to display the gross sales or the producer's profits on individual sales receipts, but the vendor will display on the sales receipts the dollar amount assumed as the result of the percentage factor used. The amount of the hidden gross taxes for the individual sale will be printed on the document, submitted to the purchaser for payment.

Commencement: This law will commence on the first day of the first quarter, which occurs more than ninety days subsequent to enactment. Within that time, the vendor will compute, from information readily available, pertinent hidden tax rate. There will be no requirement to acquire detailed back information from any prior source of supplies, services, or assets already in inventory. The vendor will compute from information available and determine the percentage indicated, and will add an additional presumed 10 percent gross sales tax for the first quarter.

Implementation: Subsequent to the commencement quarter, and within forty-five days subsequent to the end of the next quarter, the vendor will compute the actual percentage pertinent to his business or profession. The more recent quarter's percentage factor will be used (having dropped the 10 percent add-on after the first quarter), until forty-five days subsequent to the next following quarter. For the first four quarters, the vendor will use the most recent quarter. After the fifth quarter, the vendor may use the annual average, including the most recent quarter or the most recent quarter alone, whichever percentage factor he believes may best represent the reality of his business.

Enforcement: There will be no governmental enforcement agency nor enforcement procedure for this law. It is designed and intended to be self-regulatory, and its enforcement will be solely the economics and realities of the marketplace. Its enforcement will be that no document will be deemed a sufficient demand for payment without the display of the tax percentage factor used and the gross amount of the computed hidden taxes.

The failure to receive such information will not, however, constitute any defense against payment but, rather, a delay of the due date until such subsequent date as would be normal after the receipt of the corrected document containing the required information.

The buyer may, at any time, request the summary documents for the past four quarters. A vendor's failure to provide such may also constitute a defense against payment until such is received, providing that such request is made in writing not later than concurrent with the order. However, there will be no requirement for delivery of such documents by the vendor, pursuant to a demand made subsequent to the order.

In the instance of a retail vendor normally merchandising from an establishment, a posted public display of the most recent quarter and the annual average of the disclosure statements within the establishment will be deemed to suffice for computation disclosure.

There will be no enforcement agency at any governmental level for executing this law. Its enforcement, if necessary, will lie solely in the appropriate courts for collection, with the prevailing party entitled to one hundred percent reimbursement for all legal fees and court costs.

Title Taxes Paid	A Percentages Gross Sales[1]	B Paid Out Dollar Amounts[2]
W/H	_____ %	$ _____
FICA	_____ %	$ _____
Inventory	_____ %	$ _____
Suppliers	_____ %	$ _____
Depreciation	_____ %	$ _____
Import	_____ %	$ _____
Other Employers	_____ %	$ _____
Real Estate	_____ %	$ _____
Income (Corp.)	_____ %	$ _____
Dividends	_____ %	$ _____
Personal Property	_____ %	$ _____
Miscellaneous	_____ %	$ _____
Total Taxes or Percent	_____ %	$ _____

Percentage factor computed for Truth in Taxation _____
Vendor Name _____

[1] Round to two decimal points—example, 2.78%.
[2] Round to even dollars.

Sample Disclosure Document
Truth in Taxation
Disclosure Form

This report is for <u>(# of quarter), 19</u>

Vendor may use, at its discretion, either dollar amounts, percentages, or both. If Column A is used, the gross sales will be divided into the gross tax paid, to determine the percentage. That percentage will be the Truth in Taxation percentage. If Column B is used, the total of all taxes in dollar amount will be divided by the dollar amount of gross sales, to determine the Truth in Taxation percentage.

It's easy to enforce. It's not a burden on the economy. It won't even require an agency. We will enforce it ourselves, in the marketplace. The businessman will simply add the gross amount of the checks he writes to the government to the amount paid by his suppliers and divide that total by his gross sales to arrive at a percentage. That percentage will be applied to all his customers' receipts.

The receipt will say:

> $97.00
> Truth in Taxation: as per our computations, it has been determined that 60 percent of our overhead is hidden,undisclosed tax, therefore you should be aware that $58.20 of your purchase is for taxes.

No excessive effort is required of the merchant, certainly no more than is currently demanded to compute the sales taxes already in existence in most states. It's just information in the event anyone cares, and *we care*.

"Truth in Lending" bankrupted no banks, and "Truth in Insurance" broke no insurance companies. "Truth in Taxation" will certainly not break our economy, our nation, or our freedom. How could it? They're already broke.

I do not claim that "Truth in Taxation" will solve the problems of our nation. But it is a first step. It will provide information to the public, information which in turn could be used to solve the problems.

Nor do I claim to be the possessor of all wisdom. I am merely an individual who has reached certain conclusions based on the facts as I perceive them. These conclusions are mine. I can reach no others. And thus far, neither has anyone else.

But suppose I'm wrong. Suppose every one of my premises is wrong. Suppose every one of my conclusions is based on biased or faulty information. There would still be no reason to oppose "Truth in Taxation." If there is sufficient cause to require "Truth-in" laws for the other events in our lives, why not taxation? None of the other events even begin to have an equal impact on our every act.

Would it inhibit commerce? Of course not. Have you ever refused a purchase based on the disclosures of "Truth in Lending"? Or of "Truth in Advertising"? This is information to which we are entitled, all the more so given the dominant role taxes play in our lives. Withholding is taken from every one of our paychecks. We pay others' income taxes with our every purchase. Our jobs, our economy, and our freedom are affected daily. If my analysis is correct, if 60 percent of our every purchase is a result of hidden tax, name one other event that even approaches the financial magnitude of taxation's effect on us.

"Truth in Taxation" may prove me right, it may prove me wrong, but it *will* disclose the truth. And that disclosure will provide us with accurate data to help us see our problems for what they are. No one denies we have problems. No one can deny the national debt, annual deficits, negative balances of payments, industry closures, or unemployment statistics. How on earth can we deny the need for accurate data with which to attack these problems?

Actually, I believe the truth will prove the validity of my arguments. I believe "Truth in Taxation" will lead to the imposition of a consumption tax which will, in turn, resolve the problems. To those who honestly oppose such a tax and believe it to be regressive, I can only say that as a proponent I do not fear the findings of the Truth, so why should an antagonist? The Truth can disclose nothing but the truth.

Even on an interim basis, even before the actual passage of a consumption-tax law, wonderful things may happen. Perhaps, somewhere in this land, a federal judge will take note of the fact that all the hidden taxes exposed on sales receipts are unconstitutional export taxes. Perhaps he will require refunds of those taxes on that portion of our industries' production that is exported. Even with a retained income tax, the cost of products would be separated: product $X, taxes $Y. For export, the government could refund the Y portion, and our industries would again be competitive in the world market. Such an act, with such benefits, would require no new law. It would require only adherence to our own Constitution, Article I, Section 9.

When Americans are permitted to see the "Truth in Taxation" on their grocery bill, in comprehensible numbers, government purchases of unconscionable waste (those $435 hammers, $200 coffeepots, and billion-dollar cost overruns) will take on a new public meaning. Cost controls will assume accountability. Perhaps every wasteful expenditure will not be eliminated but at least the spender will be made visible, exposed to the just wrath of public awareness.

We need no more panaceas, no more patchwork, no more reforms, and no more interim measures. We cannot solve problems with data based on invalid data. We should not even try. All we need is the truth. We need "Truth in Taxation." That truth will set us free.

ENCLOSURES FOR VALIDATION

A. SUMMARY OF *U.S.* VS. *KILPATRICK*

Attached hereafter are several documents related to the IRS's conduct in *U.S.* vs. *Kilpatrick,* along with the two principal judicial rulings in the case.

HISTORY

I have, for almost twenty years, been in the capital formation business. My company puts large businesses together for the benefit of about 1,700 small investor units from all over the U.S. It permits the small investors to avail themselves of the advantages, normally reserved for large investors, as to tax treatment and profit potential.

Originally, my company addressed itself only to the question of risk versus potential profit, not to the tax consequences of the investment. In 1977 it was virtually impossible to calculate the tax consequences inasmuch as, under the current system of taxation, the middle and upper middle class had virtually no after-tax dollars to invest.

Thereafter, in an examination of the multiples of investments presented to us annually, we made two analyses: the risk versus return *and* the tax benefits resulting from Congressional legislation to induce investments in particular areas of industry.

Since the tax consequences were of such magnitude to our investors, we could not afford uncertain assumptions. We obtained advance tax opinions from major law and accounting firms, prior to any investment sale, to assure the program's compliance with not only the law but the intent of the law. Then, we sold the investment.

By 1980, my company was the largest in the U.S. specializing in this field, and regarded widely as the best at doing the very thing Congress considered so important as to require the passing of special legislation to encourage us to do it. Yet beginning in 1978, we became the IRS's "flagship case" in its campaign against abusive tax shelters. In conjunction, between 1977 and

1980, we were subjected to four SEC investigations, two FBI investigations, innumerable checks by the IRS, and one known CIA interference. Not one of these disclosed any wrongdoing on our part, and no civil charges were ever brought against us.

Then, in the summer of 1980, the IRS requested that the Department of Justice impanel a criminal grand jury. In Appendix B, "Request for a Grand Jury," the purpose of this request is stated: to collect taxes. It was, therefore, by our interpretation an illegal request. Tax collection is a civil function. A grand jury is a criminal forum and may not be used for a civil function. Listed below are more than one hundred events that were either admitted to under oath by the participants, or demonstrated by documentary evidence to have occurred, or found to be fact by at least one, if not both, of the federal judges hearing this matter. In my opinion, these events were clear violations of the law, and I shall not dignify them by referring to them otherwise. In many, many instances, my opinions were shared by either one or both of those federal judges.

No fault was ever found against us, through three court decisions also included herein, one by Judge Fred Winner and two by Judge John Kane. In the court's statement on February 23, 1983, transcript from Judge Kane's hearing, the judge noted that the charges brought against me did not constitute a crime against the government. This is important to note, because Judge Kane's decision was made *before* the words "prosecutorial misconduct" were ever uttered in any court. The numerous instances of misconduct found by both judges were merely additional reasons for the final dismissal, added seven months and nineteen months respectively, after the original dismissal for the failure to state an offense.

The government has appealed all of the decisions of the judges, but in all their appellate briefs, not one of the IRS violations is denied. The government casts them as technicalities.

B. REQUEST FOR A GRAND JURY

COMMENTS

M. Carr Ferguson, the addressee, and Robert P. Rowe, the sender, are both attorneys. Ignorance of the law is not, therefore, a defense available to either. In addition, please note the number of "Enclosures" after Rowe's signature and the august titles of the other parties participating in this act, the *illegal unconstitutional act* of using a *criminal* legal procedure for the *civil* purpose of collecting taxes.

The request is exactly that. After spending eleven and a half pages explaining how all "civil" attempts have failed to find a flaw in my operations, Rowe entitles the last three and a half pages "Use of the Grand Jury," and in the first sentence admits, "We believe the Service would have difficulty developing this case through the administrative process." *That's tough,* but it is the *only* legal procedure available. The Constitution doesn't provide the "easiest way"; it provides the "legal way." The easiest way is to shoot me, but that too is illegal for no less obvious reasons. The Constitution is written to protect citizens from these very abuses of government and limits the procedures it can use. The awesome powers of the criminal grand jury were created to protect citizens from just such abuses. Now here is Robert P. Rowe, Director, Criminal Tax Division, in the Office of the Chief Counsel (the highest lawyer in the IRS), writing a letter to the Honorable M. Carr Ferguson, an assistant attorney general of the United States, requesting that he pervert those powers for the purpose of prosecuting the very citizens they were created, hundreds of years ago at Runnymede, at the signing of the Magna Charta, to protect.

Doubt it? Then read the section entitled "Civil Considerations." This clearly explains how much, from whom, and when Rowe intends to collect these *civil* taxes after prostituting this *criminal procedure.*

Doubt it still? Read Judge John Kane's decision on the matter (see Appendix E, paragraph 3, page 292):

> . . . it is equally improper to manipulate grand jury investigations to obtain evidence for eventual civil use by the IRS. (*Federal Rules Criminal Procedures*, Rule 6(e), (e) (3) 18 USCA)

Every line of every paragraph of "Use of the Grand Jury" is rife with half truths, totally unsubstantiated allegations, and in some instances actual admissions of the error in the IRS's position. The first paragraph is, however, simply too rich to pass up.

Sentence #1: As discussed above, an admission that the service would have difficulty "developing" this case by any legal means.

Sentence #2: An allegation that I would resist administrative (civil) procedures.

Answer: How? I had sold tax shelters under the assumption that the investors would receive deductions. As every American knows, "the burden of proof for a deduction" is on him. How could we not cooperate by supplying records? My investors could not possibly get the deductions I had promised unless I supplied them. The purpose of the investment would be defeated by me stating to the IRS, "They are entitled to the deduction, but it's a secret as to why. No, you can't look at the records either, just take my word for it." The entire sentence is absurd.

Sentence #3: Alludes to my resisting subpoenas of the SEC.

Answer: There was a difference, we believed the SEC had no right to the information and was acting beyond its authority; that is not the case with the IRS. If we refused the information, the IRS would simply deny our deduction. Right or wrong, the IRS would get the information or accomplish its goal of denying the deductions, and the IRS knew it.

Sentence #4: States revenue agent Tanner requested my investor list from someone (name unknown) who was an associate of someone else (name also unknown) who refused to produce it.

Answer: If Tanner wants *my* list, ask *me*. I own it, and regardless of who was the associate of someone else, it was not his list to produce. To do so would have required the party to first steal the list (valued at over $1 million) from me, the precise act from which Tanner ultimately profited. An ex-comptroller of mine, Paul Cornwell, did steal it and turn it over to Tanner, a fact admitted under oath by Tanner in U.S. Tax Court on September 26, 1985, before the Honorable Judge Cantrell (page 632, line 24, of the transcript of the hearing).

In any case, a request for an item from a party who does not possess it says nothing as to whether or not I would have produced it.

Sentence #5: Says some "former employees" were of the opinion I would resist administrative summonses.

Answer: Again it say nothing. What former employees? Irate ones that had been fired? Again, how could I resist? The burden of proof rests on me. If I don't produce the proof, my investors lose the deduction, the IRS collects the tax, and I go out of business.

Sentence #6: The two situations—the SEC subpoenas and Tanner's requests of third parties—which prove nothing, are combined in one statement to supposedly prove everything.

Answer: A glass of water with no calories combined with another glass of water containing no calories does not become a two-glass container with many calories.

Footnote 1

Sentence #1: Alleges that I associate with organized crime figures.

Answer: I know closely only one Italian- or Sicilian-surnamed individual, a retired, multidecorated colonel from the U.S. Air Force.

Sentence #2: Omitted the names of the parties, but identifies them sufficiently for me to recognize them.

Party A—My association with the "party serving time" was that he was the owner of a national bank, to whom the same U.S. government had granted a federal charter, where I did business. I had deposits and savings accounts, and had accepted loans from the bank. His problems that caused his arrest were unknown to me. I was uninvolved and the IRS knew it. Even so, no allegation of his having organized crime connections have ever existed to my knowledge.

Parties B and C—Also no known connection with organized crime. "B" is a retired U.S. Air Force general; "C" is a British citizen. I am informed the two put together a company in California that apparently contravened California security laws. I met the two on one occasion; they introduced me to a banker.

It is rather a quantum leap to use this as proof I am involved with organized crime.

Sentence #3: Now it's alleged I have bodyguards, and know someone who carries weapons.

Answer: I do not now, nor have I ever, had a bodyguard, nor do I need one. I'm a businessman and associate with other businessmen. Our threats are limited to, "I'll see you in court." As to an associate carrying weapons, I have several friends who duck hunt, deer hunt, or pheasant hunt. All carry weapons on those occasions. I also own a deer rifle, a duck gun, and two pistols. I've never pointed any one at a human for any reason. My expertise with the weapons is the result of my military training in defense of the nation.

Sentence #4: The last sentence again connects the fallacious allegations of sentences 1 through 3 into one, assumes the proof of organized crime connections has been made and leaps to money "laundering."

The entire document is filled with this exact type of scurrilous statement, not backed by a scintilla of evidence, that then accepts the previous unfounded statement as an unqualified fact.

Since my cursory comments on this one page filled five pages, it is obvious it would take the better part of a book to address the entire document. It is a testimonial as to why the framers of the Constitution built in guaranteed rights for the people against abusive government.

It is also an excellent exercise in analytic judgment. Read it slowly. Even without my background knowledge, create your own questions, note their choice of words and their sources of information. Imagine yourself as the target. Think of how your friends, associates or passing acquaintances might be described if the IRS decided to "get" you.

Just try the first sentence of the first paragraph after the boiler plate:

These cases arose from information received from an informant [1], (Blackened out), of one of the corporations controlled [2] by Mr. Kilpatrick and was involved [3] in the methanol production tax shelter scheme [4] discussed herein.

"Informant"—What is the man's interest? Is he a paid informant? Is he an irate ex-employee informant? Is he a mentally stable informant? Does he inform weekly on people or is this a first? Is he mad at Kilpatrick for having an affair with his wife or is he a card-carrying, bank-certified, CIA–notarized, flag-waving American who stopped off in Denver, after saving 317 missing-in-action Vietnam veterans, to help apprehend the arch enemy of America, tax shelter specialist William A. Kilpatrick?

"Corporations controlled"—Who says Kilpatrick controlled the corporation? I was accused of owning not less than four, which I did not, and the record proves I did not.

"Involved"—Whoops! Why was the informant involved with Kilpatrick if Kilpatrick is so bad? So much for the red, white, and blue concept of the informant.

"Scheme"—Scheme? What scheme? How did hundreds of millions of dollars spent on coal for energy and research to convert it to liquid or gaseous fuel become a "scheme" in the first blessed sentence? Why not plan, program, concept, investment? Why choose the worst-sounding word available to start the letter? Obviously to set the tone.

From there it goes straight downhill. Read it: It's an education.

OFFICE OF CHIEF COUNSEL
Internal Revenue Service
Washington, D.C. 20224
30 JUL 1980

CC:CTGJ-11 thru 14-80
Brl:DAParis

Honorable M. Carr Ferguson
Assistant Attorney General
Tax Division
Department of Justice
Washington, D.C. 20530

In re: William A. Kilpatrick
5 Meadowlark Lane
Denver, Colorado 80221

Involving:

Pursuant to I.R.C. § 6103(h)(3)(A), we are hereby referring for grand jury investigation the above listed individuals with the recommendation that a grand jury investigation be conducted to gather additional evidence concerning violations of Title 26 and 18 U.S.C § 371 arising out of the use of various coal and methanol producing tax shelter schemes for the years 1977 through 1979 and subsequent thereto.

These cases arose from information received from an informant, ▬▬▬▬▬▬▬▬▬▬▬▬▬▬▬▬▬▬▬▬▬▬, of one of the corporations controlled by Mr. Kilpatrick and was involved in the methanol production tax shelter scheme discussed herein. As a result of the information furnished by ▬▬▬▬▬▬▬▬ certain information gathering activity was conducted concerning Mr. Kilpatrick and his tax shelter ventures and criminal investigations were begun on Mr. Kilpatrick and several of his coal shelter entities (See referral report at page two). Mr. Kilpatrick's coal tax shelter scheme has also been the subject of scrutiny by the Securities and Exchange Commission (S.E.C.) which has been involved in proceedings to enforce administrative subpoenas for almost two years (See Ex. 17).

Based on the evidence developed thus far it appears that Mr. Kilpatrick is the principal force behind certain fraudulent tax shelter schemes involving the mining and development of coal properties and the development of methanol production processes and plants. However, all of Mr. Kilpatrick's programs appear to be completely lacking in substance and economic reality and have the result of defrauding the government by causing millions of dollars of improper deductions to be reported while at the same time defrauding investors of large amounts of cash by persuading them to invest in limited partnerships with the promise of legitimate tax deductions substantially in excess of their investments.

In order to carry out his tax shelter schemes, Mr. Kilpatrick formed a number of corporate entities and limited partnerships which purportedly handle various aspects of the financing and operations. However, it appears that in reality Mr. Kilpatrick personally controls, either directly or indirectly, all of the related activities and that these activities lack economic substance. Mr. Kilpatrick's shelter schemes are further characterized by 1) the use of nonrecourse financing which appears to be handled entirely through Kilpatrick related entities in order to provide investors with a 4:1 ratio of deductions to investment, 2) the fact that no actual mining activity (in the coal shelter schemes) or methanol producing activity (in the methanol shelters) has occurred and 3) the apparent inability to actually conduct the activity which forms the basis for the shelter. These elements of the tax shelter schemes will be discussed below.

███ which is the mining company for Mr. Kilpatrick's coal shelter ventures. ███████████████████████ appears to be closely associated with Mr. Kilpatrick. The evidence reveals that ██████ company was involved heavily in the nonrecourse financing of Mr. Kilpatrick's coal shelters (Ex. 23) and that ██████ has personally accompanied Mr. Kilpatrick on his trips to the Cayman Islands (See Ex. 17, page 15). Additionally, although ███████████████ ████████████████████ is allegedly the responsible mining company in the coal shelter scheme, it appears that this company has performed no actual mining activities for Mr. Kilpatrick's entities (Ex. 23, page 20).

███████████████████████████ is another close associate of Mr. Kilpa-

trick's. ████ is known to have worked closely with Mr. Kilpatrick in a number of capacities. ██████████████████████
██████████ in various companies along with Mr. Kilpatrick (Ex. 9;11;15;16), ████████████████████████████
████████████████████████████████████
██████████████████████████ (Ex. 23, page 27; Ex. 24).
████████████████ appears to be intimately familiar with the shelter schemes particularly from the standpoint of their administration. Additionally, ██████████████
████████████████████ We believe ████
could prove to be of value as a government witness against Mr. Kilpatrick.

██████████████████████████████
████████████████ and appears to be deeply involved in the tax shelter schemes. ██████████████████████
███████████████████████████ and ████ prepares much of the offering materials and all of the tax opinion letters for Mr. Kilpatrick's entities/investors. Additionally, ████████████████████████████████
in fact for the investors in a number of Mr. Kilpatrick's coal shelter entities and has negotiated the nonrecourse financing and fund transfers through ██████████████████
(Ex. 13, page 26; Ex. 23; Ex. 42).

COAL SHELTER SCHEME

Mr. Kilpatrick's coal tax shelter scheme appears to have begun in late 1977 with the formation of ██████████████
██████████████ a Colorado Corporation owned 100% by Mr. Kilpatrick, for the purpose of developing certain coal properties in North Dakota. One fourth of the funding for ████████
██████████████ came from investors in the form of cash while three fourths of the funding came from ██████████████
██████████ as loans secured by nonrecourse notes. ████████
██████████████ could theoretically recoup the amount of the nonrecourse notes out of production. ██████████████
██████████ acted as the general partner, at least on paper, and was responsible for mining the property (or hiring contract miners to do the mining). ██████████████ and the limited partners/investors, in turn, were told that they could deduct the total of the

cash and notes which represent advance minimum royalty payments made by ███████████. This resulted in the investor receiving deductions at a ratio of 4:1 on the their cash investments. Exhibit 44 lists the potential write-off available to the investor as well as a guaranteed amount of recoverable coal covered by the investment lease.

Shortly after forming ████████████████████████████, Mr. Kilpatrick abandoned the North Dakota property in favor of certain West Virginia property leased from the ███████████ ████████████ and referred to as the L.S. I, II and III property. This property was leased by ██████████ who in turn leased L. S. I to ████████████████████████ and L.S. II to ████████████████████████████████████. Mr. Kilpatrick is an officer and 50% owner of each of these tax shelter entities. Additionally, Mr. Kilpatrick formed a number of coal tax shelter entities based on certain Tennessee property which was purported to contain at least 51 million tons of recovered coal (Ex. 51).

The coal tax shelter program provided inflated deductions to the investors in the form of advanced minimum royalties which were allegedly deductible pursuant to I.R.C. § 612 and Treas. Regs. 1.612-3(b)(3). These regulations provide that:

> The payor, at his option, may treat the advanced royalties so paid . . . as deductions from gross income for the year the advanced royalties are paid or accrued, or . . . for the year the mineral product, in respect of which the advanced royalties were paid, is sold.

Additionally, the financing arrangement allegedly was not limited by the "at risk" provisions of the 1976 Tax Reform Act, I.R.C. § 465, since the development of coal properties was not specifically covered by the section.

However, regardless of the "theoretical" property of the coal shelter scheme under the law and regulations, we believe the evidence is supportive of criminal liability in that Kilpatrick's actual shelters were nothing but shams totally lacking in economic reality and designed to defraud the government and investors while at the same time providing Mr. Kilpatrick and his associates with huge personal gains. We believe the sham nature of these shelters is evidenced by the following.

First, although nonrecourse financing would be arguably permissible in a legitimate coal shelter under the then in effect "at risk" rules (I.R.C. § 465), we believe the use of such financing in Mr. Kilpatrick's shelters was nothing more than a sham arrangement designed to induce investment in his ventures. It appears from the evidence that Mr. Kilpatrick arranged for the circular flow of nonrecourse funds through ███████████████████ ██████ an entity with which he appears to have had a close association. Through this leverage-financing scheme Mr. Kilpatrick was able to inflate the alleged advanced minimum royalty payment deductions of the investors to four times their cash investment when, in effect, it is questionable whether any real obligations were even created on the part of the Kilpatrick entities. The best example of this scheme is the ██████████████ financial arrangement whereby █████████████████████ borrowed the funds from ██████████████ to pay for their three fourths interest in ██████████████ (Ex. 23, page 25). Subsequent to the "██████████████ deal" Mr. Kilpatrick began to arrange for offshore funding of the nonrecourse notes through a Cayman Island Bank ████████████████████████████ and the ██ ████████████████████████████████████ appears to be a Cayman Island entity in which Mr. Kilpatrick has some financial interests (Ex. 23).

The evidence further reveals that the financial arrangements made by Mr. Kilpatrick, at least for the latter part of 1978, involved a "dual bank account" arrangement whereby the investors' cash contributions would be deposited to a United States bank while the nonrecourse note portion would merely be re-deposited to a Cayman Island bank. Mr. Kilpatrick would then spend most of the cash deposited by investors to pay salesmen, legal fees and management fees to ██████████████████ ██████████████████████ (which is 100% owned by Mr. Kilpatrick and is the management corporation for the tax shelter entities) leaving little or no actual cash for coal production (Ex. 23, page 30). Additionally, Mr. Kilpatrick began using ██████████████ ██████ as a middleman for the nonrecourse portion of the financing. Thus, although not crucial to the nonrecourse financing scheme, it would not be surprising to find that funds never really passed through ██████████████████ hands or ██████ ██████████████████████.

Second, there is no evidence that any actual coal mining activity was ever conducted by Mr. Kilpatrick, ██████████████ ██████████, or any other entity. In fact, ████████████████,

██████████ from July 1978 through March 1979, indicated that he was unaware of any drilling activity or any other activity on the ██████████-North Dakota property. Additionally, ████ ██████████████ questioned ██████████████ concerning its mining activities on the Tennessee property. He was told that the only thing holding up mining activity was obtaining a sales contract (Ex. 23, page 83). However, it appears that there still has been no mining activity on this property (Ex. 42).

Third, the evidence indicates that the tax shelter entities would have been unable to mine the properties even if someone had the predisposition to do so. The evidence tends to establish that the property either did not have commercially minable coal reserves to the extent represented and/or had some problem with the title which would have made it virtually impossible to enter upon the land for mining purposes.

With respect to the North Dakota property, a geological survey map at Exhibit 41, reflects that there are no known coal reserves on the property subject to the ██████████ lease and guarantee of production. Further, the fact that much of the property lies in a producing oil field would make it unlikely that coal mining operations would have ever been started on that property. Thus, it is our opinion based on this readily available survey, that it is unlikely that anyone could have reasonably anticipated successfully mining this property.

With respect to the L.S. property in West Virgina, there are recent engineering studies which indicate that no commercial mining venture would be warranted based on the limited coal reserves on that property. The first of these studies is reflected at Exhibit 49 and was performed in connection with a request for a sublease to ████████████████████. This report indicates that the coal reserves on the L.S. property do not warrant a mining venture. There is also an indication in evidence that the commercial coal on the L.S. property was mined out in the 1940s (Ex. 48–50). We believe Mr. Kilpatrick had to have known that there was a lack of minable coal on the property prior to selling the coal shelters to his investors. In this regard, we refer to a report dated February 28, 1978, from the

██. (Ex. 50) which concluded that only "salvage" reserves were present on the L.S. property. Mr. Kilpatrick received this report prior to his entering into the lease agreements with ████████████ ███████ and his other tax shelter entities (Ex. 45; 46; 47). Finally, we note that there is also some question as to whether the ████████████████████████ actually possessed the coal rights it purportedly transferred to ████████████ (Ex. 48). This factor, coupled with the fact that the lease agreements between the Kilpatrick entities (with respect to the L.S. property) executed before ████ actually transferred the property rights to ████ ███████ raises questions concerning the propriety of this entire transfer as well as Mr. Kilpatrick's control over ████.

With respect to the Tennessee coal property the file indicates that there are serious questions concerning (1) the amount of coal on the property, (2) the actual property rights transferred, and (3) whether the property actually existed as represented. In this regard the ███████████████████████ report presented to ██████████████████████████████████ Mr. Kilpatrick's management corporation) in February 1979, clearly indicated that the 9,000 acre mineral interest obtained from ███████████████████████████ was overstated in terms of both acreage and coal reserves. In fact, the report indicated that the possibility that sizable quantities of commercially minable coal was on the property was next to none (See Ex. 52). Additionally, an examination of the available records on the Tennessee property by ██████████████████████████, who was hired by █████████████████ because of his background in dealing with natural resources property, concluded that there were serious problems with the title that passed (Ex. 42, page 26) and that it appeared that no surface rights were ever acquired (Ex. 42, page 43). Consequently, it would have been virtually impossible to conduct mining operations on the Tennessee property (Ex. 42).

Mr. Kilpatrick will no doubt argue that he obtained the property based on representations from █████████████████ ██████████ President, ███████████████████████, that there were at least 51 million tons of recoverable coal represented to be on the 9,000 acres (Ex. 51). However, the following factors lead us to believe that even the Kilpatrick/████████

deal may have been a sham transaction engineered by Kilpatrick. First, ███████████████████████ appeared to be a fictitious mining company in that it had no mining equipment and its offices consisted of one desk (Ex. 42, page 29; Ex. 23, page 71). Second, there was some question concerning the passage of title as noted above. Third, even a cursory review of the available reports would have indicated major discrepancies in the ████████████████████ (Ex. 43). Fourth, Mr. Kilpatrick was advised that the ███████████████████ was not what it was purported to be prior to the issuance of ███████████'s certification letter on December 21, 1978 (Ex. 43, Ex. 51). Fifth, it appears that no legal action was pursued by Mr. Kilpatrick against ████████████ and/or his Company (Ex. 42) for what seemed to be an obviously fraudulent representation.

In short, Mr. Kilpatrick's coal tax shelter program is characterized by the creation of multiple entities under his control, the use of circular nonrecourse financing which appears to be a sham, the lack of any mining activity by any of the companies involved, and what appears to be the lack of any minable property to support the shelters. Accordingly, this program seems to be a sham transaction totally devoid of any economic reality and undertaken for the sole benefit of Mr. Kilpatrick and related parties. The magnitude of this scheme is best illustrated by the more than $11 million in royalties deducted by just four of the Kilpatrick companies and apparently passed on to the investors (Ex. 8; 9; 15; 16).

METHANOL SHELTER SCHEME

There is somewhat less information available concerning Mr. Kilpatrick's methanol shelter program. However, all indications are that it follows the same general pattern as the coal shelters in that:

1. It provides a 4:1 ratio of deductions to investment through the use of nonrecourse financing;
2. It is characterized by the apparent inability to carry out any part of the actual tax shelter activities; and
3. It is characterized by a lack of actual tax shelter activity as planned.

Mr. Kilpatrick's methanol scheme involves the extensive use of Cayman Island corporations and the formation of limited partnerships for the purpose of developing a synthetic gas process and eventually using funds contributed to finance part of the construction of a methanol production facility. Once again the limited partners contribute one fourth of the funds and the general partner, in this case ██████████████████████████ ███████████████████████████████, a Cayman Corporation, provides three fourths of the financing through loans secured by nonrecourse notes. The transaction also provides the investors with a construction contract with ████████████████████ ███████████████████████████████, a Cayman Corporation, for the construction of a methanol plant once the product is developed and the ratio of 4:1 deductions to investment typical of Mr. Kilpatrick's coal shelter scheme.

The methanol scheme devolves from analysis of I.R.C. § 174(a) which permits a taxpayer to deduct research or experimental expenditures which are paid or incurred by him during the taxable year. In this regard, the tax opinion letter prepared by ██████████████████████ indicates that the "at risk" provisions of I.R.C. § 465 are inapplicable as far as restricting the deduction to exclude nonrecourse financing by virtue of I.R.C. § 465(c)(3)(D). This subsection specifically excludes from the activities covered by the statute the holding of real property (other than mineral property) (Ex. 33).

Assuming, arguendo, that the scheme was legitimate from the standpoint of having economic substance, we believe there are legal questions which could be raised to disallow substantial portions of the research and development deductions. For instance, I.R.C. § 174(c) makes the section inapplicable to expenditures "for the acquisition or improvement of land or . . . property to be used in connection with the research or experimentation . . . which is subject to the allowance for depreciation. . . ." Since a substantial portion (if not all) of the nonrecourse funding is theoretically to be used to acquire rights in a methanol plant once a conversion process is developed it would seem that 174(a) would be totally inapplicable to this portion of the funds by virtue of 174(c). Further, Treas. Reg. 1.174-2(a)(1) defines research and development expenditures to be "expenditures incurred in connection with the taxpayer's trade or business which represent research and development costs in the experimental or laboratory sense." Since the plant is not to be built until a successful methanol process is developed it would seem that the portion of the funding earmarked for building the plant would simply not be considered research and experimental expenditures. We note in this regard that the 1.174-2(a)(2) analysis performed by ██████████████████ in Exhibit 33 finds this provision inapplicable concluding that there is no capital acquisition or business expansion purpose in the transaction. This seems to be patently inconsistent with his I.R.C. § 465 argument that the "at risk" provisions do not apply because the partnership is holding real property. I.R.C. § 465(c)(3)(D).

Additionally, we believe there is a serious question concerning the propriety of ████████████████████ conclusions with respect to the § 465 issue. ██████████████████ concludes that the partnership deductions are not limited to the "at risk" provisions of the Code pursuant to the real estate exclusion provision in 465(c)(3)(D). However, regardless of the outcome on the § 174 issue, we believe this is the type of situation where the "at risk" rules would be applied. Specifically, we point to § 465(b)(4) which provides:

> Notwithstanding any other provisions of this section, a taxpayer shall not be considered at risk with respect to amounts protected against loss through nonrecourse financing . . .

Under this provision, even if the amount of nonrecourse financing could be added to partnership basis under I.R.C. 752(a) it would not increase the amount of partnership deductions available to a limited partner under § 704(d) by virtue of the fact that it is not at risk.

By the same token, ████████████████████'s reliance on § 465(c)(3)(D) seems misplaced. The facts set forth in ████████ ██████████████s own tax opinion reveal that the partnership holds no property. Even if the partnership were conducting the tax shelter activities as planned they would, at most, hold a contingent license to use a plant which is to be built only when a successful methanol process is developed by the general partner. Thus, there is arguably no property or property right being held by the partnership. ████████████████████ § 465 argument, then, looks patently incorrect particularly when compared with his conclusion that all of the funds are deductible research expenses. Further, even if it could somehow be argued that a portion of the partnership funding fell within § 465 (c)(3)(D), we believe that there would, at least, had to have been an allocation between the real estate and non-real estate activities in order to determine the portion of the funds attributable to real estate and excludable from § 465 applicability (See Committee Reports on P.L. 95-600, Revenue Act of 1978). We note that the above discussion reflects a "results oriented" approach by ███████████████████ in formulating his tax opinions and suggests that he conspired with Mr. Kilpatrick to arrange not only a fraudulent but a legally improper tax shelter scheme. This conclusion is further supported by statements from ████ ███████████████ supporting the fact that ██████████████ worked closely with Mr. Kilpatrick developing the methanol shelter (Ex. 23, starting at page 88).

Notwithstanding the outcome on the above legal issues we believe the methanol tax shelter program was similar to the coal shelters in that it was totally lacking of economic substance and was nothing more than a fraudulent scheme perpetrated by Kilpatrick and his associates with the loser being the government.

The evidence indicates that the Cayman Island Corporations which arranged the nonrecourse financing were nothing more than Kilpatrick controlled domestic corporations which were reincorporated in the Cayman Islands sometime in 1979. Exhibit 13 indicates that ████████████████████████████ ██████████████████., ████████████████████████ in the methanol scheme was previously incorporated as ███████████ ███████████████████████.; that ███████████████████ ███████████████ was previously incorporated as ███████████ █████████████████ and that ████████████████████ ██████████████, the entity that made the ████████████████, might very well be connected with ███████████████████████ ████████████████████████.

In addition, Exhibit 13 reveals that ████████████████ ██████████████████████, the entity responsible for ████████ ████████████████████████████, was headed by one ████████████████████████. ███████████████████ was given the job by Mr. Kilpatrick and was formerly a barber. Further,

███████████████████████████ was hired as the ████████████████ ██████ of the Company in charge of building the plants. However, in the words of ████████████████████, "the only thing ██████████████████████████ did in that capacity was to build an addition onto Bill Kilpatrick's house" (Ex. 13, page 9).

Similarly, Mr. Kilpatrick hired ██████████████████████ as ███████ ██

██████████████████████ in charge of the methanol research. ██████████ ██████████████████ was told that ████████████████████ was to open a pilot methanol plant. However, ████████████████████████ was a ████████████████████████████████, not a research scientist, and, to the best of his knowledge, no plant has ever been opened.

Thus, it appears that, similar to the Kilpatrick coal shelters, the methanol shelter was arranged through the use of Kilpatrick controlled entities which were shams in and of themselves, solely designed to make it appear as if the shelter had economic substance.

USE OF THE GRAND JURY

We believe the Service would have difficulty developing this case through the administrative process. We believe it is very likely that Mr. Kilpatrick and his associates would be uncooperative and would attempt to frustrate any attempt by the Service to gain access to records through administrative means because of the fraudulent nature of the shelter schemes. In this regard, we believe the Service would face time consuming challenges to any administrative summonses issued similar to those faced by the Securities and Exchange Commission (S.E.C.) which has been attempting to gain enforcement of certain administrative subpoenas against Kilpatrick related entities for some time (See Ex. 17, relating to enforcement action by the S.E.C. against ██ and Mr. Pettingbill). We note also that in the course of the examination relative to these tax shelters, Revenue Agent Tanner requested investor lists for several of the related coal tax shelters from ████████ ██████████ an associate of ██████████████████████████ ██████ refused to produce the records pursuant to Mr. Tanner's request. Additionally, it is the opinion of a number of Mr. Kilpatrick's former employees that he would resist any administra-

tive summonses issued against the tax shelter corporations (Ex.
23, page 85, Ex. 24). We believe the response to the S.E.C.
activities as well as the activities of Revenue Agent Tanner add
credibility to these statements.[1]

We also believe that this case has significant deterrent potential. This case not only is significant in terms of potential civil
and criminal tax liabilities, it involves the area of abusive tax
shelters which has been of particular concern to the Service in
recent years. We believe the evidence developed thus far is indicative of the abusive and fraudulent nature of the Kilpatrick
shelters which have been designed to defraud the government
and the investors by offering substantial tax write-offs for shelter activities which are totally lacking of economic substance. In
this regard we note that the methanol shelter alone offered a
$50,000 tax deduction for every investment of $12,500. With
over 300 known investors the methanol program has already
produced first year deductions of over $15 million for 1979 (See
referral report, page 13).

In order to complete this investigation we believe a grand jury
would, essentially, have to develop facts to "corroborate" the
statements made by ▮▮▮▮▮▮▮▮▮▮▮▮ and ▮▮▮▮▮▮▮▮▮▮▮▮.

With respect to the coal shelters this would involve obtaining
information concerning the various Kilpatrick corporations and
partnerships as well as related banking records in order to establish that Mr. Kilpatrick, in fact, controlled all of the entities
involved. Of particular concern will be the relationship beween
Mr. Kilpatrick and ▮▮▮▮▮▮▮▮▮▮▮▮ of ▮▮▮▮▮▮▮▮▮▮▮▮.

---

[1] Mr. Kilpatrick may be involved with a number of organized crime
figures. Among his known and/or suspected associates are ▮▮▮▮▮▮▮
▮▮▮▮▮▮▮, currently serving time in a federal penitentiary for pledg-
ing worthless stock for bank loans, and ▮▮▮▮▮▮▮▮▮▮▮▮ and
▮▮▮▮▮▮▮▮▮▮▮▮, who have been indicted for grand theft and
violations of California Securities laws (Ex. 17). Additionally, Mr.
Kilpatrick is known to have hired bodyguards (ex. 24) and his associate,
▮▮▮▮▮▮▮▮▮▮▮▮, allegedly carries weapons (Ex. 13). If the
tax shelter activity is connected with organized crime and if Mr. Kilpatrick is involved in transporting cash to the Cayman Islands for purposes of "laundering" funds as suspected (Ex. 17, page 15) this might
well have an effect on his decision with respect to turning over records
pursuant to administrative actions.

Their association will have to be developed sufficiently to allow a jury to conclude that ██████████████████████ is part of the Kilpatrick conspiracy and/or that Mr. Kilpatrick actually controlled the flow of funds through ██████████████████████████ corporation. Additionally, the relationship between Mr. Kilpatrick, ████████████████████████ and ██████████████████████████ should be developed to refute any potential defensive contention that Mr. Kilpatrick might raise concerning his purchase of coal property rights from these companies. Here we note that while certain facts are available to establish that ██████ may have been manipulated by Mr. Kilpatrick (*i.e.,* the fact that all leases between Kilpatrick's companies were signed prior to the ██████/Kilpatrick lease), additional facts with respect to these relationships would still prove helpful. Additionally, any facts which would prove that ████████████████████████ and ██████████ ████████████ lacked substance as legitimate mining companies as well as facts tending to prove either that there were readily available mining reports on the properties or that no mining studies were conducted by Mr. Kilpatrick would be helpful in this case. Such facts would help establish that Mr. Kilpatrick had to have been fully aware of the nature of the transactions he was entering into and lead to the conclusion that the property acquisitions were all part of his fraudulent scheme.

In the area of nonrecourse financing the grand jury should attempt to develop facts tending to show that such financing lacked economic substance and was merely a sham to induce investors to contribute funds for the resultant tax benefits. We believe this could best be accomplished by (1) developing facts as stated above, (2) calling defrauded investors to testify as to representations made by Kilpatrick's employees and/or co-conspirators, (3) obtaining any offering materials available and (4) obtaining business and bank records concerning the fund transfers and any accompanying rights and duties. Additionally, the investor files contained in the offices of ██████████████████ ██████████████████████ would prove helpful in completing the financial picture.

We would further recommend calling current Kilpatrick employees before the grand jury to determine the extent of corporate tax shelter activity conducted to date as well as the extent of Kilpatrick's control over the various entities. Potential witnesses may include ███████████████, a coal tax shelter salesman; ████████████████████, an associate of Mr. Kilpatrick's; ██████████████████, sales manager in the Kilpatrick organization: ██████████████████, ████████████████ employed by ████████████████████████████ ████ ██████████████, who was involved in a Kilpatrick entity called ██████████████████████, and ██████████████████, the current ████████████████████████████████████ ██████. We anticipate that no material activity will be found to have occurred with the exception of Mr. Kilpatrick's manipulation of funds through the various entities.

With respect to the methanol tax shelter scheme we would recommend developing facts similar to those discussed under the coal shelters above. This would include establishing that Mr. Kilpatrick controlled all of the corporate entities involved in the financing scheme and shelter activities, that no material economic activities have been conducted to date, and, if possible, that contributed funds are being either depleted or withdrawn to foreign bank accounts to the detriment of the activity for which the shelter was designed. Additional potential witnesses in Mr. Kilpatrick's methanol shelter (in addition to those above) might include ████████████████, ████████████████████, ████████████████████████████, ████████████████████, ██████████████████████████████, and ██████████████ ██████████, ██████████████████████████████████. These individuals should have information with respect to the actual activity (or lack of activity) by the methanol shelter general partner, ████████████████████████████████, and related entities.

What may prove somewhat problematic in accepting this case for criminal prosecution is the fact that Mr. Kilpatrick made extensive use of Cayman bank accounts. Thus, it might appear that the government would have difficulty completely tracing the flow of cash through the Cayman Island banks. Additionally, recent information provided by ████████████████████ ██, indicates that Mr. Kilpatrick may now be transferring funds from Cayman Island accounts to banks in the Netherlands. However, information available in the file leads us to believe that a substantial portion of the tax shelters' records, including information relating to bank accounts, are maintained by ▬▬▬ ▬▬▬▬▬▬▬▬▬▬▬▬▬▬▬▬▬▬▬▬▬ in its Colorado suites (Ex. 23; Ex. 24). We point out also that each coal shelter company did maintain a United States bank account for investor deposits and that all of these records should be available either through the banks or corporations (Ex. 23). Further, all of the investor files, leases and correspondence should be in the corporate offices in Colorado (Ex. 24).

We also believe that the failure of the government to obtain a portion of the bank records by virtue of Cayman Island bank secrecy laws will not be fatal to this case particularly if Mr. Kilpatrick's control over the various entities can be established by witness testimony. We point out that the failure to establish circular nonrecourse financing through bank records is only one aspect of this case. What is more important here is not the fact that there was nonrecourse financing, it is the totality of the facts and circumstances which will establish that these shelters were shams and had no economic substance. *Cf. Brountas v. Commissioner,* 73 T.C. 491 (1979).

Another question which may arise is whether the attorney/client privilege would protect records which may be in ▬▬▬ ▬▬▬▬▬'s hands (See ▬▬▬▬▬▬▬▬▬▬▬▬ statements, Ex. 42). However, it is well settled that this privilege only applies to confidential communications made in the course of seeking legal advise from a professional legal advisor acting in that capacity. See *United States v. Margolis,* 557 F.2d 209 (9th Cir. 1977); *United States v. Hodge and Zweig,* 548 F.2d 1347 (9th Cir. 1977); *United States v. Ponder,* 475 F.2d (5th Cir. 1973). It would not, in our view, apply to opinion letters or offering materials prepared for public/investor use (or the backup for those products) or to any business records such as client files, corporate leases, corporate minutes, etc. which may be in ▬▬▬▬▬▬▬▬▬▬▬ possession. Accordingly, we do not believe the attorney/client privilege will pose an effective legal barrier to the grand jury.

We have also considered the possibility of joining certain investors in this grand jury investigation. However, we believe that any attempt to do so would necessarily involve some showing that the investor entered into the "tax shelter" with knowledge of Mr. Kilpatrick's fraudulent activities in order to reap the tax deductions. We further believe that this may be a difficult task particularly in light of the tax opinion letters from ███████████████ and representations made concerning the property which formed the basis for the shelter (See Ex. 27–33; 43–47). Accordingly, as a practical matter we do not envision joining the investors in the criminal conspiracy.

CIVIL CONSIDERATIONS

We are mindful of the potentially large civil tax liabilities which may be involved in this case. In fact, to date the investigation has disclosed the names and addresses of some 250 coal shelter investors (each having a minimum first year write-off of $22,500 based on Exhibit 44) and 360 methanol shelter investors (each having a minimum write-off of $50,000, Exhibit 13). In this regard we point out that the majority of the coal shelter activity did not occur until 1978 and the methanol activity did not begin until 1979. Accordingly, while the civil statute, I.R.C. § 6501, will run with respect to the 1977 year in April 15, 1981, it will not run with respect to the bulk of the civil tax liabilities until April 15, 1982, and April 15, 1983, respectively. We believe the grand jury work could be completed prior to the running of the civil statutes.

Further, the file contains a good deal of information which was developed outside of any grand jury. This information could be available to the Examination Division for the purpose of issuing statutory notices of deficiency to the investors should that need arise prior to the resolution of the criminal aspects of this case. While we do not anticipate issuing statutory notices without proper coordination, we call your attention to a recent letter from Stephen M. Miller, Deputy Chief Counsel, IRS, to Mr. Gerald Feffer, Deputy Assistant Attorney General, Tax Division, titled Criminal Cases Involving Tax Shelter Promoters, in which it was agreed that the Department of Justice would not decline prosecution of tax shelter promoters simply because the Service has taken civil action with respect to the investors or limited partners.

Additionally, we note that the various Regional Commissioners have concurred in this grand jury recommendation. Their concurring memoranda are included in this referral.

CONCLUSION

In view of the above we recommended impanelling a grand jury in the Judicial District of Colorado, where the tax shelter promoters reside and where a good deal of the corporate activity occurred, in order to gather additional evidence concerning the use of fraudulent tax shelters to violate Title 26 and 18 U.S.C. § 371.

The Office of Chief Counsel will be available upon request to assist the Attorney for the Government in evaluating any case which might emanate from the grand jury investigation. In this regard, a request for evaluation assistance should be directed to the Regional Counsel in the Internal Revenue region where the grand jury is impaneled.

Please advise Chief Counsel of your conclusion.

Sincerely,

N. JEROLD COHEN

By: _____

ROBERT P. ROWE
Director
Criminal Tax Division

Enclosures:

Volume I containing D.J. originals:
Transmittal from Assistant Commissioner Compliance to Director, Criminal Tax Division
Transmittal from Regional Commissioner, Southwest to Assistant Commissioner Compliance
Memorandum from Chief, Criminal Investigation Division to Regional Commissioner Southwest (Referral Report)
Copy Folder containing: One copy of this letter
    Copies of above documents
Volume II containing Exhibits 1–55
Volume III containing Concurring Memoranda from Regional Commissioners

cc: Assistant Commissioner (Compliance)
    Regional Commissioner (all Regions)
    Chief, Criminal Investigation Division, Denver/Cheyenne
        District
    United States Attorney

                                        TAX DIVISION
                                        December 18, 1980
                                        Washington, D.C. 20530
MCF:SFYrysa:aat
5-13-2879
8020345

CERTIFIED MAIL—RETURN RECEIPT REQUESTED

Joseph F. Dolan, Esquire
United States Attorney
C-330 U.S. Courthouse
Drawer 3615
Denver, Colorado 80294

                                Re: William A. Kilpatrick
                                    Denver, Colorado

Dear Mr. Dolan:

Reference is made to a letter dated July 30, 1980, from the Office of Chief Counsel, Internal Revenue Service, Washington, D.C., recommending that a grand jury investigate whether the above-named individuals violated Title 26 and whether they conspired to defraud the United States, in violation of Title 18 U.S.C., Section 371.

It has been determined that a grand jury investigation is warranted and you are requested to institute such action. Since this case involves issues with respect to tax shelters, the investigation must be coordinated with the Tax Division to insure that criteria established for prosecution of these cases is considered. Therefore, Steven L. Snyder of the Criminal Section, Tax Division, has been assigned to conduct the investigation. We request that an attorney from your office be assigned to jointly assist Mr. Snyder in this investigation.

No indictments or information are to be returned or filed

without the prior approval of this office. When the investigation has reached the appropriate stage, please furnish us with your views.

So that we may give proper consideration to any proposed charges, please note that unless extraordinary circumstances are present, this office will only consider those proposed charges where your views and the advice of the Service are received at least 60 days prior to the date when a determination by the Tax Division is needed as to whether prosecution should be undertaken.

For purposes of assisting you in the performance of your duties, it will be necessary to obtain the expert advice and assistance of the Internal Revenue Service personnel. You are reminded that under Rule 6(e)(3)(B), Federal Rules of Criminal Procedure, the court is to be furnished with the names of Internal Revenue Service personnel given access to grand jury material. Please advise all such Internal Revenue Service personnel that grand jury material is supplied to them on the following conditions:

1. All grand jury material will remain under the custody of the grand jury, the United States Attorney's office, and the Tax Division, Department of Justice.
2. No disclosure is to be made of this material to Internal Revenue Service personnel for other than criminal purposes and then only to personnel in the Service who are assisting in formulating the recommendation and advice of the Serivce to the Department of Justice attorneys or the United States Attorney's office.
3. All grand jury material, including any copies is to be returned to the Tax Division or retained by the United States Attorney when it is no longer needed for use in advising and assisting the Tax Division or the United States Attorney's office in the investigation of the matter under consideration.

Please acknowledge receipt of this letter and its enclosures.

Sincerely yours,
M. CARR FERGUSON
Assistant Attorney General
Tax Division

By:

STANLEY F. KRYSA

Chief, Criminal Section

Enclosures

cc: Chief Counsel
  Attn: Dir., Criminal Tax Division

C. LISTING OF VIOLATIONS

Background Comment: After three years of investigations using the legal civil and administrative procedures available, the IRS was unable to find anything wrong with the investment programs of my company. But instead of declaring those programs legal and deductible, it requested a grand jury as a resort to accomplish illegally what it had been unable to do within legal civil and administrative procedures. This interpretation of illegality is based on the substance of the "Request for a Grand Jury." The first two thirds of it lists all the ways the IRS tried, to that date, to find something wrong. It describes what we did, admits our procedures were correct, and finally concludes that is was impossible for the IRS to make a case using civil or administrative means, the only legal means available to them. It is illegal and unconstitutional to use a criminal procedure to accomplish a civil purpose. The collection of taxes is a civil matter; the purpose of a grand jury is criminal. The last third of "Request for a Grand Jury" is entitled "Use of the Grand Jury." It details the acts the IRS desired the grand jury to perform and how the benefits of these acts would be used to accomplish the IRS's goals. Immediately following the "Request" is the signed agreement of the Department of Justice.

A grand jury is constituted to protect citizens against an oppressive government abusing its powers. Once impanelled, its authority is almost limitless. Regardless of the specific purpose of its calling, it can totally change the direction of its efforts and commence an investigation of the sheriff, the prosecutor, even the judge that impanelled it. It can, in fact, indict them all, instead of the accused. Its powers are vast and unsurpassed in our system, and for good reason. It is the citizens' greatest barrier against any violation of their rights. The potential of such a runaway grand jury turning on the government is the subject of much concern in prosecutorial circles.

In this case, the IRS usurped those awesome powers and used the grand jury, not as an unbiased jury to protect the citizen,

241

but as a prosecutor's tool to perform its investigation. The IRS, together with the Tax Division, Department of Justice, took the powers designed to protect the citizens and turned them against a citizen.

Each event listed below occurred and was either admitted or otherwise proven. After the description of each, I cite the source of the information and the law which I believe it violates, and in some instances, I add a comment which explains further the basis of my belief.

1. The IRS requested a criminal grand jury to help collect civil taxes. (Proven in "Request for Grand Jury.") *Violation*— Federal Rules Criminal Procedure (FRCP) Rule 6(e),(e)(3) 18 USCA.

2. The Department of Justice agreed to perform the services. (Proven in "Request for Grand Jury.") *Violation*—FRCP 6(e),(e)(3) 18 USCA.

Comment: The fact that none of the information developed by the grand jury proved valuable in making their case is irrelevant. It was the act itself that was important.

3. Records were stored across the street from the U.S. attorney's office. (Admitted.) *Violation*—Rules for Grand Jury Procedures as stated in the U.S. Attorney's Manual and FRCP 6(e).

Comment: All grand jury records are secret. The law requires they must be maintained in a separately locked room within the local U.S. attorney's office. Access is forbidden even to other employees of the U.S. attorney's office not engaged in the case. It is specifically forbidden to the IRS or any other third party. The party being investigated is not, yet, even charged with a crime, much less convicted of one. His reputation can be destroyed by just the publicity that he is being investigated, as in my instance. This is the purpose of the secrecy laws of grand juries.

4. Records were in an office rented by the IRS. (Proven by GSA records.) *Violation*—FRCP 6(e).

5. The office was equipped with IRS telephones, paid for by the IRS. (Proven by GSA records.) *Violation*—FRCP 6(e).

6. The office was staffed solely by IRS personnel. (Admitted.) *Violation*—FRCP 6(e), the secrecy requirement of grand juries.

7. Special locks were put on the doors, and the only keys were maintained by IRS personnel. The U.S. attorney did not even have access without IRS permission. (GSA records, admitted.) *Violation*—FRCP 6(e).

8. The door was routinely left unlocked and open, witnesses and other parties regularly walked in and availed themselves of the "secret by law" documents and invaded my privacy. (Testimony and court records.) *Violation*—FRCP 6(e), as well as Fourth Amendment rights to privacy.

9. IRS civil personnel were used to perform audits on the bank accounts for civil purposes. The civil purpose was proven by their failure ever to present the audits to the criminal grand jury. Plus, the bank audits were valueless in relation to the charges against me. The IRS was forbidden such access with or without a grand jury. (Admitted.) *Violation*—FRCP 6(e) and Fourth Amendment.

10. Seventy-eight IRS agents were documented as having been permitted full or partial access to the documents. (Admitted.) *Violation*—FRCP 6(e) and Fourth Amendment.

11. The IRS maintained the administration of all records at all times. (Admitted.) *Violation*—FRCP 6(e).

12. IRS personnel performed the entire computer-programming procedure, thus gaining additional access. (Admitted.) *Violation*—FRCP 6(e) and Fourth Amendment.

Comment: It was decided to computerize the records.

13. The local IRS shared the documentations with personnel from the Dallas and Ogden IRS offices and, thus, further spread the illegally gained information. (Admitted.) *Violation*—FRCP 6(e) and Fourth Amendment.

14. On completion, the program was placed on IRS computers. (Admitted.) *Violation*—FRCP 6(e) and Fourth Amendment.

15. Only the IRS had computer code access, not the U.S. attorney. (Admitted.) *Violation*—FRCP 6(e) and Fourth Amendment.

16. Every IRS agent in the U.S. had total and perpetual access to our secret records. (Admitted.) *Violation*—FRCP 6(e) and Fourth Amendment.

Comment: Why else did they put it on the computer? This was a violation of my Fourth Amendment rights against unreasonable search or seizure of my papers and effects. Since the entire investigation was for illegal purposes, none of the subpoenas to acquire my documents attained the status of warranted. The continued disclosure also violated my Fourth Amendment right to privacy in my affairs.

17. Two minutes after the judge completed the swearing in of the jury and departed from the room, the prosecutors added two IRS agents to the jury as "Agents of the Grand Jury." (Grand jury records, admitted.) They are quoted as boasting about doing it in every case, in every circuit, as a matter of routine procedure. *Violation*—Fifth Amendment right to be indicted by an impartial grand jury of my peers.

18. The jury was informed that, since the IRS agents were the jury's agents, the jury could totally depend on them to be unbiased. They would help the jury reach a fair decision. (Records of the grand jury and admitted.) *Violation*—Fifth Amendment, Sixth Amendment, and possibly perjury.

19. The agents were sworn in by the assistant U.S. attorney, who had no authority to administer the oath in that court. (Admitted, proven by grand jury transcript.) *Violation*—FRCP.

Comment: Grand juries do not have agents. They certainly do not have prosecutors as agents; and especially, they do not have as agents the very IRS agents that initiated the request for the grand jury.

20. The IRS agents routinely sat in on grand jury deliberations. (Records of grand jury.) *Violation*—FRCP.

Comment: Grand juries have severe limitations on who may appear before them. They are: (1) the attorney for the government, (2) sworn witnesses (one at a time; two witnesses may not appear together), (3) the recorder or stenographer, and (4) an interpreter, if necessary. No other party may even *enter* the room, nor may any of the parties who do enter be acting in any capacity other than the above.

21. The IRS agents routinely testified *together* before the grand jury. (Records of grand jury and admitted.) *Violation*—FRCP 6(d).

22. The IRS agents, at times, testified alone and together without being sworn in. (Records of grand jury and admitted.) *Violation*—FRCP 6(d).

Comment: The agents' statements described in 23 and 24 below are unquestionably lies. If the agents were sworn on these occasions (which they were not on many occasions—another violation within itself) the agents perjured themselves, though to this date they have not been prosecuted for perjury.

23. The IRS agents testified to having evidence which they did not have by virtue of the fact that the witness who supposedly conveyed the testimony *did not exist.* (Records of grand jury and admitted.) *Violation*—Perjury.

24. The IRS agents testified to having evidence (testimony) from two witnesses that did exist, but that never, in their testimony, even alluded to the subject of the agents' testimony. Nor did the agents ask them any questions about it. (Records of grand jury.) *Violation*—Perjury.

Comment: In order to acquire testimony from a reluctant witness, prosecutors in a grand jury may grant *immunity* to a witness in order to obtain that which might otherwise be unavailable. There is an exact statutory procedure that must be used, called Statutory Immunity, and it was not observed in my case, leading to several of the violations that follow. Its provisions:

A. The prosecutor (that is, the assistant U.S. attorney) in charge first must make the determination that it is necessary to give immunity in order to obtain the testimony.

B. Certification must be made that the witness has refused, or is likely to refuse, to testify because of his privilege against self-incrimination.

C. Prosecutors must then acquire the approval of the local U.S. attorney for the district and his concurrence of the necessity.

D. The prosecutor and the U.S. attorney must obtain further approval of no less an authority than the Attorney General of the U.S., a deputy attorney general, or an assistant attorney general.

E. A U.S. District Court judge must then perform the ministerial act of signing the order and memorializing the exact terms, limits, and purposes of the immunity.

F. A record must be kept for Congress, in order to determine if the extraordinary act accomplishes the effect desired and if the forced waiving of the Fifth Amendment right achieves sufficient beneficial effects to warrant the procedure.

The purposes of this procedure are manyfold, not the least of which are (1) Congressional supervision; (2) court supervision of the terms of the immunity and its correct fulfillment; (3) court determination of the exact acts that are forgiven; (4) court ascertainment of the validity of the prosecutors' reasons, and the truthfulness of the testimony (there is a strong chance that a party, subject to prosecution for a serious felony, might be willing to lie in order to acquire immunity); (5) assurance that the prosecutors cannot badger a witness into perjurious testimony by threats of withdrawal of immunity, if the testimony is not sufficiently incriminating to the target; and (6) certainty that prosecutors do not gain long-term control over a witness by future threats of withdrawal of any unmemorialized immunity.

25. The prosecutors unilaterally issued letters of immunity by only their signatures. (Letters signed by the prosecutors.) *Violation*—18 USC 6002 and 6003.

26. No determination was ever made that any witness would have been any less willing to testify without the immunity. (Admitted.) *Violation*—18 USC 6002 and 6003.

27. U.S. attorney was never even asked for approval and, in fact, was not aware immunity was being given. He certainly had not given his required approval. (U.S. attorney testimony.) *Violation*—18 USC 6002 and 6003.

28. Letters were issued on U.S. attorney stationery that the U.S. attorney was unaware the agents possessed. (U.S. attorney testimony.) *Violation*—Theft, fraudulent use of government documents and 18 USC 6002 and 6003.

29. Letters were signed by the prosecutors on the U.S. attorney's stationery, thus implying an approval and authority they did not possess. (The letters.) *Violation*—Fraud and forged authority.

30. Neither the Attorney General nor his assistant was ever notified of the letters, nor did they give any approval. (Testimony.) *Violation*—18 USC 6002 and 6003.

31. No judge was ever utilized in connection with the granting of immunity; thus, no order of immunity ever existed. (Statement from the bench by the only judge authorized to grant it.) *Violation*—18 USC 6002 and 6003.

32. No records were maintained; therefore, Congress lost its ability to supervise. (Admitted in testimony.) *Violation*—18 USC 6002 and 6003.

33. Threats of withdrawal of the immunity were made to witnesses when the testimony turned out to be favorable to the

accused's and not the prosecutor's case. (Records of the grand jury and the court hearings.) *Violation*—Obstruction of justice by threats, badgering and intimidation.

34. The witnesses first offered immunity were indicted if their testimony was not "good enough" or if they refused to make up testimony to the agents' and prosecutors' liking. (Court records.) *Violation*—Obstruction of justice.

35. Witnesses not given immunity were called before the jury and forced to take the Fifth Amendment, prejudicing the jury against them and the targets. (Admitted by prosecutors.) *Violation*—Rules for Grand Jury Procedures.

Comment: In essence, every procedure intended to ascertain the correct use of Statutory Immunity was avoided, and the exact abuses the procedures were designed to prohibit were then committed by the prosecutors. One such witness, who succumbed to the threats, was described by the judge as "lying by the clock." The witness couldn't remember his story line, and he contradicted himself on eleven subjects in less than forty-five minutes. Others were equally and obviously false, if not as blatant.

36. Seventy-eight sessions of the grand jury, their testimony numbering in the hundreds of pages, were withheld from the court in direct violation of three court orders. (Court records, admitted.) *Violation*—Contempt of court and obstruction of justice.

Comment: During the trial and subsequent hearings, many of the abuses were admitted by the guilty parties after evidence made denial impossible. Judge Winner then ordered the entire transcripts of the two grand juries turned over to him in order that he might see what other abuses may have occurred.

On his retirement at mid-hearing, he issued a second order that the same entire transcript be turned over to the defendant's attorneys for their determination of other violations that might be more apparent to them than to him.

On taking the bench for the continuation of the hearings, Judge Kane issued a third order, that the entire transcript also be turned over to him.

37. Finally, after the third court order, fifty-five of the seventy-eight sessions were turned over. (Court records, admitted.) *Violation*—Contempt of court and obstruction of justice.

38. The fifty-five sessions were not sequential, but random;

and they were the very documents which contained the majority of the evidence of the 102 acts referred to herein. (Transcripts.) Twenty-three of the sessions are still withheld, in violation of the court orders, with the excuse that they were lost. (Court records and admitted.) *Violation*—Either additional acts of contempt, obstruction, perjury, violations of the rules of procedures for grand juries, or all of the above.

Comment: As was noted in the judge's decision, losing the transcripts was a per se violation. The law required that the transcripts be maintained in the U.S. attorney's office under lock and key. Had they been kept there, they would not be lost and the other disturbing questions raised by the losing would not exist, including the fact that 2 of the missing 23 were miraculously found two years later when the prosecutors wanted to quote statements beneficial to them in connection with their appeal of the decision in my favor.

39. The records disclosed, on numerous occasions, that the clerk/recorder was ordered to cease recording and not to start again until commanded to do so. (Grand jury transcripts.) *Violation*—Rules for Grand Jury Procedures and the Fifth Amendment.

Comment: All proceedings *must* be recorded. Having considered the content of the fifty-five found and wondered about the content of the twenty-three lost, though presumably at least recorded, one has to speculate on what occurred during those hours, and occasionally days. If the agents/prosecutors permitted the dozens of violations to be recorded that were recorded, what were they doing that was so much worse that they feared even grand jury secrecy might not protect them?

40. At the noon recess, the prosecutor informed a witness, Professor Roland Hjorth, that he was a disgrace to his profession and implied he could be fired by the university if his testimony did not improve. (Testimony of Hjorth and a disinterested third-party attorney witness.) *Violation*—Obstruction of justice.

Comment: Abuse, badgering, and threatening of witnesses was not limited to those with pocket immunity. Roland Hjorth, a professor at the University of Washington Law School and a recognized academic expert on tax law, was called as an expert witness. He testified that the deductions were not only legal, but that they were precisely the intent of Congress and deductible.

41. The prosecutor at one point addressed Professor Hjorth: "I will see you in court," implying a personal indictment if he did not change his testimony. (Testimony, same as 40.) *Violation* —Obstruction of justice.

42. Richard Birchall, an ex–assistant U.S. attorney, possessed Sixth Amendment protected attorney/client privileged information sought by the government. He was taken to a bar by the prosecutors, who attempted to get him drunk and obtain the documentation while he was intoxicated. (Testimony of Birchall, event—not purpose—admitted.) *Violation*—Sixth Amendment attorney/client privilege.

43. When intoxication failed, the prosecutors threatened to indict Birchall as a co-conspirator if he didn't yield the documents. (Testimony of Birchall, denied by the prosecutors, though admitting that they had considered prosecuting Birchall and may have mentioned this to Birchall.) *Violation*—Sixth Amendment attorney/client privilege and obstruction of justice by threatening a witness.

44. When both attempts at intimidation failed, the prosecutor claimed that he had testimony from a female witness as to an affair with Birchall. (Birchall's testimony, prosecutor denied threat but admitted discussion of the female witness.) *Violation* —FRCP 6(e), disclosure of grand jury evidence.

Comment: Even if true, which Birchall denies, this was an illegal disclosure of secret grand jury information.

45. The prosecutor told Birchall that if he did not yield the document the prosecutor desired, the sex story would be given to Birchall's wife's attorney in his then-current divorce proceedings. (Birchall's testimony, prosecutor denied.) *Violation*—Obstruction of justice.

46. The privileged documents desired by the prosecutor were stored for safekeeping with the government during a court hearing held to determine if they were to be given to the government. Although the court denied access to the government, thereafter the prosecutor had the information. *Violation*— Theft, contempt, obstruction of justice and the lawyers' code of ethics.

47. At the time of Birchall's concern over the sex story, he was permitted free access to the grand jury's document room, an illegal disclosure of secret grand jury evidence. (Birchall's testimony: Prosecutor first said Birchall lied, then said Birchall

shouldn't have taken advantage.) *Violation*—FRCP 6(e) and Fifth Amendment.

Comment: The security of the documents was the prosecutor's responsibility.

48. Wilson Quintella was arrested as a material witness to be held in jail until trial. (Court records.) *Violation*—Tampering with a witness known to be favorable to the defendant.

Comment: Wilson Quintella, a retired Admiral in the Brazilian Navy and an attorney, was a witness critical to the defendant's defense. Mr. Quintella is now a paraplegic and had, at the time, a serious stomach ailment. He was in the U.S. for medical treatment over periods of time, during one of which the prosecutors seized him in the hope of converting him to their side. A federal judge ordered Quintella to be released, but also instructed him to return to testify. Quintella delayed stomach surgery for four months to ensure his availability at the trial to testify for me.

49. Three days before the trial, the agents notified Quintella, through the American Embassy in Rio de Janeiro, that the subpoena was cancelled and his testimony was not needed. The witness submitted to surgery and was not available for testimony at the trial. (The letter was a court exhibit. Agent admitted sending it.) *Violation*—Witness tampering, contempt of court by dismissing a court order.

Comment: The subpoena was not the agent's to cancel, it was the court's. The witness was not agent's, he was the defendant's.

50. Arrest warrants were issued for two witnesses through U.S. Customs by the agents/prosecutors, in case these men attempted to enter the U.S. in order to testify for me. (Warrants were in evidence, admitted by issuers.) *Violation*—Witness tampering, obstruction of justice.

Comment: C. S. Gill and Michael Alberta, attorneys in Grand Caymen, were witnesses critical for me, against whom no charges existed.

51. Richard Bell, a respected accountant in the U.S. and Costa Rica and a citizen of the U.S., was given immunity in exchange for testimony about financial transactions. When his testimony was described as "not good enough" and it became obvious it was more beneficial to the defendant than to the government, he and his attorney were told, "All bets are off if you ever testify for Kilpatrick." This was apparently in reference to

his pocket immunity. (Testimony of Bell and his attorney. Statement admitted but the presumed intent denied.) *Violation*—Obstruction of justice, blackmail.

Comment: These were acts committed against, or in the presence of, lawyers, presumably trained in their rights and knowledgeable of the law. The effect on the lawyers was unremarkable—they reported the incidents almost immediately. If the arrogance of the government attorneys/agents extended to the belief that they could do this with qualified officers of the court, one can imagine their acts on untrained and unknowledgeable citizens. Indeed, several such acts were revealed later, after some protection of the court was availed the individuals. It is known that still other acts remained unreported out of residual fear.

52. The agents identified the accused in dozens of letters to dozens of witnesses over four continents. (Letters in evidence and admitted.) *Violation*—FRCP 6(e).

Comment: No one may be availed of any evidence obtained by the grand jury, or given the identity of the accused target, unless he is admitted to the 6(e) list. That list must be submitted to a judge before the information's disclosure. Once admitted to the 6(e) list, a person may not disclose information to *any* other party. The only parties supposed to be admitted are those necessary to the prosecutor to perform his duties before the grand jury, and for *no other purpose*. Only the prosecutor may appoint them, and this authority may not be delegated. It is required by law that the identity of the target of a grand jury remain secret to others than those on the 6(e) list until after indictment, if any, in order to avoid tainting the target with implied guilt associated with the investigation and to avoid tainting his reputation or slanting witness testimony.

53. Letters were written on stolen U.S. attorney stationery to render greater credibility. (Letters in evidence.) *Violation*—Theft, unauthorized use of federal documents, FRCP 6(e).

54. Letters were signed by IRS agents who were not attorneys and who were not authorized to sign such documents. (Letters in evidence, showing the signature, testimony of U.S. attorney's representative.) *Violation*—Unauthorized usurpation of a federal authority, impersonation of an officer of the court.

55. Dozens of IRS agents traveled all over the U.S., inter-

viewed hundreds of investors, and disclosed to each the identity of the targets. (Admitted.) *Violation*—FRCP 6(e).

56. Many of the IRS agents were not on the 6(e) list and should not have known, themselves, much less disclosed such information to others. (Records of the court.) *Violation*—FRCP 6(e).

57. The 6(e) list was prepared by the agents, who made the decisions as to who would receive the information, and not the prosecutors. (Court records proved and admitted.) *Violation*—FRCP 6(d).

Comment: The prosecutors did not know many of the people and were unaware as to why they were on the list. It was obviously for the agents' own purposes of collecting taxes, a civil act illegal in the course of grand jury proceedings.

58. The 6(e) list was habitually not submitted *prior* to disclosure, but rather after. (Court records and admitted.) *Violation*—FRCP 6(e).

59. One 6(e) list was not submitted until three weeks after the grand jury adjourned. (Court records and admitted.) *Violation*—FRCP 6(e).

60. Many IRS employees who were given grand jury information were never placed on the list before, during, or after the grand jury. (Court records and admitted.) *Violation*—FRCP 6(e).

61. Records were illegally transferred to Lowery Air Force Base, by the agents, to parties not on the list. The agents testified that the judge had given his permission, but the judge denied it. The agents were unable to find the supposedly signed order. (Court records, court testimony.) *Violation*—FRCP 6(e).

62. The records were again transferred by the agents to other IRS offices in Ogden and Dallas. The agents did not even allege to have had permission. (Admitted.) *Violation*—FRCP 6(e).

63. IRS Civil Division supervisors, of no conceivable benefit to the jury or prosecutors, were placed on the 6 (e) list and given grand jury information. (Grand jury records.) *Violation*—6(e) and rules of jurisprudence governing criminal and civil procedures.

64. Grand jury information was given even to student clerks, who were not on the 6(e) list. (Admitted.) *Violation*—FRCP 6(e).

Comment: This was probably not a damaging act to the defendant, but is indicative of attitude.

65. The agents illegally presented evidence in tandem, when not more than one could be in the room at any one time. (Admitted.) *Violation*—FRCP 6(d).

66. The agents and their IRS superiors admitted their awareness of the grand jury being used for civil purposes. (Testimony and documented in court.) *Violation*—Civil/criminal rules of procedure.

67. The questionnaire used by the agents for potential witnesses contained dozens of questions with absolutely no relevance to any grand jury procedures, though of great importance to the purpose of collecting taxes. (Questionnaire in evidence of court records.) *Violation*—Civil/criminal rules of procedure.

68. Civil employees of the IRS were used to perform audits of investors which were of no benefit to the grand jury, nor were they ever presented to the grand jury. (Testimony.) *Violation*—Civil/criminal rules of procedures.

69. Hundreds of letters were sent to the investors by the Civil Division of the IRS notifying them that their returns were either to be audited or their deductions were already denied. The letters stated that these actions were based on "a report soon to be issued containing facts as presented to the Federal Grand Jury." (Letters in evidence in the court records.) *Violation*—Civil/criminal rules of procedure.

70. The prosecutor decided to interrogate an employee of the Bank of Nova Scotia without his attorney's presence. (Admitted.) *Violation*—Conspiracy to commit a violation of the Sixth Amendment.

Comment: No indicted party may be interrogated by a prosecutor without the permission of that party's attorney or the attorney's presence. Numerous court cases have held that the same privilege is extended to employees of an indicted corporation.

The Bank of Nova Scotia was indicted as a co-conspirator. The bank was represented by an attorney who advised the prosecutor that an employee the prosecutor wished to interrogate had been transferred from Puerto Rico to Canada. He further advised that the employee would be made available upon request and that the attorney intended to be present.

71. The prosecutor and an IRS agent surreptitiously followed the employee's wife for five days through the streets of Puerto Rico. (Admitted.) *Violation*—Fourth, Fifth, Sixth amendments and the Canons of Professional Ethics of the American Bar Association.

Comment: The prosecutor discovered that the employee's wife and daughters, ages ten and eight, were still in Puerto Rico (the school term was imcomplete). He journeyed to Puerto Rico with and IRS civil agent, with no notice to the attorney.

72. The prosecutor and the agent interrogated the employee's ex-secretary without the attorney's knowledge. (Admitted.) *Violation*—Sixth Amendment.

73. The prosecutor and the agent interrogated the employee's replacement without the attorney's knowledge. (Admitted.) *Violation*—Sixth Amendment.

74. The prosecutor and the agent interrogated the bank's chief executive officer without the attorney present. (Admitted.) *Violation*—Sixth Amendment.

75. The prosecutor and the agent interrogated miscellaneous other employees without the attorney present. (Admitted.) *Violation*—Sixth Amendment.

76. The prosecutor and the agent attempted to interrogate the employee's children at school without the mother or attorney present. They did, in fact, interrogate the children's teachers and principal. (Admitted.) *Violation*—Sixth Amendment and the laws of common decency.

Comment: Children's evidence is normally inadmissible.

77. The prosecutor and the agent shadowed the children after school, until they met up with their mother. (Admitted.) *Violation*—Fourth, Fifth, and Sixth amendments.

78. The prosecutor and the agent shadowed the three to their home. (Admitted.) *Violation*—Fourth, Fifth, and Sixth amendments.

79. The prosecutor and the agent then interrogated the wife and children before friends and neighbors, without the attorney, as to the husband's whereabouts. (Admitted.) *Violation*—Fourth, Fifth, and Sixth amendments.

Comment: They apparently believed the employee was hiding out, still in Puerto Rico.

80. When informed that the employee was, indeed, in Can-

ada, the prosecutor and the agent attempted to induce the wife to influence her husband to submit to secret interrogation without the attorney. (Admitted.) *Violation*—Conspiracy to violate Sixth Amendment.

81. When questioned about these activities, the prosecutor admitted his awareness of the infractions. He stated that no case had ever been dismissed for such violations, that the only penalty normally imposed by the courts was the suppression of the evidence so gained, and that he hoped to avoid even that. And if he did, and if he happened to get some good information, he would use it to try to develop the same information from another source and use it in the same way. (Admitted.) *Violation*—Miranda, Massiah, Fourth, Fifth, and Sixth amendments.

Comment: The arrogation of an authority he did not possess and the intentional, admitted violation of citizens' constitutional rights were symptomatic of the entire investigation.

82. Early in the hearings regarding IRS and prosecutorial misconduct, Judge Winner ordered all government employees who were potential witnesses or targets sequestered—that is, they were not to be permitted any information as to testimony, nor were they to discuss together their own past or future testimony. The purpose was to ensure that their testimony would be pristine, spontaneous, truthful, and not colluded. Within an hour after the order, one such witness, an attorney, ordered the entire past transcript. (Admitted.) *Violation*—Contempt of court.

83. The Department of Justice thereupon immediately relieved all possible witnesses of court duties in the case for the balance of the proceedings. It replaced them with Charles Alexander, a senior trial attorney, Tax Division, Department of Justice. On Sunday evening, with the testimony of the sequestered witnesses due Monday through Wednesday, Alexander conducted a three-hour meeting with all of the witnesses. (Meeting admitted, purpose denied.) *Violation*—Contempt, possibly collusion to perjure.

Comment: This was in direct violation of the order. The only conceivable purpose was to collude in the precise testimony the judge had ordered sequestered.

84. When caught, Alexander's excuse was that they weren't discussing their testimony, they were discussing the facts of the

case. To which the judge responded, "To what are they proposing to testify, the nonfacts?" (Record of court testimony.) *Violation*—Obstruction of justice.

85. The prosecutor had a temper tantrum in response to a ruling against him, resulting in the mouthing of obscenities at the judge and a coat-throwing incident in the courtroom. He subsequently denied its occurrence against the contrary testimony of five disinterested witnesses. (Testimony.) *Violation*—Obstruction of justice by colluding to perjury and possibly perjury.

86. Five agents and assistant U.S. attorneys restrained the prosecutor. Afterward, all testified exactly the same way, "I don't remember." (Testimony.) *No violation*—Memory not provable.

Comment: Each of the disinterested witnesses had variations as to the details, but they were fairly consistent in their description of the overall incident. That is normal of truthful testimony: Different witnesses, possessing no collusion in their testimony, routinely describe scenes differently. The Department of Justice had the gall to suggest that, since their testimony so perfectly coincided and was more consistent, it should be given more weight and credibility than testimony with variations!

87. Robert Grossman, an attorney for the defendant, requested and received a pre-indictment review and was given one by Jared Scharf, a man represented to be, but who was not, a reviewer. Rather, he was a trial counsel for the department. (Admitted.) *Violation*—Deception, deceit, and fraud.

Comment: The Department of Justice has an announced procedure that the target of a grand jury may request a review, prior to an indictment. The supposed purposes are: (1) A target is allowed to present his proposed defense; (2) If the defense has merit, the case or proposed indictment may be dropped if the higher echelon unbiased judge is convinced that no crime has been committed or that the evidence is insufficient to warrant a conviction; (3) The procedure reduces costs for senseless prosecution; (4) The defendant saves the expense of a trial; (5) Needless embarrassment is eliminated, and (6) The defendant's reputation that otherwise could be destroyed by an indictment for a nonexistent or unprovable crime can be salvaged. The reviewer supposedly occupies a quasi-judicial, unbiased position and passes judgment on whether the case should be prosecuted.

In such hearings, the defense lawyer is led to believe he can be fully candid about his theory of defense and his plans, with no concern that his words will be thrown back at him or that he has forewarned the other side of his tactics.

88. Scharf, it later developed, was not only a trial counsel, he was *the* ranking investigator in the very case he was now reviewing. (Admitted.) *Violation*—Fraud.

89. Scharf was not only the ranking investigator, he was also the *lead* prosecutor in charge in this case. (Admitted.) *Violation* —Fraud.

Comment: Scharf's behavior was tantamount to the judge first hearing the case, then leaving the bench, taking sides, and becoming the prosecutor. The statement of the prosecutor was that they did it all the time. Thus, the defendant's counsel was tricked into disclosing his entire plan of defense to his opponent, months in advance of the trial. This permitted the prosecutor to arrange his case in anticipation of the defense.

90. An agent shredded 3,500 documents in his possession that were potentially favorable to the defendant. (Admitted.) *Violation*—Destroying documents related to an ongoing trial.

91. Jared Scharf, the reviewer/prosecutor who was involved but not actually trying the case, yelled at the judge from the spectator section behind the bar as the judge left the courtroom. He demanded an explanation of the decision and then entered into an argument with the judge over his wisdom and/or bias. (Court transcript.) *Violation*—Contempt of court.

Comment: The Judge showed the greatest restraint by not responding to this obvious attempt to obtain a mistrial in the, by then, obviously lost case of the government.

92. The prosecutors habitually crossed the forbidden line between prosecutors and investigators. (Admitted.) *No violation*— They simply lost their otherwise absolute immunity from civil suit in the pursuance of their duty.

93. The prosecutors filed a brief stating that the defendant's objections to all their misconduct were "silly and frivolous." (Brief is record.) *Violation*—Contempt of court, law, and defendant's rights.

94. Despite hundreds of grand jury secrecy violations by the prosecutor, he acted to the contrary when beneficial to him. He imposed secrecy on the only two witnesses to the jury on which secrecy could not be imposed, the defense attorneys. Thus, I

was deprived of an attorney/client consultation, to which I was absolutely entitled. (Grand jury transcript.) *Violation*—Sixth Amendment.

95. Numerous witnesses testified to the prosecutors statements that, even if the defendant wasn't guilty, the government would break him with the cost of the defense and that the prosecutor intended to do so. (Court records.) *Violation*—Fourth Amendment, the confiscation of my property and assets without due process.

96. The prosecutors discovered a proposed merger of my corporation with another international company, a deal that would presumably save my company from destruction. They subpoenaed my comptroller to learn the details in order "to shoot the deal in the ass." (Court testimony.) *Violation*—Fourth Amendment.

97. The prosecutors in the grand jury allowed a witness to hear the testimony of other witnesses, a violation of secrecy and prejudicing of supposedly independent testimony. (Testimony of numerous witnesses.) *Violation*—6(e).

98. A former U.S. attorney, whose testimony was favorable to me, was called a liar by an agent concerning a fact about which it was impossible for the agent to have had *any* knowledge of its truth of untruth. (Testimony of former U.S. attorney.) *Violation*—Badgering of a witness.

99. A witness, hesitant to testify without counsel, was told by the prosecutor that his attorney had given his permission when the prosecutor knew that he had not. (Testimony.) *Violation*—Fifth and Sixth amendments.

100. That same witness, an attorney, was thus induced to violate his own client's attorney/client privilege at the same time he was tricked into relinquishing his own. (Testimony.) *Violation*—Sixth Amendment.

101. When the grand jury agents summarized evidence for the jury to seek indictment, their statements contained numerous inaccuracies which led to misconceptions by the jury. Those statements led to the indictments, which the eventual evidence did not support. (Grand jury transcript and judge's order.) *Violation*—Perjury and Fifth Amendment.

102. Agents and prosecutors had been informed that the business transactions to which they objected were not illegal; but they requested the indictments nonetheless, presumably to ac-

complish their stated goal: "We may not convict, but we will destroy." (Court records.) *Violation*—Fourth Amendment and wrongful prosecution.

103. An IRS agent who was not an attorney, nor in any other manner qualified to be, was represented as the expert in the field to summarize the prosecutor's legal theory to the jury. It was a theory totally alien to the law, but impressive to the layman jury members, who were dependent on the agent of the grand jury as the expert on whose knowledge they had been told they could rely. (Grand jury transcripts.) *Violation*—Wrongful prosecution, Fourth Amendment.

104. The agents and prosecutors accepted and prosecuted the indictment even though they knew it was tainted. (Court records.) *Violation*—Fourth, Fifth, and Sixth amendments.

105. The agents and their 6(e) list assistants threatened potential witnesses with grand jury subpoenas if they did not voluntarily render the desired information. (Court testimony, admitted.) *Violation*—Obstruction of justice.

106. The prosecutors habitually asked employees of my company who were testifying favorably to me to name who was paying their attorneys. This left the jury with the impression that I was financing their testimony. The question was not asked of those helpful to the prosecutors, whose attorneys I was also paying. (Grand jury transcript.) *Violation*—Fifth Amendment.

Comment: They were *all* employees, and companies routinely pay employees' legal fees for acts performed in the course of their duties.

107. When Judge Winner attempted to publish his memorandum opinion concerning these violations, Tax Division, the Department of Justice, attempted to gag his order by forbidding its publication. (Appeal to 10th Circuit.) *Violation*—First Amendment, guarantee of freedom of the press against prior restraint; also the principle of the separation of powers: an Executive Branch agency attempting to impose control over the Judicial Branch.

SUMMARY COMMENT

In this listing of violations, some acts were repeated under a different number. This was done to clarify the act's implication to either the preceding or succeeding act. So it should be made clear that the total types of violations number only 102, not the 107 shown.

On the other hand, I must point out that most of the 102 were committed time and again, some well over a hundred times. A few were committed in the thousands of times during the course of this seven-year nightmare.

1. Violations #3–#8 and #11 were recommitted daily for over eighteen months.
2. Violation #10 was committed a proven seventy-eight times, with known but undocumented others.
3. Violation #16 was *potentially* committed 88,000 times (since there was no way to prevent all 88,000 employees of the IRS from availing themselves of the information).
4. Violations #25–#32 were committed at least a proven twenty-eight times, with known but undocumented others.
5. Violation #36 was committed seventy-eight times.
6. Violation #38 was committed twenty-three times.
7. Violation #52 was committed twenty-eight times.
8. Violation #55. Although the exact number of instances is unknown, it is estimated to be in the hundreds.

Finally, it would be a mistake to assume that *U.S.* vs. *Kilpatrick* was an isolated case conducted by one or two misdirected individuals outside the approval of the IRS. The record proves and the courts have found that the acts were accomplished in the full light and knowledge of, and in complicity with, dozens if not hundreds of IRS and Department of Justice employees on the orders of their superiors.

D. DECISION OF JUDGE FRED WINNER*

UNITED STATES of America, Plaintiff,

v.

William A. KILPATRICK, et
al., Defendants †

No. 82-CR-222.

United States District Court,

D. Colorado.

Aug. 25, 1983.

Following jury verdict of guilty of obstruction of justice, defendant moved for dismissal or new trial with pending dismissal motions resting on accusations of Internal Revenue Service and prosecutorial misconduct during grand jury proceedings and during trial. The District Court, Winner, J., held that: (1) there was a more than adequate showing that grounds may have existed for motion to dismiss indictment and accordingly entire grand jury transcript dealing with indictment would be made available for study by defense counsel, and (2) one defendant was entitled to new trial.

Ordered accordingly.

1. Criminal Law—627.6(6)

There was a more than adequate showing that grounds may have existed for motion to dismiss indictment because of Inter-

* Synopsis and headnotes copyright © by West Publishing Company; 1983; reprinted with permission from Volume 575 of the Federal Supplement, page 325.
† This opinion which was originally published at 570 F.Supp. 505 was withdrawn from the bound volume on order of the United States Court of Appeals for the Tenth Circuit that further publication be temporarily delayed. The order so providing has now been vacated by the Court of Appeals.

nal Revenue Service and prosecutorial misconduct during grand jury proceedings; accordingly, entire grand jury transcript dealing with indictment would be made available for study by defense counsel. Fed. Rules Cr.Proc. Rules 6, 6(e)(3)(C), 18 U.S.C.A.

2. Witnesses—8

Lawyers cannot substitute themselves for the court to release a witness for subpoena.

3. Criminal Law—919(1)

Defendant was entitled to new trial because of alleged improprieties including government counsel's releasing a witness from subpoena.

———————

William Waller and Richard K. Rufner, Wagner and Waller, Englewood, Colo., for defendant Kilpatrick.

James L. Treece, Treece, Zbar, Webb & Kenne, Littleton, Colo., for defendant Declan O'Donnell.

James Nesland, Ireland, Stapleton & Pryor, Denver, Colo., for defendant Bank of Nova Scotia.

H. Alan Dill, Dill & Dill, P.C., Denver, Colo., for defendant Sheila Lerner.

Linda Surbaugh and Robert Miller for U.S. Atty's. Office, D. Colo., Denver, Colo., and Charles J. Alexander, Dept. of Justice, Tax Div., Washington, D.C., for U.S.

WINNER, District Judge.

This case was started with a multiple count, multiple defendant indictment returned after an investigation spanning the lives of two grand juries. Judge Kane dismissed all except one count, which left a one defendant charge of obstruction of justice case to try. It was prosecuted by three attorneys employed by the Tax Division of the Department of Justice in Washington. The single remaining count of the indictment had absolutely nothing to do with tax law, and the trial could have been handled competently and with aplomb by any assistant United States Attorney living in Denver, but the administrative decision of the Department of Justice was to send three lawyers from the

Tax Division to try an obstruction of justice case, a prosecution unrelated to their professed area of expertise.

I mention this fact for one very important reason. Following a jury verdict of guilty, defendant moved for dismissal or a new trial, and the pending dismissal motions rest on accusations of IRS and prosecutorial misconduct during the grand jury proceedings and during trial. There is absolutely no suggestion of any improper conduct on the part of the United States Attorney for the District of Colorado or on the part of any of his assistants. Defense counsel carefully point out that neither they nor their client complain about anything other than acts of the IRS and Department of Justice Tax Division lawyers who ran the grand jury and tried the case. Based upon my review of the record and participation in the trial, I share their view that the Colorado United States Attorney's Office is absolutely blameless in this case so fraught with problems. Also, it should be emphasized that no one is critical of government counsel now handling the post trial motions.

To fully cover all of the headaches of this case would require a volume, and I don't plan to write that book for reasons which will appear presently. Instead, I shall highlight some of the things which occurred during the investigation and during the trial of the case. But, there are so many things to cover that this opinion won't be short. Many of the accusations are disputed by the accused government counsel and agents, but they are forced to admit a few instances of "mistake," and their denials of facts run contrary to testimony of a large number of witnesses. To accept the testimony of government witnesses at full value would require that I effectively decide that quite a few reputable lawyers and citizens of this community and other communities are guilty of perjury, and I make no such determination. The record made to date is incomplete. A full evidentiary hearing was scheduled, but, as will be explained later, present government counsel was not able to prepare for the first hearing, and the testimony of essential government witnesses was put over for three weeks. It was ordered that a summary of the testimony of government witnesses be furnished in advance of a hearing scheduled some three weeks later. The summary was furnished, but the government witnesses weren't called although I and defense counsel wanted them called. Therefore, at this point, all I have to rely on is the summary of proposed testimony, but the witnesses have not been sworn nor have they been cross-examined.

With that, then, I set the stage for some of the bizarre happenings in this case, and I do so by mentioning a frequently quoted case. In 1935, in *Berger* v. *United States,* 295 U.S. 78, 55 S.Ct. 629, 79 L.Ed. 1314, Justice Sutherland, speaking for a unanimous court, criticized the misconduct of the prosecutor in that case. The prosecutor had injected his personal belief concerning the facts of the case (so did a prosecutor here) and he had unfairly cross-examined witnesses. That which the court said concerning reliance by a jury on a prosecutor's integrity is even more applicable to the reliance of a grand jury on a prosecutor. As to a prosecutor's duties, the Court said:

> The United States Attorney is the representative not of an ordinary person to a controversy, but of a sovereignty whose obligation to govern impartially is as compelling as its obligation to govern at all; and whose interest, therefore, in a criminal prosecution is not that it shall win a case, but that justice shall be done. As such, he is in a peculiar and very definite sense the servant of the law, the twofold aim of which is that guilt shall not escape or innocence suffer. He may prosecute with earnestness and vigor—indeed, he should do so. But while he may strike hard blows, he is not at liberty to strike foul ones. It is as much his duty to refrain from improper methods calculated to produce a wrongful conviction as it is to use every legitimate means to bring about a just one. *It is fair to say that the average jury, in a greater or less degree, has confidence that these obligations, which so plainly rest upon the prosecuting attorney, will be faithfully observed* . . .

Perhaps the thing which disappoints me the most is the forgetfulness of the grand jury itself in going along with having two IRS agents in charge of the IRS investigation sworn as "agents of the grand jury." Yet, I can understand, as Justice Sutherland said in *Berger* v. *United States,* that grand jurors rely on Justice Department lawyers for their legal advice. They should do this, but because I impanelled the first of these two grand juries, I know what those jurors were told, and I strongly suspect that the second grand jury was told about the same thing. I orally, and on the record, stressed that a grand jury has a duty to protect the innocent and I emphasized that a grand jury is an independent body, separate and apart from investigative agencies and that grand juries are not an arm of the prosecution but instead, they have a duty to examine the government's case carefully. I didn't tell them that they couldn't appoint IRS agents as their own "agents," because it never occurred to me that there could be such a blurring of the "investigative agency," "prosecuting attorney" and "grand juror" function. However, I did supply each grand juror with a copy of the recommended instructions to grand jurors authored under the auspices of the Judicial Center, and I urged each grand juror to read the instructions frequently to be sure that they adequately performed their duties. (I now urge that Justice Department prosecutors read them.) Those instructions say in important part:

> You will recall from my earlier remarks that the grand jury developed in England as an entity independent from the king to protect a subject from an unwarranted prosecution. The king could not charge a subject with a serious crime without first submitting evidence and witnesses to a grand jury, which then decided whether to return an indictment against the accused person.
>
> Just as the English grand jury was independent of the king, the federal grand jury under the United States Constitution is independent of the United States Attorney, the prosecutorial agent of the executive branch of the federal government. The grand jury is not an arm of the Federal Bureau of Investigation; it is not an arm of the Internal Revenue Service; just as it is not an arm of the United States Attorney's Office. There has been some criticism of the institution of the grand jury for allegedly acting as a mere rubber stamp approving prosecutions that are brought before it by government representatives. Similarly, you would perform a disservice if you did not indict where the evidence warranted an indictment.
>
> As a practical matter, you must work closely with the government attorneys. The United States Attorney and his assistants will provide you with important service in helping you to find your way when confronted with complex legal matters. It is entirely proper that you should receive this assistance.
>
> However, you must remember that you are not the prosecutor's agent. Your role is related to but clearly distinct from

that of the government attorneys who will assist you, and it is important that you keep the distinction between the roles clearly in mind. Although you must work closely with the government, you must not yield your powers nor forego your independence of spirit.

These comments are meant to be cautionary in nature. The government attorneys are sincere men and women, and you will develop ordinary human feelings as you work with them during your term of service. If past experience is any indication of what to expect in the future, then you can expect candor, honesty, and good faith efforts in every matter presented by the government. However, it is because you may tend to expect such high quality from the government's agents that there is a potentially grave risk to your independence of thought and action, which may cause you to lapse into reliance when you should be dubious or questioning.

You should also remember that the government attorneys are advocates of the government's interests. They are prosecutors; you are not. While they will usually balance fairly the government's interest against the interest of a citizen's personal liberty, it is your responsibility to ensure that the proper balance is achieved in every case brought to your attention. You must exercise your own judgment, and if the facts suggest a different balance than that advocated by the government attorneys, then you must achieve the appropriate balance even in the face of their opposition or criticism.

In the face of these instructions, the grand jury wasn't two minutes into its investigation when one of the Justice Department lawyers personally administered an "oath" to an IRS Special Agent, and that "oath" was:

> Mr. Mendrop, do you swear to carry out the duties as directed by the Foreman and Members of the Grand Jury, keep all proceedings of matters and documents which are received pursuant to your work with this grand jury secretive? (sic).

In its brief the government says: The government concedes that Mr. Snyder had no authority to administer oaths to agents. However, Mr. Snyder will testify, and the record will reflect, that the agents were first given an oath by the foreman. It was only after they had been sworn in by the foreman that Mr. Snyder gave the agents what purported to be an additional oath directing the agents to maintain secrecy. [As has been noted, this testimony hasn't been presented yet, and on

the sworn record made to date, it is not clear who gave an oath
to testify truthfully.]

The government then "quotes" from the transcript which
shows that those were the facts. That's not what the transcript
which was supplied to me shows, and I am concerned about the
validity of someone's transcript. It is true that other "oaths"
administered by Mr. Snyder do appear to have followed an oath
administered by someone to testify truthfully, but if any such
oath was administered to Mr. Mendrop at the first session, it
doesn't show up in my copy of the transcript.

Six months later, the Special Agents of the IRS were each
sworn as an "agent" of the second grand jury, and if there could
be any doubt as to the mingling of the investigative agency/
prosecutorial/grand jury functions, the hash which results from
the following proceedings eliminates that doubt. After a statement by government counsel that he wanted the agent sworn as
an "agent of the grand jury," this job description was furnished
by Mr. Snyder:

> . . . when he interviews people and he looks at this stuff, he
> is not looking at it so much as a special agent of the criminal
> investigation division of the Internal Revenue Service, and he
> is looking at (it) as your agent and he is amendable to you and
> he is amendable to Rule 6. Do you recall Rule 6, the Grand
> Jury secrecy?
> *What it is, is very, very plain, and it states in what capacity he is
> operating in this investigation so there is no question about it.*
> (The agent was then sworn as a witness by someone, and the
> transcript continues)
>
> MR. SNYDER: Do you have the oath to make him a—they
> don't have the oath. Raise your right hand. Do you solemnly
> swear that the information and evidence which you receive
> pursuant to the Grand Jury you will keep secret to yourself
> *except as provided by the foreman of the Grand Jury* or federal
> judge? . . . In the course of your *duties as a special agent and also
> as an agent of a previous grand jury* have you conducted an
> investigation into the affairs of one William A. Kilpatrick?

I don't know how it could be any clearer than in Mr. Snyder's
eyes, the agent's investigation was a combined IRS and Grand
Jury investigation conducted by a single "agent," and, of course,

under Rule 6 he was the prosecuting attorney's little helper. That isn't what the stock instructions to grand jurors say should be done, and, although the government argues that other grand juries have had agents, it fails to come up with a case approving the practice and it fails to mention any case discussing the blurring of functions. The government relies on *United States* v. *Cosby,* (1979) 5 Cir., 601 F.2d 754. There, the court itself challenged the practice of appointing an "agent of the grand jury," but it "assumed" that the practice was proper because it reversed the case on other grounds. The opinion cites several cases where "the use of third parties to assist grand juries has been considered and approved," but it is to be noted that those cases were decided before the amendment of Rule 6(e) which makes no mention of grand jury "agents" and which says that disclosure may be made to government lawyers for use in the performance of duty, and to other governmental personnel "as are deemed necessary by an attorney for the government *to assist an attorney for the government in the performance of such attorney's duty to enforce federal criminal law.*" The rule doesn't permit the grand jury to have an "agent," and it categorically says that Rule 6(e) permits disclosure to non-lawyers for the single purpose of assisting the "attorney for the government." The rule doesn't mix up the separate functions of prosecutor and grand jury, and with Rule 6(e) clarified, those functions cannot be blended.

My thoughts on this score are in full accord with those of the Advisory Committee, because its note to the 1972 amendment to Rule 6(e) says:

> Federal crimes are "investigated" by the FBI, the IRS, or by Treasury agents, *and not by government prosecutors or the citizens who sit on grand juries.*

Here, the "Grand Jury Agents" investigated and they testified, all the while being special agents of the IRS, and, as will be detailed later, a government prosecutor "investigated" on the streets of Puerto Rico.

The government concedes the obvious. A lawyer employed by the Tax Division of the Department of Justice can't administer oaths, but, sworn, or unsworn, I don't think that an IRS special agent can act in the combined capacity of IRS Agent, "Agent for the Grand Jury" and recipient of grand jury information supplied under Rule 6(e) for the sole purpose of helping out the prosecutor. This is a confusion not of apples and oranges. It is confusing apples, oranges and bananas.

Admitting impropriety in the conduct of counsel, the government's brief argues that the error wasn't serious and that it resulted from good motives of Mr. Snyder. The error may or may not be serious, and I express no opinion as to the gravity of the error. However, the government is playing with fire in arguing that good motive excuses making one's own law. I discussed my thinking of this argument at quite some length in *United States* v. *Best,* (1979) 476 F.Supp. 34, where I ruled that a belief that blocking some railroad tracks would save the world from nuclear devastation didn't excuse the offense, and the Tax Division has surely heard tax protestors say that their motives in refusing to obey the tax laws are pure as the driven snow. Mr. Snyder's good intentions don't excuse his arrogation of a power he didn't have. And, even if the illegal "oath" doesn't amount to serious error, it started the case downhill on a course of repeated excesses on the part of the prosecution. Good intentions or ignorance of the law don't make those errors go away. The creation of the "office" of grand jury agent is harder to excuse when the impartial jurors' "agent" is a chief investigator of the IRS case against the defendants and is receiving grand jury information under Rule 6(e) only to help out the attorney for the government charged with the supervision of presentation of the government's case to the grand jury.

What has been said thus far, and much of that which is to follow, bear in no way on the trial itself, and, therefore, those things can't enter into a decision of whether a new trial should be granted. That which took place during the grand jury proceedings and most of that which took place outside the presence of the jury couldn't poison the jury verdict, and these alleged transgressions are argued in support of the motion to dismiss because of prosecutorial misconduct and in support of claimed lack of professionalism of government counsel. Therefore, insofar as possible, I shall try to discuss the arguments bearing on the new trial motion in a separate part of this memorandum.

In a brief filed by trial counsel (not signed by present counsel for the government and not adopted by Colorado's United States Attorney whose typewritten signature does appear) the many accusations were described as "silly," but they aren't either silly or frivolous. Indeed, the brief filed by trial counsel was couched in language far different from that which the court is accustomed to reading. When asked, Mr. Scharf said that higher authority in the Justice Department Tax Division had approved the brief and its phraseology, and that higher authority thought the whole thing was a ploy of defense counsel. If that be so, the lawyers in the upper echelon of the Tax Division have adopted a style of brief writing markedly different from that Justice Department lawyers have filed with this court in the past, and I have had my fair share of experience in dealing with Tax Division lawyers for whose ability and ethics I have the highest regard. And, if the overlords of the Tax Division think this whole mess is just a ploy, I recommend that they take a second look.

Since I started this with the grand jury proceedings, I think that I should continue with them and with matters which occurred during the trial which don't impact on the new trial motion but which are aimed at the dismissal motion and lack of professionalism. I think that the place to start is with Rule 6(e), F.R.Cr.P. itself, because that is the rule which governs grand juries and it is the rule which was violated here. I quote from Rule 6(e) and I italicize the phrases in that section which are of importance to this case:

> (e) Recording and Disclosure of Proceedings.
>
> (1) All proceedings, except when the grand jury is deliberating, shall be recorded stenographically or by an electronic recording device. An unintentional failure of any recording to reproduce all or any portion of a proceeding shall not affect the validity of the prosecution. *The recording or reporter's notes or any transcript prepared therefrom shall remain in the custody or control of the attorney for the government* unless otherwise ordered by the court in a particular case.
>
> (2) A grand juror, an interpreter, a stenographer, an operator of a recording device, a typist who transcribes recorded testimony, *an attorney for the government, or any person to whom disclosure is made under paragraph (3) (A) (ii) of this subdivision shall not disclose matters occurring before the grand jury* except as otherwide provided by these rules. *No obligation of secrecy may be imposed on any person except in accordance with this rule.* A known violation of Rule 6 may be punished as a contempt.
>
> (3) (A) Disclosure otherwise prohibited by this rule of mat-

ters occurring before the grand jury, other than its deliberations and the vote of any grand juror, may be made to—

> (i) an attorney for the government for use in the perfor-
> mance of such attorney's duty; and
> (ii) such government personnel as are deemed necessary
> *to assist an attorney for the government in the performance of*
> *such attorney's duty to enforce criminal law.*
> (I don't know how it can be argued that this language
> permits disclosure to IRS agents to work as "agents for
> the grand jury" unless it is argued that the grand jury is
> simply an arm of the prosecutor's office, and if that be the
> argument, almost 800 years of history is going to have to
> be forgotten. The document King John signed at Run-
> nymede contains no such concept, nor does our Consti-
> tution.)
> (iii) such government personnel *as are deemed necessary by*
> *an attorney for the government to assist an attorney for the gov-*
> *ernment in the performance of such attorney's duty* to enforce
> federal criminal law.
> (It seems pretty clear to me that the IRS agents to whom
> disclosure was made were hired guns of the prosecutor
> and the IRS—not of the grand jury.)

(B) . . . An attorney for the government shall promptly provide the district court, before which was empanelled the grand
jury whose material has been so disclosed, with the names of
the persons to whom such disclosure has been made. (The
language of the rule is this clumsy.)

(C) Disclosure otherwise prohibited by this rule of matters
occurring before the grand jury may also be made . . .

> (ii) when permitted by a court at the request of the defen-
> dant, upon a showing that grounds may exist for a motion
> to dismiss the indictment because of matters occurring
> before the grand jury.
> If the court orders disclosure of matters occurring before
> the grand jury, the disclosure shall be made in such man-
> ner, at such time, and under such conditions as the court
> may direct.

I first mention something not raised by defense counsel, but
defense counsel had no way of knowing anything about it. I
found out about it from a scanning of the full file drawer of
grand jury transcript. A while back, it was the practice to make

grand jury witnesses take an oath of secrecy, and this is still the rule in some state court systems. Because of public outcry, the rule was changed, and, as has been seen, this is now verboten because of the language of rule saying, "No obligation of secrecy may be imposed on any person except in accordance with this rule." This language has been uniformly interpreted to prohibit any instruction to a witness that his testimony is secret. *In re Langswager,* (1975) D.C.Ill. 392 F.Supp. 783; *In re Grand Jury Witness Subpoenas* (1974) D.C.Fla. 370 F.Supp. 1282; *In re Alvarez* (1972) D.C.Cal. 351 F.Supp. 1089; *In re Minkoff* (1972) D.C.R.I. 349 F.Supp. 154; *In re Investigation before April 1975 Grand Jury* (1976) D.C.Cir. 531 F.2d 600; *In re Vescovo Special Grand Jury* (1979) 473 F.Supp. 1335, and many other cases. In spite of this express command of Rule 6(e), secrecy obligations were imposed on several witnesses, and, to make the violation more disturbing, secrecy obligations were imposed on lawyers called to furnish information concerning their clients. That makes the violation gravely beyond the pale, because of the impossible position the lawyer-witness is placed in, but that's what the grand jury transcript discloses. No "oath" of secrecy was administered, but an obligation of secrecy was imposed by instructions from government counsel to witnesses. This foolishness may or may not have been intentional, but ignorance of the law is not a defense available to a prosecutor. This misconduct is established by the record, and it will prove difficult for the government to deny, just as the government had to admit the attempted administration of an "oath" by Mr. Snyder. The government surprisingly defends the proven mishmash of function of the IRS Special Agent/Grand Jury Agents/Assistants to the Attorney for the Government appointed under Rule 6(e), but maybe it thinks that admitting that this was error would confess the motion to dismiss.

I come now to other accusations made by defendant and pretty much denied by the prosecutors and IRS agents. I make no finding as to whether most of the charges are proven or unproven, but I do find that as to all assertions made by defendant there is cause for concern that the prosecutor's conduct before the grand jury may require dismissal of the indictment. The accusations are made sincerely; there is some evidence to support all of them, and there is quite a bit of evidence to support some. However, before factual findings can be made, a further hearing permitting participation by all parties interested in the grand jury proceedings is necessary—something which will be explained later. Most importantly, of course, the testimony of government counsel is essential, and it is still missing although all three of the lawyers were in Denver during the last hearing.

Because that additional hearing is required, I shorten discussion of most of the claims of prosecutorial misconduct, but I shall comment briefly on them. Frequently I will phrase the charges as if the facts had been established, but I emphasize that I am not saying that the facts have been proven. I am just adopting the practice of the government in phrasing an indictment in language saying that thus and so are the facts. I am only phrasing the defendant's charges against the goverment in the same way the government phrases its charges against a defendant, and the fact that the charges are made is not evidence that they are true, nor do I find that they are.

Richard Birchall is a lawyer formerly with the Tax Division who practices in New Jersey and who did some work for defendant and his company. He was subpoenaed to testify before the grand jury, and he showed up in Denver pursuant to the subpoena. He says that he met Mr. Snyder and the agents in a bar and they downed a few drinks paid for by Mr. Snyder. During this session Mr. Snyder supposedly disregarded the secrecy rules and, having done so, he told Mr. Birchall he was a potential target. He added that there was testimony about a personal relationship of Mr. Birchall's, a comment which was bothersome to the witness because of marital problems of Mr. Birchall. These communications are of a nature (if they were were made) designed to bring about hurried cooperation from a witness, and especially from a witness who is a former Tax Division lawyer practicing tax law in the private sector. While in Denver, Mr. Birchall was left in a room with some grand jury transcripts and material lying on a table in plain sight. Mr. Birchall scanned some of the material trying to locate that which dealt with the matters discussed by Mr. Snyder. Perhaps he shouldn't have done this, but this is a matter of morals while grand jury secrecy is a matter covered by Rule 6, and Mr. Snyder was under it, but Mr. Birchall wasn't. Moreover, Mr. Birchall testified that he thought that he was being threatened by Mr. Snyder, and he was reacting to the threats. I pass no moral judgment on what happened because that's not the question to be decided in this case.

This doesn't end the accusations made through Mr. Birchall's testimony. He said that Mr. Snyder tried to persuade him to breach his ethical duty of confidentiality and he attributed to Mr. Snyder a remark that even if the defendant wasn't guilty, the government would "break him" with the cost of the defense. These accusations go to the heart of our system of justice, and it was no ploy on the part of defense counsel to bring the accusations out for public scrutiny.

Professor Roland Hjorth teaches tax law at the University of Washington Law School, and he is a recognized expert who was employed by defense counsel on the recommendation of the professor of tax law at the University of Michigan. At the request of defendant, Professor Hjorth was permitted to testify as an expert before the grand jury. His views of tax law differed markedly from those of Mr. Snyder, who bragged on frequent occasions that he had never taken a course in taxation and knew almost nothing about it. Nevertheless, Professor Hjorth was brow-beaten and ridiculed by Mr. Snyder, and some of the conversation so out of place for an ethical prosecutor took place during a recess in the hearing of some grand jurors. The government's post trial brief says as to this breach of ethics and standards of common courtesy:

> It was poor judgment on the part of Mr. Snyder to carry on a conversation with Professor Hjorth while two grand jurors were present. However, the record fact is that there was no disclosure of Grand Jury material during the conversation.

I'm not so sure about that. The record shows that the argument and ridicule was as to that which Professor Hjorth had testified to, and that persons other than grand jurors could hear the argument. However, even if the government is correct in this statement, the fact is that the argument begs the real question. Professor Hjorth also testified that as a result of Mr. Snyder's conduct, he would never again appear as an expert witness. Intimidating witnesses by telling them that their testimony disgraces them and implying that the Tax Division of the Department of Justice will take after the witness and will complain to the University of Washington Law School because an expert testified to his expert opinions does no credit to our government. I think that the government's argument in its post trial brief is unconvincing, and, seemingly, the professor's testimony isn't seriously contested. I hope that we haven't gotten to the point that disagreement with the legal concepts of the IRS provides grounds for attacks by that bureaucracy because sometimes the IRS is wrong. *U.S.* v. *Sells Engineering* (1983)—U.S.—, 103 S.Ct. 3133, 77 L.Ed.2d 743 and *U.S.* v. *Baggot*, —U.S. —, 103 S.Ct. 3164, 77 L.Ed.2d 785.

Peter Parrish is a former IRS agent who is now employed as an accountant and who worked for defendant. He said that when he responded to a subpoena, he was interviewed by Mr. Blondin and matters which took place before the grand jury were discussed. He also said that the discussions could be heard by outsiders. I don't approve this casual approach to witness interviews, but I think that the incident is picayune. It doesn't deserve discussion.

To further muddle the status of the Special Agent/Grand Jury Agent/Assistant to the Prosecutor matter, letters were written on the letterhead of the United States Attorney for the District of Colorado, and they were signed by the IRS agents with an explanatory line under their signature saying that they were "Special Agents." The letters were authorized by Justice Department attorneys, but they were not authorized by the United States Attorney in Colorado. Apart from the fact that IRS agents who claim to be "agents of the grand jury" shouldn't be using the U.S. Attorney's letterhead, the identity of the persons and the transactions which were under grand jury scrutiny shouldn't be disclosed to anyone by letter or otherwise, but these startling letters did precisely that. I can't fault the IRS agents for this because the government's brief says as to these singular letters:

> Mr. Blondin and Mr. Snyder on these occasions asked the agents to send out correspondence and to sign the letters for them, after having the contents of the letter read to them over the phone. On no occasion, did the agents who were acting under the direction and control of Mr. Snyder, Mr. Blondin

and the United States Attorney's Office sign any such letters
without advance authority from the government's attorneys.

The United States Attorney for the District of Colorado has
disavowed the letters written on his letterhead, and he has seen
to it that this won't happen again.

Thus, the disclosures were made with knowledge of Tax Division lawyers and the IRS agent signatures on U.S. Attorney
stationery were approved by them. The government has cited
no authority for this novel procedure by which the nature of
that which was going on before the grand jury and the identity
of a target was certified to in writing on the letterhead of the
U.S. Attorney who was not running the investigation. Once
more, I attribute no fault to the U.S. Attorney.

In recent years, the use of "pocket immunity" has become
prevalent. The phrase, for the benefit of the uninitiated, refers
to a practice of ignoring the Congressional mandate as to how
immunity can be granted and instead of doing what Congress
commands, informally substituting a "deal" struck between a
prosecutor and a witness. The enforceability of the side agreement in the federal court is an open question, but I have never
heard it even argued that federal pocket immunity applies to a
state court prosecution. However, when it is coyly suggested that
a lawyer's client is a target of a grand jury inquiry and that the
client can escape the range of fire by incriminating himself
along with someone else, the carrot proffered by the prosecutor
is hard to resist. Not unimportant, of course, is the fact that the
pocket immunity need not be included in statistical reports
showing the number of immunities granted in federal prosecutions. (These statistics have been of interest to Congress in the
past, and I believe that they still are.)

The deal is a good one for both sides, but it skirts the law. It
can be granted on a local level by lawyers not authorized to
approve the grant of formal immunity, and no report of its use
is required. Formal immunity would have required the approval
of the United States Attorney and a designated Assistant Attorney General. But pocket immunity can be granted at the whim
of any lawyer running a grand jury, and there is no public
record of the side deal. Here, the United States Attorney didn't
authorize nor did he approve the immunities. In fact, he didn't

know anything about them, although statutory immunity requires his okay.

The history of immunity statutes, colonial, state and federal, is set out in footnotes to *Kastigar* v. *United States* (1972) 406 U.S. 441, 92 S.Ct. 1653, 32 L.Ed.2d 212, and the present immunity statute enacted in 1970 is there discussed, as is the Congressional intent in its enactment. The intent as to the formality of grants of immunity is quite plain. 18 U.S.C. §6002 effectively recognizes privilege against self-incrimination up to the point "the person presiding over the proceeding communicates to the witness an order issued under this part," to testify. The preliminaries to obtaining such an order are spelled out in 18 U.S.C. §6003, and they are:

1. There must be a request for the order *made by "the United States attorney for such district."*
2. The request by the United States Attorney for the immunity grant *must then be approved by "the Attorney General, the Deputy Attorney General, or any assistant Attorney General."*
3. There must be a certification that the testimony may be necessary for the public interest and that the witness has refused or is likely to refuse to testify because of his privilege against self-incrimination.

At that point, a district judge performs the ministerial act of signing the immunity order. *In re Corrugated Container Antitrust Litigation* (2nd Cir. 1981) 644 F.2d 70, *In re Daley,* (7th Cir. 1977), 549 F.2d 469. The order typically tracks § 6002 and says that "no testimony or other information compelled under the order . . . may be used against the witness in any criminal case, except a prosecution for perjury, giving a false statement, or otherwise failing to comply with the order." This was the statute which was analyzed in *Kastigar* v. *United States* (1972), 406 U.S. 441, 92 S.Ct. 1653, 32 L.Ed.2d 212, in which the old case of *Counselman* v. *Hitchcock* (1982) 142 U.S. 547, 12 S.Ct. 195, 35 L.Ed. 1110, was explained and distinguished. In *Kastigar* it was held that the statute did not grant transactional immunity and that the grant was limited to use. "The statute, like the Fifth Amendment, grants neither pardon nor amnesty. Both the statute, like the Fifth Amendment allow the government to prosecute using evidence from legitimate independent sources."

When the statute is followed, there is a formal, understandable record of the immunity granted and its extent, but, with pocket immunity, no one is sure what the deal is, and there is no adequate record—statistical or otherwise. An underlying purpose of the statute is to reduce to written record the identities of persons granted immunity to permit necessary comparison at a later time of their relative guilt, as compared with persons not let off the hook. With the informal pocket immunity only a few of the grants come to light, and clear Congressional purpose behind the law is defeated. The statute cannot be read to mean anything other than a limitation on immunity grants to requests made by a "United States Attorney," approved by "the Attorney General, the Deputy Attorney General, or any assistant Attorney General." Congress did not delegate to Tax Division Assistants any right to formally or to informally deal out immunity to the objects of their bounty, but here persons identified as targets of the grand jury were later bargained out of the case by Messrs. Snyder and Blondin. Whether there was any approval of the gifts of pocket immunity, and if so, by whom, I know not, but I do know that there was not compliance with 18 U.S.C. §§ 6002-6003, and I do know that the United States Attorney did not authorize the pocket immunities granted by Tax Division lawyers.

This is especially troublesome in this case in light of the record made concerning the witness Richard Bell who was allegedly targeted by the grand jury (or at least by Mr. Snyder and Mr. Blondon). Mr. Bell was represented by his brother, Malcolm, an attorney practicing in New York City, and a witness I found to be straightforward, fair, convincing, and most generous to Mr. Snyder. Malcolm Bell succumbed to the carrot of pocket immunity for his brother, but later he was told by Mr. Snyder that if Richard "testified for Mr. Kilpatrick, all bets are off." Maybe this meant that if Mr. Bell perjured himself he would be prosecuted for perjury, but if the immunity statute had been followed, the nagging question of the meaning of "all bets are off" wouldn't confront us. Under the statute, all bets weren't off if Richard Bell testified for Mr. Kilpatrick, although he could have been prosecuted for perjury if he testified falsely, but incriminating testimony given by him couldn't be used in a prosecution of the charges with which he was threatened. If the statute had been followed, the government couldn't welch on the bet of not using any incriminating testimony and I doubt that it can welch on that bet when the immunity grant is in pocket form. All too often, pocket immunities are carelessly granted, and sometimes they grant transactional immunity which Congress has not authorized. It is not surprising that there was uncertainty and misunderstanding in this instance. Grand jurors can't be expected to know the requirements of law concerning lawful immunity grants, and if the prosecutor ignores the statute, the grand jury should be told that witnesses are testifying under a side deal made with the witness by the prosecutor. The nature and informality of the immunity grant might bear on a grand juror's evaluation of the credibility of a witness, especially if the grand juror knew of the short cut used by the prosecution.

James Treece is a former United States Attorney for the District of Colorado. He was representing one of the targets of the grand jury investigation, and he was served with a subpoena duces tecum to produce records before the grand jury. He told the IRS Special Agent/Grand Jury Agent/Assistant to the prosecutor who served him that he had no such records in his possession, to which the agent, speaking in which capacity I know not, responded, "You're a liar." I guess that at this point this "man of many occupations" decided to act as a grand juror and pass on credibility. That this was said is denied, but I cannot disregard the testimony. I have no knowledge that any such comment was communicated to the grand jury, but Mr. Treece was required to testify after being called a liar by the "grand jury agent," and although I doubt that Mr. Treece was intimidated, other witnesses would have been.

We have not one but two problems under *Massiah* v. *United States*, 377 U.S. 201, 84 S.Ct. 1199, L.Ed.2d 246. With full knowledge that he was represented by counsel, Declan O'Donnell appeared before the grand jury against the advice of his counsel, and that advice was known to the prosecutors. The government argues that O'Donnell was a lawyer and that he appeared voluntarily. I don't think that this is any answer to *Massiah* although I concede that the case deals with an indicted defendant and O'Donnell was not then indicted. The government excuses its conduct saying it is permitted under *Edwards* v.

Arizona, 451 U.S. 477, 478, 101 S.Ct. 1880, 1881, 68 L.Ed.2d 378. I don't think that *Edwards* v. *Arizona* is apposite. That case has to do with *Miranda* rights, and, although the government asks that I read footnote 9 of the opinion, I think that footnote 8 has more to do with the *Massiah* problem. I do not rule that there was or was not a violation of *Massiah* in the case of Mr. O'Donnell's testimony before the grand jury because such a ruling is not necessary to this memorandum, but defendant's argument isn't frivolous.

Robert G. Morvillo is a prominent lawyer practicing in New York City, and his testimony was taken by telephone. He represented the Bank of Nova Scotia, and he testified concerning the activities of Mr. Scharf in going to Puerto Rico to play cop in a further and total blurring of the distinction between prosecutor and investigator. In its brief, the government sees no impropriety in this conduct, but I remind of the Advisory Committee's comment that "Federal crimes are 'investigated' by the FBI, the IRS or by Treasury Agents and not by *government prosecutors* or the citizens who sit on grand juries." (They surely aren't investigated by "reviewers," something next to be discussed.) In any event, I have no doubt that when a prosecutor turns cop, he loses his *Imbler* v. *Pachtman,* 424 U.S. 409, 96 S.Ct. 984, 47 L.Ed.2d 128 prosecutorial immunity.

While in Puerto Rico, Mr. Scharf conducted a surveillance of some little girls and tailed them to their home. This let him question their mother as to the whereabouts of his prey who happened to be her husband, and who is a Bank of Nova Scotia employee. Of course, Mr. Scharf must have known that the wife couldn't have been compelled to testify to her husband's whereabouts, even under the lessened privilege adopted in *Trammel* v. *United States,* 445, U.S. 40, 100 S.Ct. 906, 63 L.Ed.2d 186. As an investigative technique tailing the little girls and quizzing the wife may have been brilliant police work, but I am quizzical as to the propriety of a lawyer questioning someone he knows he couldn't question in court because of an absolute privilege which, according to *Trammel,* can be waived only with full knowledge of the incompetence to testify. It seems to me that whatever may be the obligations of an IRS agent, a prosecutor owes a duty not to question a wife about her husband's whereabouts unless *Berger* v. *United States,* 295 U.S. 78, 55 S.Ct. 629,

79 L.Ed. 1314 has been overruled, and it hasn't been. Totally apart from the propriety of Mr. Scharf's actions in Puerto Rico under *Trammel,* the witnesses were employees of the Bank of Nova Scotia, well known to Mr. Scharf to be represented by Mr. Morvillo. He says that interviews conducted by Mr. Scharf violate *Massiah;* the government says they don't, and I express no judgment as to who is right or wrong, but, undeniably, there is a problem, and I think that the problem was well known to Mr. Scharf when he visited Puerto Rico.

Next we come to still another confusion in who occupied what job. It seems that within the administrative procedures of the Department of Justice sometimes conferences can be arranged with "reviewers" who are higher ups in the Tax Division. Many lawyers are of the impression that the "reviewers" occupy a sort of quasi-judicial capacity to pass judgment on whether a case should be prosecuted, and that they are pretty much like the Appellate Staff on the civil side of the Tax Division. Experienced tax lawyers think that a "reviewer" is someone with whom compromise can be discussed. Moreover, from time immemorial, lawyers have dealt with one another in trying to settle cases in the belief that they can be straightforward without having their words thrown back at them at time of trial. The IRS hasn't always shared this view, and problems with the IRS played no small part in the enlargement of the coverage of the common law rule by the enactment of Rule 408 of the Federal Rules in Evidence. That rule now provides, "evidence of conduct or statements made in compromise negotiations is likewise not admissable."

During the troubled history of this case, some lawyers were and some were not afforded the luxury of a conference with a "reviewer." Experienced tax lawyers think that a conference with a Reviewer offers a last ditch opportunity to avoid a criminal prosecution through negotiation, and memoranda are submitted to the Reviewer to analyze defense counsel's legal position. Conferences are then set up, attended by IRS agents, trial attorneys for the government, and defense counsel to present arguments pro and con for more or less impartial consideration by the Reviewer. Counsel for some targets were and some were not favored with a conference with a Reviewer, but those who were so favored met with one Jared Scharf acting as the Reviewer. Something which was not disclosed to defense counsel was that he was behind the scenes prosecutor, and, not only was he a behind the scenes prosecutor, he was actually an investigator in the case.

Rule 6(e) says that the grand jury transcript shall "remain in custody or control of the attorney for the government." The transcript of this grand jury was in the custody and control of the IRS. After the indictments were handed down, the transcript was stored away from the United States Courthouse in a room obtained from the General Services Administration by the Internal Revenue Service. It was a room assigned to the IRS, and, if the United States Attorney wanted in, he would have had to get a key from the IRS Special Agents. One cannot help fretting about this violation of the express language of the rule, and *United States* v. *Sells Engineering, Inc.,* —U.S. —, 103 S.Ct. 3133, 77 L.Ed,2d 743, coupled with *United States* v. *Baggot.* — U.S. —, 103 S.Ct. 3164, 77 L.Ed.2d 785, decided a few weeks ago, don't lessen the concern as to why the IRS retained custody of the transcripts which the rule unambiguously says should be under the control of the United States Attorney and only the United States Attorney.

There is testimony that Mr. Snyder threw his jacket on the floor and mouthed obscenities at me as I left the bench. I didn't see anything like that, and the conduct is denied. I don't know whether he did or didn't do any such thing.

When I recessed court one day, the players were in their usual positions. Mr. Snyder, Mr. Blondin, Ms. Surbaugh, and an IRS agent were seated at plaintiff's table. Mr. Scharf was in his bleacher seat, a couple of rows back in the spectator's section where he always sat while the jury was in the courtroom. It was only when the jury left the courtroom that he sat at the counsel table and became an active trial participant. Because of suspicions I had based on testimony in the case (suspicions enhanced by post trial testimony) I was concerned about possible violations of *Massiah,* and I cautioned one and all that I didn't want the rule violated. I started to leave the bench, and Mr. Scharf yelled at me (he says that he spoke in a loud voice, but the dictionary I have suggests that the difference between a loud voice and a yell is quibble). Mr. Scharf's discourtesy amused me more than it offended me, but, according to that which has been said in the post trial hearings, members of the public were distressed that a government lawyer would shout at the judge from the spectator's section of the courtroom. I thought that my court reporter's comment as we left the courtroom was discerning. She said that if her five year old son did something like that he would be sent to bed without his supper.

Rule 6(e) was amended to change the procedure for disclosure of grand jury information to "such government personnel as are deemed necessary by an attorney for the government to assist an attorney for the government in the performance of such attorney's duty to enforce the criminal law." No court permission for the disclosure is required, and the rule is complied with if the attorney for the government "promptly provide(s) the district court . . . with the names of the persons to whom such disclosure is made." As I read it, any "attorney for the government" can promptly provide the information, and any "attorney for the government" can make the decision to disclose. I have no fault to find with the paper trail left in this matter insofar as the disclosure requirements are concerned. I am troubled about testimony suggesting that authority to make the disclosure decisions was delegated to the IRS Special Agent/ Grand Jury Agents/Prosecutor's helpers. Under common law rules of agency, this authority couldn't be delegated to a subagent, and, especially it couldn't be delegated to an IRS agent whose fellow workers were aiming at the defendants from a different angle. My worry on this score is not lessened by an IRS letter in evidence saying that making a civil tax case under the administrative process would be difficult. *United States* v. *Sells Engineers* and *United State* v. *Baggot,* both *supra,* which settle the question of using a grand jury to collect taxes.

At the post trial hearing, Donald D'Amico, a witness called by the government, testified as to his appearance before the grand jury. He said that in the presence of the grand jury, Mr. Snyder threw his arm around his shoulder and whispered, "Don't let them cut you up." Then Mr. Snyder introduced him to the grand jury with a glowing recitation of Mr. D'Amico's war record and said, "we have a genuine war hero." After that, Mr. Snyder read off a list of names and asked if the witness would take the Fifth Amendment if inquiry was made concerning those persons. Upon receiving an affirmative answer, the witness was excused from further testimony, and it was not until the post trial hearing that Mr. D'Amico received oral pocket immunity. From what was said at the hearing I glean that counsel for Mr. D'Amico had discussed the grand jury testimony before the witness was called, and why he was called just to claim his privilege remains unexplained.

Bernard Bailor was called as a witness by the government. He is a lawyer of long experience with the Tax Division of the Department of Justice, and I was impressed with his knowledge and with his candor. He said that if a case is being prosecuted by a United States Attorney, it is not unheard of to have a Reviewer assigned to assist in a trial if the United States Attorney so requests, but that when a case is being prosecuted by Tax Division lawyers, it would be most unusual to have a Reviewer act as a trial attorney. He also summarized the security given grand jury material in a major case he handled, and that security was far greater than the security in this case. He made the statement that abuse of the grand jury process should bring about a dismissal of the indictment.

[1] I think that I have talked enough about the grand jury to explain why I think there has been more than an "adequate showing that grounds may exist for a motion to dismiss the indictment because of matters occurring before the grand jury." There is such a motion, and, accordingly, I act under the provisions of Rule 6(e)(3)(C) which says that disclosure of grand jury matters may be made "when permitted by the court at the request of the defendant, upon a showing that grounds may exist for a motion to dismiss the indictment because of matters occurring before the grand jury." The Advisory Committee note to Rule 6 requires a "preliminary factual showing of serious misconduct" and I am convinced that the requirement has been met. I guess that technically, the requisite "request" to examine the entire grand jury transcript hasn't been made, but in light of this memorandum, I am sure it will be. I have scanned the transcript, but I haven't had time to study it, and, even if I had the time, nuances recognizable by counsel wouldn't be apparent to me. Because of the showing made as to the claims of prosecutorial conduct, and without finally ruling that there was or was not any such misconduct, I order that the entire grand jury

transcript dealing with this indictment be made available for study by defense counsel. Defense counsel say that a grand juror who is also a lawyer, if permitted, would testify that Mr. Snyder oppressed witnesses before the grand jury and that he was overbearing and discourteous. I leave to another judge to decide whether this evidence should be received.

The rules says, "If the court orders disclosure of matters occurring before the grand jury, the disclosure shall be made in such manner, at such time, and under such conditions as the court may direct." The conditions follow: Disclosure shall be made to counsel and only to counsel. Paralegals shall not be used as substitute lawyers, and only members of the bar shall examine the transcript. They shall hold secret matters they learn, and they shall discuss them with no one other than co-counsel, and, insofar as necessary to the preparation of their arguments, with their clients. Typists given direct or indirect information concerning the content of the transcript shall receipt for a copy of a written order commanding that they hold secret any information learned by them as to what took place before the grand jury, and those receipted orders shall be filed with the clerk. During the time a transcript is being used to prepare arguments in this case, counsel shall be personally responsible for its secrecy, and when not in actual use, the transcript shall be placed in locked storage to which only counsel have access. When need for the transcripts no longer exist, all copies of it shall be returned to the United States Attorney to remain in his custody and control. All briefs disclosing grand jury testimony shall be sealed.

I make this ruling because I think that disclosure of the transcript is necessary in the interest of justice, and I make it because of recent action by the United States Court of Appeals for the Tenth Circuit. I also have in mind that which I anticipate the future holds in store for me. I noted earlier that Judge Kane has dismissed all except one count of the indictment, and the government has appealed his ruling. Because the prosecutorial misconduct, if proven, may result in a dismissal of the entire indictment, the Court of Appeals has ordered a partial remand to permit full development of the facts by all defendants. The remand is of such recent date that other defendants cannot be adequately prepared, and they should be permitted to participate in the matter to whatever extent they desire. They may be satisfied with the record made, or they may want to expand on it. Even defendant Kilpatrick's lawyers may want to expand the record after reading the full transcript. I cannot, and I do not rule on the motion to dismiss. I earlier asked for suggestions as to remedy, and the government has said that such suggestions are premature. I think that is correct. Dismissal is a possibility under a theory of a totality of the circumstances, and it is because proof of repeated misconduct is necessary to order dismissal that I have discussed the many accusations. See, *U.S.* v. *Gold,* (1979) D.C.Ill. 470 F.Supp. 1336. But dismissal is a last resort seldom used. *U.S.* v. *Narciso* (1976) D.C.Mich. 446 F.Supp. 252. Contempt is a possibility, and it is the remedy usually suggested. See, *U.S.* v. *Hoffa* (6th Cir.1965) 349 F.2d 20, *U.S.* v. *Dunham Concrete Products* (5th Cir. 1973) 475 F.2d 1241, *U.S.* v. *District Court* (4th Cir.1956) 238 F. 2d 713. Disciplinary proceedings are a possibility, and the government has advised that "all of the allegations under consideration have been referred to the Office of Professional Responsibility" of the Department of Justice. Our local committee on conduct would also have jurisdiction of some of the matters.

Because further hearings are essential to a ruling on the motions to dismiss, and, perhaps, because Rule 605 of the Rules of Evidence, but more importantly because I plan to quit the judging business before the hearings can be completed, I make no ruling on and I intimate no belief as to what should be done with the dismissal motions. This decision will have to be made by Judge Kane, as will all other decisions concerning remedy.

No defendant other than defendant Kilpatrick is interested in the motion for new trial, and I am the only judge who should rule on it because I was there and watched in amazement the trial's conduct. But little discussion is necessary to this ruling. I have talked about the testimony of Richard Bell and his brother. I heard that testimony outside the presence of the jury, and I wouldn't let the jury hear it. I think that was an error, and I don't think that I should put the parties to the expense of having the Court of Appeals tell me it was error. The witness was a key to the prosecution's case, and testimony as to the alleged pressures was important to an evaluation of his credibility. The pocket immunity and the circumstances of its grant bear on credibility. I initially thought that the testimony went only to prosecutorial misconduct which is for the court to determine, and I overlooked the credibility aspect of the implied threat coupled with the pocket immunity grant just as I overlooked the right of the jury to know that immunity wasn't granted the way Congress says it shall be. The jury should have heard the testimony and it might have changed some juror's mind. As a trial lawyer I didn't like the phrase "harmless error," and as a trial judge I don't use it when the error has any substance at all. This error has substance.

[2.3] One Wilson Quintela was subpoenaed by the government, and he was arrested as a material witness. The prosecutors exercised a power possessed only by the court, and they released the man from subpoena. He promptly returned to his home in Brazil. Lawyers can't substitute themselves for the court to release a witness from subpoena. *U.S.* v. *Sanchez* (2nd Cir. 1972) 459 F.2d 100. At the time of trial, the government admitted that their conduct was in error, and every effort was made to get the witness to come back from Brazil when defense counsel said that he was relying on the availability of the witness. After the trial started, the government said that the witness would return, but defense counsel said at that point he had developed his trial strategy on the basis of the release of the witness from the subpoena. He may have correctly thought that an interruption of the trial to permit travel from Brazil would be detrimental. That the government was guilty of no evil intent I am sure, but that the defendant suffered no harm I am not sure. Standing alone, this is one mistake I might reluctantly say was "harmless error," but coupled with other things, I can't so rule.

If there is any one thing that Tenth Circuit has been vehement about it is expressions of personal opinions by counsel as to whose testimony they believe. That rule was violated here, and I suggest that a review of the grand jury transcript may show frequent violations of the rule during grand jury proceedings. My thinking on this score goes immediately to the appearance of Professor Hjorth before the grand jury. I jumped in during final argument to try to lessen the error of the comment, but I doubt that I cured it.

It is argued that in the presence of the jury one of the agents stared at and laughed at the defendant. The prosecution says that this didn't happen, and that if it did, I would have seen it. I didn't see it, but that doesn't mean that it didn't happen, because no judge sees everything which goes on in a courtroom. This is especially so because I was concentrating my attention on Mr. Scharf's glowering as he sat in the second row of the spectator's section, and I doubt that defense counsel could see him. I mention this only because it is one more tiny aspect of the atmosphere of the trial. It was an atmosphere of unfairness and overreaching illustrated in small degree by ex parte telephone calls to my law clerk made by government counsel inquiring through the back door to learn my thinking as to some legal situations in the case. (Colloquy about this appears in the records, and, consistent with their denials of what so many others say, government counsel deny my law clerk's statements as to the conversation.) The case is the only trial I have ever conducted in which the courtroom deputy complained about discourtesy on the part of counsel, and I suppose that it goes without saying that it was not defense counsel who were discourteous. (An apology by government lawyers was extended later.)

Other arguments are advanced supporting the new trial motion, but I don't think that I need extend this opinion by discussing them. I have taken them into account in my thinking. Usually, when a case goes to the jury, there are no more difficulties to be encountered, but that's not so in this ill-starred case which had its first questionable conduct during the opening two minutes of grand jury investigation and which had conduct suspect under the Canons of Professional Responsibility lasting into post trial hearings. While the jury was deliberating a note was received. I notified counsel on both sides, and a hearing was held in open court with the defendant present, defense counsel present. Ms. Surbaugh of Colorado's United States Attorney's Office, and Mr. Blondin were there on behalf of the government. (Messrs. Scharf and Snyder didn't show up, although when the jury retired all counsel had been told to stand by for jury questions or a verdict.) We discussed the answer which should be given to the jury, and we all agreed on it. The answer was written, and a copy was given to both sides.

I was more than a little surprised when a telephone call from

Mr. Scharf was received a few minutes later. He had decided that he wasn't satisified with that which those who saw fit to come to the hearing all agreed to. He demanded a further hearing, and I told him we would have one right away. He then made the most ridiculous demand I have ever heard in the almost 50 years since I graduated from law school. Mr. Scharf directed that I instruct the jury to "cease its deliberations" until he could have his hearing. This direction was made on the telephone and it was obviously not made in the presence of defendant or defense counsel. To accede to this absurd demand would have created irretrievable error under Rule 43 and under *Rogers* v. *United States,* 422 U.S. 35, 95 S.Ct. 2091, 45 L.Ed.2d 1. That error I avoided because I told Mr. Scharf I wouldn't even consider obeying his command to instruct the jury to quit deliberating. We did have the hearing and it didn't take long. Exactly what was said at that time is part of the record in the case.

After the jury verdict, timely motions were filed, and it was apparent from a reading of them that Mr. Scharf, Mr. Blondin and Mr. Snyder were going to have to testify about matters raised in the motions. Their recognition of the factual dispute is clearly shown in the flippant brief filed in opposition to the motions. At the outset of the hearing I inquired concerning the ethical bind in which the prosecutors found themselves, and I asked if other counsel should not be handling the hearing. I admit to surprise when I was told that top lawyers in the Tax Division of the Department of Justice saw nothing wrong with the continued participation in the case of lawyers whose testimony was quite obviously going to be required. We started the hearing with participation by two of the lawyers who were essential witnesses. (One was said to be in trial somewhere else.) The hearing went for a little while, when, suddenly, there was a 180 degree change of direction, and government counsel announced that they wanted to withdraw. They were permitted to do so, and the hearing recessed. Mr. Alexander took over, and he has performed ably and ethically. However, he was handicapped by lack of time to prepare, and the hearing which I had hoped to complete weeks ago had to be continued for later testimony. We are still waiting for that testimony.

This brings us down to date. I have already explained that I cannot and I do not rule on the motion to dismiss, but I do grant the motion for a new trial. I deny the motion for judgment of acquittal, but I do so without intent that this is the "law of the case," and leave it to another judge to take a fresh look at the motion if the case is tried again.

ORDER

Rule 6 of the Federal Rules of Criminal Procedure provides that matters occurring before a grand jury shall be secret, subject to a few exceptions. One exception is that there may be disclosure when directed by a court in connection with a judicial proceeding. I have directed that there be some disclosure of grand jury matters, and undoubtedly, typists will have to learn what is contained in grand jury transcripts in the performance of their secretarial work for lawyers who read the transcripts. Accordingly, such disclosures as may be necessary to the accomplishment of secretarial duties is authorized, but any typist who so learns of any such grand jury matters is ordered to keep secret such information. Rule 6 itself provides that violation of the secrecy requirements of the rule may be deemed contempt of court, and violation of this order may be deemed contempt of court.

E. DECISION OF JUDGE JOHN KANE*

UNITED STATES of America, Plaintiff,

v.

William A. KILPATRICK, Declan J. O'Donnell, John Pettingill, Sheila C. Lerner, Michael L. Alberga, C.S. Gill, C.M. Smith, Bank of Nova Scotia, Defendants

Crim. No. 82-CR-222.

United States District Court,
D. Colorado.

Sept. 24, 1984.

Defendants were charged with conspiracy, mail fraud, and tax fraud, and one defendant with obstruction of justice. The United States District Court for the District of Colorado dismissed all except one count, and the Government appealed. The Court of Appeals, after briefing but before oral argument, partially remanded case for determination of whether prosecutorial misconduct and irregularities in grand jury process constituted additional grounds for dismissal. Before and immediately after the partial remand, the District Court, 575 F.Supp 325, Fred M. Winner, Senior District Judge, ordered that the Government provide defendant with copies of transcripts of all grand jury proceedings. On remand, the District Court, Kane, J., held that indictment had to be dismissed because of totality of circumstances, which included numerous violations of federal criminal rule pertaining to grand juries, violations of statutory witness immunity sections, violations of the Fifth and Sixth Amendments, knowing presentation of misinformation to the grand jury and mistreatment of witnesses.

Indictment dismissed.

---

1. Grand Jury—23

Prosecutor's description to grand jury of role of "grand jury agent" in connection with office of "agent of the grand jury" created for Internal Revenue Service special agents misled grand jury, which was consistently reminded of agents' uniquely created and described role and urged to rely on special agents as their "agents," as to appropriate role of IRS agents in investigation in violation of criminal rule relating to grand juries, especially since agents did not view their role and conduct their investigation as agents of independent unbiased grand jury. Fed.Rules Cr.Proc.Rule 6, 18 U.S.C.A.

2. Grand Jury—41

Responsibility and decision-making authority that criminal rule relating to grand juries vests in government attorneys was relinquished to and exercised by Internal Revenue Service, which undertook policy of determining whether and to whom disclosure of confidential grand jury material would be made and whether notifications of disclosure would be made. Fed.Rules Cr.Proc.Rule 6(e), 18 U.S.C.A.

3. Grand Jury—41

Disclosure of grand jury information is only one of forbidden purposes and it is equally improper to manipulate grand jury investigations to obtain evidence for eventual civil use by the Internal Revenue Service. Fed.Rules Cr.Proc.Rule 6(e),(e)(3), 18 U.S.C.A.

4. Grand Jury—41

Government's publicizing of names of individuals and entities that were being investigated as well as nature of grand jury's inquiry breached grand jury rule's imposition upon government attorneys of obligation to secure grand jury information from improper disclosure. Fed.Rules Cr.Proc.Rule 6(e), 18 U.S.C.A.

5. Grand Jury—41

Government's imposition of unauthorized secrecy obligations upon two witnesses, in order to prevent suspects from determining nature and extent of any communication that might have been revealed and to foreclose challenge to testimony based upon applicable privilege, violated a grand jury rule. Fed.Rules Cr.Proc.Rule 6(e)(2), 18 U.S.C.A.

6. Grand Jury—36

General instructions, months prior, that grand jurors not draw inferences from individual's invocation of privilege against self-incrimination cannot correct practice of calling witnesses only to have them invoke their Fifth Amendment privilege before the grand jury. U.S.C.A. Const.Amend. 5.

7. Grand Jury—1

Most important function of grand jury is to stand between government agents and suspect as unbiased evaluator of the evidence.

8. Grand Jury—39

Indictment and Information—144.1(2)

Events which occurred in grand jury room while special agents assigned by Internal Revenue Service to assist prosecutors were present as "agents" of the grand jury and not under oath as witnesses under examination violated grand jury rule provision concerning who may be present before grand jury and required dismissal of indictment charging conspiracy, mail fraud, tax fraud and obstruction of justice. Fed.Rules Cr.Proc.Rule 6(d), 18 U.S.C.A.

9. Indictment and Information—144.1(2)

When grand jury provision concerning secrecy is violated recklessly and systematically, dismissal of indictment is appropriate; when knowing violations of rule prejudice and embarrass targets whose identities the government reveals, contempt remedy is not always wholly adequate and under those circumstances it is not necessary for defendant to show that he has been prejudiced by violations. Fed.Rules Cr.Proc.Rule 6(e), 18 U.S.C.A.

10. Indictment and Information—144.1(2).

Violations of grand jury secrecy requirements and directions to witnesses not to disclose fact or substance of their grand jury testimony based on prosecutors' relinquishment to Internal Revenue Service of their responsibility to determine persons to whom disclosure would be made, and IRS's failure to provide mandated prompt notification of disclosure and improper manipulation of secret material to obtain information and data for use during civil litigation required dismissal of indictment charging conspiracy, mail fraud, tax fraud and obstruction of justice. Fed.Rules Cr.Proc.Rule 6(e), (e)(2,3), 18 U.S.C.A.

11. Witnesses—304(1)

Pracitce of bestowing informal or pocket immunity through letters of assurance rather than following congressionally authorized procedure for conferring grants of immunity is illegal; when granting immunity, Department of Justice must comply with statutory requirements. 18 U.S.C.A. §§ 6002, 6003.

12. Indictment and Information—10.1(4)

Witnesses—304(1)

Prosecutors' repeated use of letters of assurance or so called "pocket immunity" for grand jury witnesses violated applicable witness immunity statutes and tainted grand jury indictment with its illegality. 18 U.S.C.A. §§ 6002, 6003.

13. Indictment and Information—144.1(2)

Calling of seven witnesses before grand jury to take advantage of impermissible inferences that arose from their invocation of privilege against self-incrimination did not require dismissal of indictment per se but was a factor to be considered in determining whether grand jury had been overreached or usurped. U.S.C.A. Const. Amend. 5.

14. Grand Jury—36.4(2)

Improper efforts to prejudice defendants by impermissible inferences from seven witnesses' assertions of their privilege against self-incrimination was compounded by questioning before grand jury concerning payment of witnesses' legal fees, since no legitimate purpose for such questioning exists. U.S.C.A. Const. Amend. 5.

15. Grand Jury—36.8

Mischaracterization of testimony before grand jury and unidentified use of questionable hearsay information with regard to vital issues intrudes upon independent role of grand jury particularly where misrepresentations could not be expected to be readily apparent to grand jury and relate to material issues in prosecution.

16. Criminal Law—662.1

Guarantees of Sixth Amendment apply to corporate defendants with same force as to individual defendants. U.S.C.A. Const.Amend. 6.

17. Indictment and Information—144.1(2)

Dismissal of indictment was inappropriate remedy for *Massiah* violations as result of interrogations of bank employees in absence of counsel where bank's counsel performed ably and adequately throughout litigation and no prejudice was demonstrated, but *Massiah* violations entered into qualitative assessments of prosecutors' and grand jury's conduct in determining whether indictment should be dismissed based on totality of the circumstances.

18. Indictment and Information—144.1(2)

Totality of circumstances concerning grand jury investigation, from inception of 20-month grand jury investigation when prosecutors divined office of "agent of the grand jury" on Internal Revenue Service agents through time agents' improper "summaries" were presented shortly before indictment was returned, usurped indicting grand jury and required dismissal of indictment charging conspiracy, mail and tax fraud, and obstruction of justice. 18 U.S.C.A. §§ 2, 371, 1341; Fed.Rules Cr.Proc.Rule 6, 18 U.S.C.A.

———

Charles Alexander, Trial Atty., U.S. Dept. of Justice, Tax Div., Washington, D.C., and Robert N. Miller, U.S. Atty., Linda S. Surbaugh, Asst. U.S. Atty., Denver, Colo., for U.S.A.

William C. Waller, Richard K. Rufner, Wagner & Waller, P.C., Englewood, Colo., for Kilpatrick.

James L. Treece, Littleton, Colo., for O'Donnell.

David L. Hiller, Duboskey & Hiller, Denver, Colo., for John Pettingill.

Thomas French, Dill, Dill & McAllister, Denver, Colo., for Lerner.

Donald E. Van Koughnet, Naples, Fla., for Alberga & Gill.

C. M. Smith, No Appearance.

James E. Nesland, Ireland, Stapleton & Pryor, Denver, Colo., and Robert J. Anello, Obermaier, Morvillo & Abramovitz, New York City, for Bank of Nova Scotia.

FINDINGS OF FACT, CONCLUSIONS OF LAW AND ORDER

KANE, District Judge.

PROCEDURAL BACKGROUND

After a twenty month investigation conducted before two successive grand juries, the instant proceeding was commenced on September 30, 1982 by the filing of a twenty-seven count indictment charging seven individuals and The Bank of Nova Scotia with conspiracy, mail fraud and tax fraud and also charging William A. Kilpatrick with obstruction of justice (Count 27). The bank was charged in ten counts with conspiracy to defraud (18 U.S.C. § 371) (Count 1) and aiding and abetting mail fraud (18 U.S.C. § 1341 and § 2) (Counts 13 through 21).

On February 21, 1983, I dismissed the first twenty-six counts of the indictment for failure to charge a crime and as improperly pleaded. Additionally, upon separate motion by the bank, I dismissed the charges in which the bank was named upon the ground that the indictment failed to allege that the bank or any of its representatives had the requisite knowledge and intent to commit the crimes charged. The government appealed the dismissals.

On August 8, 1983, after briefing but before oral argument, the Tenth Circuit entered an order partially remanding the case to me so that all defendants could participate in hearings to determine whether prosecutorial misconduct and irregularities in the grand jury process constituted additional grounds for dismissal.

Before and immediately after the partial remand by the Tenth Circuit, the Honorable Fred M. Winner, Senior United States District Judge, presided over post-trial motions hearings following a guilty verdict against Mr. Kilpatrick on Count 27. On August 25, 1983, at about the time of his retirement from the bench, Judge Winner issued a memorandum decision which, among other things, summarized the status of the hearings which were being reassigned to me. Further, Judge Winner ordered that the government provide defendants with copies of transcripts of all proceedings that occurred before the grand juries. After some bizarre episodes of procedural novelty, Judge Winner's opinion was finally published. *See United States* v. *Kilpatrick*, 575 F.Supp. 325 (1983). The instant Findings of Fact, Conclusions of Law and Order must be read in conjunction with Judge Winner's opinion.

The government attorneys failed to provide defendants with complete transcriptions as ordered. They apparently overlooked, and did not transcribe, dozens of proceedings before the grand jury. The latter proceedings—which converted into hundreds of pages of transcripts and, more significantly, disclosed clear violations of Rule 6—were not produced until the defense detected the lack of compliance with Judge Winner's order. Even now, the government remains unable to provide transcripts of all the proceedings and was unable to produce a single Rule 6(e) order (which government attorneys testified they obtained) authorizing several major disclosures of grand jury matters. The government asserts that it has turned over such transcripts as could be had as soon as they were received from the court reporter. Such, in my view, does not excuse the failure to produce complete and accurate transcripts. If the assertion minimizes the inference of dissimulation, it exacerbates stronger ones of confusion and indifference.

FACTS ESTABLISHED BY THE RECORD[1]

A. Grand Jury Agents

[1] Despite detailed instructions from the impaneling court that the grand jury should maintain its independence and not

develop into a "prosecutor's agent," shortly after both grand juries involved in the investigation leading to the instant indictment were sworn, the prosecutors created the office of "agent of the grand jury" for Messrs. Mendrop and Raybin, Special Agents assigned by the IRS to assist the prosecutors.[2] Several months later an IRS agent assigned to the civil division and who the prosecutors relied upon as an expert was also sworn in as an "agent of the grand jury." G.J. Tr. Schneider, May 3, 1982, 1:34 p.m., at pp. 2–3. The prosecutors divined the office of "grand jury agent" by personally administering oaths before the grand jury to Raybin, Mendrop and Schneider.[3] The government concedes that the prosecutors possessed no authority to administer such oaths. Indeed, the prosecutor who administered the oaths now concedes he created the oath and was "shooting from the hip" when he did so. K.Tr. 501.

The government argues that this event should be viewed as a technical mislabeling of no great import. It is, however, more than a misnomer.

First, the prosecutor's description to the grand jury of the role of a "grand jury agent" clearly misled the grand jury as to the appropriate role of the IRS agents in the proceedings. *See* Winner opinion, 575 F.Supp. at 329. As conceded by the prosecutor, there is simply no basis for his description to the grand jury of the role of grand jury agents.[4] K.Tr. 501.

Second, the grand jury was consistently reminded of the agents' uniquely created and described role and urged to rely upon the IRS special agents as their "agents." Thus, on many occasions when Raybin and Mendrop appeared as witnesses the government attorney reiterated that they were appearing as "agents of the grand jury."[5] *See e.g.,* G.J. Tr. Mendrop, August 4, 1981, 9:25 a.m., at p. 2, August 5, 1981, 4:04 p.m., at p. 2, September 29, 1982, 9:32 a.m., at p. 2; G.J. Tr. Raybin, July 8, 1981, 9:11 p.m., at p. 5, March 3, 1982, 1:19 p.m., at p. 2, September 29, 1982, 2:32 p.m., at p. 2. Further, the government attorneys assigned special importance to identifying the IRS agents with the grand jury. When conducting interviews in connection with the investigation, Raybin and Mendrop were directed by the prosecutor to inform witnesses that they were "assisting a grand jury investigation in the Judicial District of Colorado." K.Tr. 619; *see also* G.J. Tr. Mendrop, August 5,

1981, 4:04 p.m., at p. 2; G.J. Tr. Raybin, July 8, 1981, 9:11 a.m., at p. 5, September 29, 1982, 2:32 p.m., at p. 2.[6]

Third, contrary to the role of the IRS agents described to the grand jury by the prosecutors, Mendrop and Raybin *did not* view their role and conduct their investigation as agents of an independent, unbiased grand jury. Rather, they viewed their role as agents of the Department of Justice, not the grand jury. When asked if his function as an agent of the grand jury was to assist the grand jury, Raybin testified:

> A: My duties were designed to assist the Department of Justice in its investigation . . .

K.Tr. 232.

Mendrop similarly interpreted his role as agent of the grand jury to be "primarily" to assist the prosecutors:

> Q: . . . Mr. Mendrop, who were you really assisting in this matter during the grand jury investigation?
> A: Well, *primarily, I was assisting the attorneys for the government* and indirectly I'm sure that I must have been assisting the grand jury through the work that I was doing for the investigation that they were, that they had under consideration.
> Q: Well, in fact, you directly represented to the grand jury that you were assisting them, did you not, sir?
> A: I'm not sure how you meant that.
> Q: In fact, you represented to the grand jury that you were their agent and Mr. Snyder also represented to the grand jury that you were their agent; is that correct, sir?
> A: I believe those words were used, yes, sir.

K.Tr. 401-02 (emphasis supplied).

Ironically, the government attorneys who created the grand jury agents and described their role are confused themselves as to whether the "agents" roles should be considered aligned with that of independent grand jurors or the prosecutors.[7] K.Tr. 534-35; 1126.

Fourth, the government attorneys used the "grand jury agents" to do more than assist the attorneys in the investigation. They used them to summarize evidence in front of the grand jury. On the first day that the second grand jury convened, after his pseudo-investiture as a grand jury agent, Raybin summarized the investigation so far conducted, explained tax shelters to the jury, and opined that the circular financing utilized in the tax shelters under investigation was illegal. *See* G.J. Tr. Raybin, September 29, 1982, 2:32 p.m.; Mendrop, September 29, 1982, 9:32 a.m.; Raybin, September 30, 1982, 10:40 a.m. Similar kinds of substantive testimony were given by Raybin on September 9, 1981 and March 3, 1982. *See* G.J. Tr. Raybin, September 9, 1982, 10:02 a.m.; March 3, 1982, 1:19 p.m. On September 29 and 30, 1982, when the government attorneys, and apparently the "agents of the grand jury," were seeking the indictment, Raybin and Mendrop purported to summarize the evidence for the grand jury to support the 27 count indictment presented by the government attorneys. On September 30, 1982 Schneider appeared as "the expert" in the field of tax shelters to summarize the legal theory. G.J. Tr. Schneider, September 30, 1982, 9:22 a.m. These summaries contained numerous inaccuracies and were misleading in several respects. Although the government attorneys were quick to inform the grand jury of their role as advocates, the grand jurors were never informed that their "agents" were "primarily" representing the interests of the Department of Justice attorneys.

Finally, the prosecutors' creation and use of grand jury agents resulted in many other abuses and Rule 6 violations. Most notably the agents made many joint appearances before the grand jury, without the presence of government counsel, and read transcripts to the jurors. K.Tr. 483–87; 636–39; 691–92; 707–12.

Raybin and Mendrop appeared before the second grand jury to give testimony regarding the investigation. Each time they appeared alone, were sworn, and were examined by the government attorneys. When they appeared to read testimony from the first grand jury to the second grand jury, they appeared together, were apparently not sworn, and were not examined by government attorneys because the latter were usually absent. It is not clear in what capacity they were appearing to read testimony. The confusion was exacerbated by two other IRS agents—Burke and Shea—also appearing together to read testimony to the second grand jury. In what capacity they were appearing is even less evident since they were not made "grand jury agents" and the record of their appearance does not support a finding that they were witnesses.

The transcripts of the agents' simultaneous appearances establish that they were not present as witnesses. They appear not to have been sworn; they appeared together; they were not examined; and they were mostly unaccompanied by government attorneys. The testimony of the prosecutors and agents that the agents were sworn, even if evidenced by a transcript, would not authorize their simultaneous appearances under Rule 6(d). The recollection of the prosecutors and agents that the oath was administered is challenged by the almost dozen transcripts showing the oath was not administered on any single occasion where the agents appeared together.

The record reveals that the agents' many appearances before the second grand jury, whether sworn or unsworn, were largely unsupervised. The agents were frequently unattended by government attorneys and, in some instances, may have convened the grand jury sessions without government counsel in order to read testimony. K.Tr. 483-87; 636-39; 691-92; 707-12.

In other instances the transcripts do not make clear precisely when the agents entered or left the grand jury room. It appears that they may have been present while the prosecutors engaged in colloquy with grand jurors. G.J. Tr. Remarks of Prosecutor, February 2, 1982, 1:07 p.m. at p. 18; Remarks of Prosecutor, February 4, 1982, 3:30 p.m. at pp. 2–3; Remarks of Prosecutor, April 6, 1982, 9:08 a.m. at p. 8.

Both prosecutors acknowledge that the agents "*were not* under examination" when they read to the grand jury. K.Tr. 485 (emphasis supplied); *see also* K.Tr. 707. The conclusion that they were not under examination is inescapable because no attorney was present to conduct an examination. Further, the grand jurors were under instructions *not* to question the agents during such appearances. K.Tr. 481-87.

B. Improper Disclosure, Improper Use and Secrecy Violations

[2] During the course of the grand jury investigation, the government representatives systematically disregarded the strictures of Rule 6(e). The record demonstrates that the responsibility and decision making authority that Rule 6(e) vests in government attorneys was relinquished to and exercised by the Internal Revenue Service. Members of that agency under-

took a policy of determining whether and to whom disclosure of confidential material would be made and whether notification of such disclosure would be made pursuant to the Federal Rules. Moreover, the evidence suggests that information was disclosed to other IRS agents for use in civil cases. Grand jury secrecy was repeatedly breached by those with a duty to remain silent and secrecy obligations were imposed upon others of whom the law does not require confidentiality.

(1) Disclosure

The disclosure notices filed pursuant to Rule 6(e)(3)(B) indicate that numerous individuals at all levels of the Internal Revenue Service, many of whom were assigned from the civil division of that agency, were permitted access to grand jury material. DX Q; *see* K.Tr. 26, 29–36, 40, 43, 50. The hearings have demonstrated that numerous other IRS personnel (all of whom were civil personnel), were given access to grand jury material, that these people were never identified on a disclosure notice and that they remain unknown even now.

That the decision as to which individuals should be privy to the grand jury material was frequently made by the IRS, rather than by the prosecutors, was admitted by the agents.[8] K.Tr. 241. That it was the norm is confirmed by several additional facts. Disclosure was made liberally and often before obtaining attorney approval, an act the prosecutors acknowledged violates Department of Justice rules. K.Tr. 57–69; 754. Notice of such disclosure was not made "promptly" as required by Rule 6(e). The decision as to which names to include on the disclosure lists was largely left up to the IRS agents. The integrity of the lists themselves, as well as the decisions to make disclosure to the listed personnel, is lacking. The government attorneys admitted that they were unable to identify a substantial number of those named on the disclosure notices. K.Tr. 498–99. Further, these notices were frequently filed by attorneys having little relationship to the investigation. *See* K.Tr. 15–67; DX Q. The IRS agents were likewise unable to identify many of the persons on the list or why they were listed. K.Tr. 14–22, 30, 36–38, 39, 43–44, 56, 60–61, 65, 69, 106–09.

Perhaps the best illustration of the insouciance with which grand jury disclosures were made and recorded appears in the circumstances surrounding the post-indictment notice. The agents were directed by the government attorneys to pick their brains and prepare a catch-all disclosure notice listing any individuals whom they could recall may have had access to secret grand jury materials but who were not listed as required. Thus, on October 20, 1982, approximately three weeks after the indictment was returned, a final notice of disclosure adding sixteen names of IRS employees was filed. K.Tr. 57–59.

The agents' post hoc attempt to determine to whom disclosure had been made in order to supplement the disclosure notices was not entirely successful. Numerous persons with access to grand jury material were forgotten and never included on the notices. The discovery of these forgotten people occurred only because, during the hearings, government representatives testified at length concerning two computer programs compiled from grand jury documents, ostensibly for purposes of assisting in the grand jury's investigation. *See, e.g.,* K.Tr. 71–79, 87–91, 157–61. The performance of this function was riddled with Rule 6(e) violations.

Although the prosecutors testified that a court order was obtained permitting the transfer of the derivative grand jury information for that purpose to Lowry Air Force Base, the government was unable to produce such an order at the hearings. K.Tr. 494–99; 517; 755; 807. The prosecutors acknowledge that no order was obtained permitting transfer of similar information to Dallas and Utah, a failure caused by their unawareness even at the hearing that the IRS agents had taken it upon themselves to arrange for the computerwork to be done at those locations and because the prosecutors left the "details" of the computer work to the IRS. K.Tr. 87–88, 494–96, 523, 807.

Many IRS employees with access to information used in compiling the computer program were eventually listed on the disclosure notices. *See* K.Tr. 34, 40, 43, 61, 72, 76, 78. Just as many, however, apparently never found their way onto the lists. Although the computer programs were created by computer "groups" in Dallas and Ogden (K.Tr. 74–76), the Disclosure Notices list few, if any, of the computer personnel from Utah or Texas. The indifference of the government attorneys is further revealed by the fact that a student clerk assisting the prosecutors was not listed as having had access to grand jury material although it was revealed at these hearings that she did. K.Tr. 1085–87.

Whatever instructions there were, if any, concerning disclosure and use of the grand jury material was apparently passed on by the staff of the Internal Revenue Service itself and not by the Department of Justice attorneys. Little or no instruction concerning the strictures of Rule 6(e) is included in the training of many of those IRS employees who had access to the information. K.Tr. 155.

Further, when the IRS agents acting as "agents of the grand jury" undertook the task of explaining the secrecy provisions to other employees of the IRS, it is clear that the information was of little practical use. For example, one such agent testified that, although he informed the supervisor of the computer program that he should disclose information only to one whose name was listed on the disclosure notices, only a few of the names on those lists were revealed to the supervisor. K.Tr. 155.

(2) Improper Use

The free rein given the IRS by the Department of Justice attorneys in this investigation and in the use and disclosure of grand jury material presents a serious possibility that the extraordinary powers of the grand jury were manipulated in order to obtain evidence useful in later civil litigation. The record reveals that such a danger was real and that substantial investigative activities disclosures were made for purposes other than "to assist an attorney for the government in the performance of [his] duty to enforce federal criminal law." *See* Rule 6(e)(3), Fed.R.Crim.P.

[3] IRS institutional intent to take advantage of the grand jury investigation in civil audits was confirmed by Richard Gullion, a civil IRS agent assigned to the examination division in Denver, who freely acknowledged that the IRS hoped to take advantage of the facts developed by the criminal investigation after conclusion of the criminal proceedings. W.Tr. 836–38. The government, in resisting this claim, has asserted that no improper disclosure to IRS civil agents has occurred. K.Tr. 150–51, 413–14, 416–17, 645–46. Disclosure is only one of the forbidden purposes. It is equally improper to manipulate the grand jury investigation to obtain evidence for eventual civil use by the IRS.

United States v. *Sells Engineering, Inc.*, 463 U.S. 418, 103 S.Ct. 3133, 77 L.Ed.2d 743 (1983). As is discussed below, the record confirms that the grand jury's extraordinary powers and resources were, in part, initiated and channeled for just such a purpose.[9]

The government's investigation of defendants originated at the IRS in 1979. From August, 1979 to July, 1980, the IRS conducted a joint civil and criminal investigation. In July, 1980, the IRS referred its investigation to the Tax Division of the Department of Justice with the recommendation that a grand jury investigation be conducted because its administrative processes were potentially ineffective. DX M.

The agents' testimony that they abandoned all civil interest when the grand jury commenced reminds me of Joel Chandler Harris' story about Bre'r Rabbit asking the fox not to throw him in the briar patch. At least one witness believed that the government was anxious to build civil cases through the use of grand jury information. W.Tr. 73–74. Several facts confirm that the IRS agents did not abandon entirely IRS civil interest in recouping taxes.

For example, agents of the IRS interviewed numerous tax shelter investors. The interviewees were threatened that if they did not speak voluntarily a grand jury subpoena might be obtained. Thus, they were informed that the interview was being conducted in lieu of a grand jury appearance. K.Tr. 191. In connection with these investor interviews the IRS agents assisted in the creation of "Investor Questionnaires." These questionnaires instructed interviewers to ask numerous questions concerning the tax shelters. Several of the questions involved investor motives, a subject of no conceivable relevance to a criminal investigation of the targets but highly relevant in a civil audit of the investor. DX W; G.J. Tr. Raybin, January 6, 1981 at pp. 4–7. That this interviewing program had no criminal investigation purpose is demonstrated by the fact that no investor, let alone any investors interviewed, appeared before the grand jury. None of the interviews, nor the results of the interviews, was presented to the grand jury. K. Tr. 149. The government offered no explanation at the hearings of why and for what purpose such interviews were conducted.

Civil IRS employees, armed with grand jury information,

were brought into the investigation to prepare audits of the tax shelter investors. These audits, like the interviews, were not presented to the grand jury and no reasons or explanations for their preparation were offered at the hearings. K.Tr. 149.

IRS activity since the return of the indictment confirms its intent to utilize the grand jury investigation and information for civil litigation purposes. Since return of the indictment the IRS has issued civil audit letters to the investors interviewed, notifying them that their returns were being examined. The letters read in part: "[a] report will be issued in the near future containing a position consistent with *facts* as presented in the Federal Grand Jury Indictment of September 30, 1982, for the United States District Court for the District of Colorado." DX L (emphasis supplied); *see also* K.Tr. 176–78, 344–48.

Finally, several statements attributed to the prosecutors by witnesses during the course of the investigation confirm that the grand jury proceedings, at least in part, were conducted for other than legitimate federal criminal purposes. Richard Birchall, a former attorney with the Department of Justice, testified that "[t]here was a vengeance to the manner in which [the prosecutor] conducted the investigation." W.Tr. 69. Mr. Birchall also reported that on one occasion the prosecutor indicated that even if he were unsuccessful on the merits, the defense would be excessively expensive to the defendants. W. Tr. 133.

A similar improper motive was testified to by Donald Morrison, a witness who made numerous grand jury appearances. With regard to a proposed business activity of some of the defendants, Morrison testified that a prosecutor indicated they were going to "shoot in [the] ass [the] coal deal." W.Tr. 192. These statements were vigorously denied by the prosecutors. I am in no position to resolve the obvious conflict in the testimony by assessing the credibility of witnesses appearing before Judge Winner with those appearing before me. Thus, I do not find as a fact that the statements were actually made. I describe them here because they illustrate the infusion of hostility and vitriol which permeates this entire case—a condition which I attribute to the frequently rude, consistently arrogant, and occasionally obnoxious conduct of some of the government attorneys assigned to the prosecution of this case.[10]

(3) Secrecy Violations

[4] Several instances demonstrate blatant disregard for the time-honored tradition of grand jury secrecy. As discussed below, such violations were utilized by the government, not only to gain what was certainly perceived as an advantage in connection with the intended prosecution but were also apparently part of an improper attempt to embarrass the targets and hinder the ongoing operation of their business during the course of the grand jury investigation.

Throughout the course of the grand jury investigation the government widely publicized the names of the invididuals and entities that were being investigated as well as the nature of the grand jury's inquiry. The dissemination of information concerning the proceedings before the grand jury was undertaken without the circumspection normally afforded such disclosure by government attorneys. Such disclosures were particularly egregious insofar as the recipients of the information were known customers and business associates of the targets.

With the knowledge of Department of Justice attorneys, numerous letters were sent out identifying the targets, the related entities and the nature of the criminal investigation. The letters were sent to individuals beyond the subpoena power of the grand jury and with whom it was understood the targets had ongoing business and professional relationships. The letters, which were written on the letterhead of the United States Attorney, but signed by supposed agents of the grand jury, were not only misleading in terms of the capacity in which they were sent, but also clearly posed a danger of adversely affecting the acknowledged business and professional relationships. K.Tr. 121–25, 597–98, 969–75; DX V–1 through V–15; DX Y.

The text of the letters read in part as follows:

> *The United States Department of Justice is conducting a Grand Jury investigation of the business activities of William A. Kilpatrick, Declan J. O'Donnell, John Pettingill and Sheila C. Lerner* for the years 1977 through 1980. The Grand Jury is attempting to determine whether these individuals, through United Financial Operations, Inc., P & J Coal Company, Inc., Marlborough Investments, Ltd., International Fuel Development Corp., Ltd., and International Block Construction Company, Ltd.,

have committed violations of Title 18 and Title 26 of the United States Code.

The Grand Jury has obtained information whcih indicates that you have had and/or currently do have a business relationship with one or more of the individuals and/or entities listed above. It has been determined that your testimony will be helpful in resolving questions which still face the Grand Jury. Subsequently, the United States Department of Justice cordially invites you to appear and testify before the Federal Grand Jury in Denver, Colorado (U.S.A.) at your convenience. Transportation, lodging and meals will be arranged for and paid by the United States Department of Justice.

• • • • • •

We look forward to your response,

Sincerely yours,
STEPHEN L. SNYDER
Trial Attorney
Criminal Section
Tax Division
By: PAUL E. RAYBIN
Special Agent

(emphasis supplied)

The impropriety of publicly identifying targets in these letters was readily apparent to Judge Winner:

[T]he identity of the persons and the transactions which were under grand jury scrutiny shouldn't be disclosed to anyone by letter or otherwise, but these startling letters did precisely that.

575 F.Supp. at 334.

The prejudicial disclosure of the targets and the nature of the grand jury's investigation, however, was not limited to these "startling letters." During the course of the investigation, the "agents of the grand jury," and other employees of the IRS, ostensibly in connection with the ongoing criminal investigation, interviewed numerous investors in the tax shelters. Those investors, too, were informed of the nature of the grand jury's inquiry and the names of those being investigated. K.Tr. 93–94.

Rule 6(e) imposes upon government attorneys the obligation to secure grand jury information from improper disclosures. That obligation was breached several times. The disclosure of secret grand jury material was not limited to identification of the targets of the investigation. Grand jury information was also shared with Richard Birchall, a witness and one-time potential target.[11] Details of the investigation were revealed to Birchall during a meeting in which one of the prosecutors attempted to persuade him to assist in the government's investigation by suggesting that the grand jury had received evidence warranting his consideration as a target. W.Tr. 44–52, 983–84; 575 F.Supp. at 332–33.

Moreover, Birchall, who apparently was led to believe that he might face criminal exposure, was left unattended in a room housing grand jury material. He admittedly utilized the opportunity to rummage through the grand jury documents. 575 F.Supp. at 332–33. In further disregard of the secrecy provisions of Rule 6(e) another witness, Bernard Bailor, noted that the room in which the grand jury material was housed was generally left open. W.Tr. 1130–31. Judge Winner commented that he found Mr. Bailor's testimony to be knowledgeable and candid during the hearings. 575 F.Supp. at 338–43.

Whatever may be said as to the impropriety of Richard Birchall's rummaging through grand jury testimony and documents when he was left alone in the grand jury storage room, it does not excuse the government attorney's impropriety in availing him of that opportunity. Before leaving him alone in the grand jury storage room they accused Birchall of making several extortion threats to O'Donnell, a target of the investigation. K.Tr. 377, 381, 422–23, 425–26. Birchall obviously took advantage of the opportunity improperly provided to him to search through the grand jury records and documents.

(4) Improper Imposition of Secrecy Obligations

[5] For what the record reveals was clearly an improper strategic purpose, secrecy obligations in clear violation of Rule 6(e)(2), Fed.R.Crim.P., were imposed upon two grand jury witnesses. On January 5, 1982, David H. Hoff and David R. Major appeared before the grand jury. When Hoff appeared separately before the grand jury he was advised:

> Q: You are also aware that the proceedings of this Grand Jury are secret and that is covered by Rule 6 of the Federal Rules

of Criminal Procedure, that is, any questions I put to you today, questions that the Grand Jury may have, any discussion we have in this room at your appearance, that your appearance should be kept secret by you; do you understand that?

A: Yes, sir, I do.

G.J.Tr. Hoff, January 5, 1982, 9:50 a.m., at p. 4. A similar directive was given to David R. Major, G.J.Tr. Major, January 5, 1982, 11:13 a.m., at p. 5.

These confessed violations of Rule 6(e) were neither innocent nor inadvertent. Rather, the record reveals the improper obligation to keep the information and fact of their appearance secret was imposed for a strategic purpose.

Both witnesses occupied positions as attorneys who had formerly represented Defendants Kilpatrick and O'Donnell in previous SEC proceedings involving the same tax shelters under investigation before the grand jury. *See* G.J.Tr. Remarks of Prosecutor, January 5, 1982, 9:09 a.m., at p. 8. The government attorney explained to the grand jury the purpose of calling them as follows:

> The primary focus of our investigation involving the financing is the factual representations made concerning Marlborough Investments Limited, IFDC; we want to know what the lawyers were told by the principals, and what information they related to the parties.

G.J.Tr. Remarks of Prosecutor, January 5, 1982, 9:09 a.m., at p. 12. Thus, the government attorney imposed the unauthorized secrecy obligations upon these two witnesses to prevent defendants from determining the nature and extent of any such communication that might have been revealed and to foreclose a challenge to such testimony based upon an applicable privilege.

Such a conclusion is buttressed by the fact that the same government attorney examined four other witnesses that same day, several witnesses two days later on January 7, 1982, and approximately fifteen witnesses on other occasions. *None* of those witnesses were given the same directive. The prosecutors were fully cognizant that Rule 6(e) prohibits the imposition of secrecy obligations on grand jury witnesses.[12]

Indeed, during these hearings, the Department of Justice attorney involved acknowledged that at the time he imposed the improper obligations he was aware of the United States Attorneys' Manual provisions prohibiting the imposition of an obligation of secrecy upon a witness. Yet, although provided with ample opportunity, he was unable to offer any legitimate reason for his transgressions. K.Tr. 697–99.

C. Use of Pocket Immunity

During this investigation, Department of Justice Attorneys ignored entirely the federal immunity statute (18 U.S.C. §§ 6001, *et seq.*) which prescribes the congressionally authorized procedure for conferring grants of immunity and, instead, secured testimony by engaging extensively in what I have previously described as the "damnable practice" of bestowing "informal immunity" through "letters of assurance." *United States* v. *Anderson,* 577 F.Supp. 223, 233 [13] (D.Colo.1983). The testimony of 23 witnesses in this investigation was secured by means of such "immunity" conferred by Snyder and Blondin. K.Tr. 513. Not one witness was given statutory immunity.

The profligate issuance of such "letters of assurance" had its inception shortly after the investigation commenced, in a telephone call between one of the prosecutors and Bernard Bailor, Esq., who, with his firm, represented many of the witnesses who later received such letters. K.Tr. 476. Bailor explained that his clients would not testify voluntarily before the grand jury. In response, the prosecutor suggested that in lieu of statutory immunity he would be willing to issue letters of assurance. Mr. Bailor accepted the offer and at that point a procedure for issuing the so-called informal "immunity" was inaugurated. K.Tr. 476–77.

After reaching his agreement with Bailor, the prosecutor apparently consulted with senior assistant chief Edward Vellines of the Tax Division. According to the prosecutor, Vellines indicated that the prosecutor had the authority to issue such letters of assurance provided he abided by the instructions of a Department of Justice memorandum *and* the United States Attorneys' Manual *and* provided further that the recipient was not a target of the investigation. K.Tr. 514–15; 602; 623.

Thereafter, the prosecutors undertook, without seeking specific approval from any superior, what was characterized as a "liberal" policy of distributing this type of informal immunity to witnesses. At no point was an effort made to obtain statutory immunity for any witness, nor was the United States Attorney's Office for the District of Colorado informed of the issuance of such letters though written on United States Attorney's stationery. K.Tr. 476–77, 720, 731–32; 575 F.Supp. 335–36; Remarks of Prosecutor, February 2, 1982 at 1:07 p.m. at p. 5–8; DX U-1-U-17.

No witness who testified pursuant to this form of informal "immunity" bestowed by the prosecutors indicated that he or she would have been less cooperative or unwilling to testify had he or she been granted statutory immunity. Rather, the government attorneys readily concede that they chose the method they did simply for the sake of expediency—to by-pass the review procedure established by Congress in the statutory scheme. K.Tr. 476, 721–22; 724–28. Among the vehicles for review avoided by the unauthorized method chosen here was the statistical compilation that Congress indicated as among its purposes for establishing the statutory procedure. Indeed, the government acknowledged that, unlike grants of statutory immunity on which central records are maintained, there is no realistic way for the Department of Justice to determine the number of letters of assurance executed. K.Tr. 729; 839. Despite what the prosecutor explains were his specific instructions, informal immunity was bestowed upon individuals once considered targets of the investigation (*i.e.*, John Jewell and Richard Bell). Moreover, one of the prosecutors admitted having conferred immunity upon an individual who it was later learned had failed to file tax returns for several years. K.Tr. 734–35; *see also* G.J.Tr. Kitrick, May 5, 1981, 10:36 a.m., at p. 3–4; Stephenson, April 6, 1981, 301 p.m., at p. 3–4; 575 F.Supp. at 335.

In their deliberate efforts to avoid the review process and the certainty that Congress intended in the granting of witness immunity, the prosecutors injected serious ambiguity in the critical area of witness credibility. Several facts demonstrate the seriousness of the ambiguity created by this unauthorized procedure.

Despite alleged explanations of letters of assurance,[14] the grand jurors whose job it was in this investigation to assess witness credibility were presented with conflicting descriptions of the effect of these letters upon the witnesses and, consequently upon the value to place upon their testimony. On some occasions, the witnesses were advised before the grand jury that the letters gave them "immunity" and that they had no Fifth Amendment privilege. *See, e.g.,* G.J.Tr. Stanley, April 6, 1981, 4:27 p.m., at p. 5; Stephenson, April 6, 1981, 3:01 p.m., at p. 4; Kitrick, May 5, 1981, 10:36 a.m., at p. 4; Miller, June 2, 1981, 9:28 a.m., at pp. 3–4. On other occasions, witnesses were advised that although they were testifying after receiving a letter of assurance, they retained their Fifth Amendment privilege and could refuse to testify. *See, e.g.,* G.J.Tr. Jewell, February 4, 1982, 1:19 p.m., at pp. 2–3; Caddell, February 4, 1982, 10:50 a.m., at p. 3; Folsom, April 6, 1982, 11:42 a.m., at p. 4; *see also,* G.J. Tr. Remarks of Prosecutor, February 2, 1982, 1:07 p.m. at pp. 5–8.

Moreover, the prosecutors' avoidance of statutory immunity in this investigation left every witness in the posture of testifying with the impression and fear that unless the witness' testimony pleased the government, the government might withdraw its assurances. That such a fear was more real than imagined was apparent to Judge Winner in his review of the events surrounding the grand jury appearance of Richard Bell, a witness who testified with a "Letter of Assurance."

> Mr. Bell was represented by his brother, Malcolm, an attorney practicing in New York City, and a witness I found to be straight-forward, fair, convincing, and most generous to Mr. Snyder. Malcolm Bell succumbed to the carrot of pocket immunity for his brother, but, later he was told by Mr. Snyder that if Richard "testified for Mr. Kilpatrick, all bets were off." Maybe this meant that if Mr. Bell perjured himself he would be prosecuted for perjury, but if the immunity statute had been followed, the nagging question of the meaning of "all bets are off" wouldn't confront us.

575 F.Supp. at 335.

The meaning of the admonition of the prosecutor was a "nagging question" to Malcolm Bell, who as an experienced attorney ultimately determined that the prosecutor must have meant that the deal was not withdrawn but that Richard Bell was subject to perjury. More significantly, however, Richard Bell, as would most lay witnesses, believed it meant the "Letter" would be withdrawn. T.Tr. 460-63.

D. Witness Invocation of Privilege Against Self-Incrimination

The prosecutors pursued their course of distributing letters of assurance "quite liberally" until, in the words of one of them, it was decided "all good things come to an end." G.J.Tr. Remarks of Prosecutor, February 2, 1982, 1:07 p.m. at p. 5. At that point they replaced the unauthorized procedure with the equally abusive and dubious practice of calling witnesses who had not been issued letters and having them invoke their Fifth Amendment privilege before the grand jury regarding the targets and the transactions under investigation; knowing in advance that they would do so. K.Tr. 515.

In all, seven witnesses were called to invoke their privilege in February and March, 1982. That the purpose was to prejudice the grand jury against the targets and the tax shelter transactions under investigation, and not to lay a statutory predicate for immunizing the witnesses (which the prosecutor never did) cannot be denied. First, the prosecutor who called the witnesses admitted that he did not do so to obtain congressionally authorized grants of immunity. K.Tr. 515. Second, the uniform questions posed to the witnesses evidence the intention to utilize the witnesses assertion to prejudice the grand jurors against the targets:

> Q: Now, Mr. Drizin, if I would ask you any questions concerning any relationship you may or may not have had with William A. Kilpatrick, John Peddingill [sic], Shiela Lerner or Declan J. O'Donnell or United Financial Operations, would you assert your right against self-incrimination on those questions?
>
> A: Yes, sir.

G.J.Tr. Drizin, March 2, 1982, 9:29 a.m., at p. 4. Third, the prosecutor did not limit his questioning merely to have the witness invoke his Fifth Amendment privilege but rather questioned several of the witnesses to elicit that Kilpatrick's company, United Financial Operations, was paying their attorneys' fees, leaving the grand jury with the impression that their refusal to testify was being financed by the targets.[15] *See e.g.,* G.J.Tr. D'Amico, February 4, 1982, 12:35 p.m., at pp. 6–7.

[6] That the prosecutor's conduct in this regard (which occurred before the second of the two grand juries impanelled in connection with this investigation) was known to him to be improper and prejudicial is revealed by his statements to the first grand jury several months earlier:

> Immediately all the witnesses I had subpoenaed today decided that they would not want to come in here and testify and they said they would assert their Fifth Amendment rights.
>
> I could force them in here under their Fifth Amendment rights, but under the Department of Justice guidelines *I should not do that except in exceptional circumstances should I bring a person in here and have them assert their Fifth Amendment rights because it serves no purpose and it only serves to prejudice, and it can prejudice a layman.*

G.J.Tr. Remarks of Prosecutor, February 2, 1981, 9:40 a.m. at pp. 2–3 (emphasis supplied). Indeed, the prosecutor did to the second grand jury precisely what he told the first grand jury he could not and should not do. The only difference is that, when he did it anyway, he did not tell the grand jurors that he was doing it to them. General instructions, months prior, that jurors not draw inferences from an individual's invocation of the privilege against self-incrimination cannot correct such corruptions of the grand jury process. G.J. Tr. Remarks of Prosecutor, July 8, 1981, 10:50 a.m., at p. 6; January 5, 1982, 9:09 a.m., at pp. 22–23.

E. Government Summaries of the Evidence

Although the investigation of the instant case covered almost two years, the transcripts reveal that the case against The Bank of Nova Scotia was, for the most part, presented on a single day, September 29, 1982, the day before the indictment was returned. It was done, moreover, almost exclusively by having Mendrop summarize the "evidence" against the bank. The government seeks to explain these summaries as nothing more than legitimate use of hearsay testimony by the grand jury. *See United States* v. *Rogers,* 652 F.2d 972, 975 (1981).

During the course of the September 29, 1982 proceedings, the grand jurors expressed concern that The Bank of Nova Scotia was being singled out for prosecution while other banks that allegedly permitted similar banking activity were not being named as defendants. In response, the prosecutor suggested that the Bank of Nova Scotia was a more appropriate target because, unlike the other institutions involved, it was a large internationally known bank doing business in the United States and its prosecution could be expected to deter others. *See* G.J.Tr. Mendrop, September 29, 1982, 9:32 a.m., at p. 50–52. The prosecutor erroneously suggested that the "evidence" indicated that The Bank of Nova Scotia representatives were familiar with the operation of Kilpatrick's business and that the IRS was to be defrauded by virtue of the banking activity. *See* G.J.Tr. Remarks of Prosecutor, September 29, 1982, 8:52 a.m. at pp. 8, 13.

No evidence of the kind suggested by the prosecutor had been presented to the grand jury. The discussion of these points was heard for the first time during the testimony of Mendrop. Instead of being presented as a witness who was to present hearsay investigative information concerning the Bank's role, Mendrop was introduced to the grand jurors as one who was to "summarize" and "just walk through, one more time, and refresh your memory." G.J.Tr. Remarks of Prosecutor, September 29, 1982, 8:52 a.m. at p. 5. Mendrop then proceeded to "summarize the evidence relating to each of the individuals involved" and "the evidence pertaining to The Bank of Nova Scotia." *See* G.J.Tr. Mendrop, September 29, 1982, 9:32 a.m., at pp. 40, 52, 64, 66, 72. On the vital issue of the bank's knowledge and intent, however, it is clear that Mendrop's testimony was both misleading and inaccurate. In particular, Mendrop purported to "summarize" in connection with the bank's role the testimony presented by three witnesses: Messrs. Waters, Ros and Charles. An examination of the grand jury testimony, however, reveals that it was not a summary of the evidence before the grand jury. One of the witnesses whose testimony was "summarized" never appeared before either grand jury. The other two witnesses whose testimony was "summarized" did not give testimony even remotely resembling that supposedly "summarized" by Mendrop. The grand jury was never informed of these mischaracterizations or of any alternative basis for Mendrop's summary.

The inaccurate "summaries" of the evidence before the grand jury concerning the role of The Bank of Nova Scotia was particularly abusive for several reasons:

(i) The misleading "summaries were presented by an individual upon whom the grand jurors had been urged to rely as their "agent";

(ii) The investigation spanned 20 months and two successive grand juries. Much of the testimony of the 27 witnesses who appeared before the first jury was read to the second grand jury in an improper and unsupervised manner;

(iii) The grand jurors had not previously focused on The Bank of Nova Scotia as a target since the bank was not mentioned as a target until the month the indictment was returned;

(iv) The reading of testimony from the first grand jury (which included the testimony of Ros and Charles) occurred early in the presentation of the case to the second grand jury. The grand jurors and the prosecutors frequently commented upon the monotony and difficulty of listening to the readings and, indeed, the grand jurors expressed confusion as to which transcripts had been read. *See, e.g.,* G.J.Tr. Remarks of Prosecutor, November 4, 1981, 9:12 a.m. at p. 5; Remarks of Prosecutor, February 2, 1982, 1:07 p.m. at p. 20; and

(v) The improper summaries related to vital issues concerning the Bank's knowledge and intent. Unbeknown to the grand jurors, the government attorneys contemporaneously entertained serious doubts as to the accuracy of certain critical "facts" contained in the summaries.

In sum, the mischaracterizations reasonably could not have been expected to be picked up by the grand jurors and, undoubtedly, formed a substantial basis for the indictment against the bank. The examples of improper mischaracterizations of the evidence are detailed below.

(1) Mr. Waters

Asserting that he was discussing a "few of the pieces of evidence" and "the summary of the evidence pertaining to The Bank of Nova Scotia," Mendrop purported to summarize what the prosecutor characterized as the "evidence" provided by

Waters about a trip supposedly made by defendant Monte Smith, the bank's Cayman Island branch manager, to Kilpatrick's offices in Denver. (Smith was vital as it is upon his activities that the bank has been claimed vicariously liable.) G.J.Tr. Mendrop, September 29, 1982, 9:32 a.m., at pp. 36, 64, 65–72; *see also* G.J.Tr. Remarks of Prosecutor, September 29, 1982, 9:07 a.m., at p. 10. According to Mendrop and the prosecutor, this claimed trip by Monte Smith was important because it demonstrated that Smith was familiar with Kilpatrick's tax shelter operations. Apparently unbeknown to the grand jurors, Waters never testified before either of the grand juries. The grand juries were never informed of the actual source of Mendrop's testimony which apparently was an interview of Waters or testimony of Waters at a contempt hearing involving Kilpatrick.

Whatever the source, it is clear that Mendrop's supposed "summary" of Waters' testimony is an inaccurate recitation of "facts" in several significant respects. At the time Mendrop was supposedly summarizing the "facts" of Monte Smith's trip to Denver, the government attorneys entertained serious doubts about its accuracy because Waters' description of the individual he met at Mr. Kilpatrick's offices did not resemble Monte Smith.[16] The testimony of Waters during the 1983 obstruction trial of Mr. Kilpatrick confirms the inaccuracies of Mendrop's testimony. During that trial Waters testified that when picking up some checks from Kilpatrick for payment due him, he was informed by Kilpatrick that one of the people present was Mr. Smith who was the manager of the Bank branch on which the checks were drawn. Mr. Waters' description of that individual during trial does *not* resemble Monte Smith. T.Tr. 311–12. In fact, at these hearings, commenting on Mr. Waters' somewhat unusual description of Monte Smith, one of the prosecutors admitted that at the time "[t]here was a real question as to whether or not it was the same person." K.Tr. 742–43. Despite the facts that Waters was not called as a witness before either grand jury, that the grand jurors were never informed that transcripts of taped interviews of Waters existed and that a "real question" existed as to the accuracy of Waters' identification, Mendrop was permitted to represent to the contrary that there was "considerable confirmation that Mr. Smith did actually come out here and visit with Mr. Kilpatrick." G.J.Tr. Mendrop, September 29, 1982, 9:32 a.m., at pp. 66–68.

(2) Mr. Ros

Raul Ros, a "chauffeur" for Mr. Kilpatrick, testified before the first grand jury. He did not appear before the grand jury that returned the indictment; his testimony was read to the second grand jury. G.J.Tr. Mendrop, September 9, 1981, 8:44 a.m., at p. 3. A year after Mendrop read his testimony to the grand jurors, Mendrop purported to summarize it. According to Mendrop, Ros' evidence confirms the testimony of Waters with regard to Monte Smith's appearance in Denver. G.J.Tr. Mendrop, September 29, 1982, 9:32 a.m., at p. 66. Mendrop indicated that Ros commented that during Smith's claimed visit to Denver, he and Kilpatrick discussed funding for the tax shelters. No such testimony can be found in Raul Ros' grand jury transcript. Mendrop gave absolutely no explanation of an alternative source, but rather erroneously led the grand jurors to believe that he was simply relaying information contained in the Ros testimony before the prior grand jury.

(3) Mr. Charles

Mendrop's "summary" also mischaracterizes the testimony of Barry Charles. Like Raul Ros, Charles testified before the first grand jury not the second grand jury. As he did with Raul Ros' testimony, Mendrop attributed "testimony" to Charles that the bank fulfilled virtually all of Mr. Kilpatrick's requests and that it "appeared" to Charles that the bank officers knew what was being done. G.J.Tr. Mendrop, September 29, 1982, 9:32 a.m., at p. 68. The "summary" given by Mendrop is at odds with Charles' testimony. G.J.Tr. Charles, June 2, 1981, 8:40 a.m. Again, Mendrop did not identify any alternate source for the comments attributed to Charles.

In his testimony before the first grand jury Charles indicated that he was not present during most of the transactions in the bank. Charles, who traveled to the Cayman Islands with Kilpatrick, Pettingill and O'Donnell, was the least involved in the group and observed less than Oliver Hemphill who himself testified that he had witnessed little of the banking activity. See G.J.Tr. Hemphill, May 5, 1981, 9:28 a.m., at p. 12. Thus, Mendrop's suggestion to the grand jurors of the "evidence" to be gleaned from Charles' "testimony" is contradicted by the actual testimony of Charles and others.

(4) Comments by the Prosecutor

In addition to presenting Mendrop's summary of the "important evidence" against the bank on the day before the indictment, the prosecutors also argued in favor of an indictment of the bank. Once again, the evidence against the bank on the essential issue of knowledge of the claimed object of the conspiracy was seriously mischaracterized by the prosecutor, who asserted:

> [A]s my agents will tell you there is evidence that the Bank knew it was the IRS—*they were in fact told that it was the IRS they were defrauding.*

G.J.Tr. Remarks of Prosecutor, September 29, 1982, 8:52 a.m. at p. 13 (emphasis supplied). No such evidence was ever presented. Indeed, even the misleading summary of Mendrop provides no basis for such a statement.

F. Interrogation in Absence of Counsel

In February, 1983, during the period between indictment and dismissal of the charges against The Bank of Nova Scotia, one of the prosecutors departed from the traditional role of a government trial attorney in order to travel to Puerto Rico and engage in investigative activity. The prosecutor undertook his journey with the intention of interviewing bank employees concerning the whereabouts and reasons for transfer of another bank employee, Malcolm Haynes, who the prosecutor understood was the second in command at the bank's Cayman Island branch during the period covered by the indictment. No attempt had been made to talk to this potential witness before indictment. The prosecutor's purpose was to interview him concerning matters underlying the indictment. W.Tr. 642–49, 694, 709–10.

Although the prosecutor was fully aware that the bank, an indicted defendant, was represented by counsel, he did not feel constrained by the Supreme Court's dictates in *Massiah* v. *United States,* 377 U.S. 201, 84 S.Ct. 1199, 12 L.Ed.2d 246 (1964) to inform counsel of his intentions to interview high ranking bank employees.[17] Instead, he undertook this investigative exercise with the "hope" of eventually interviewing Malcolm Haynes "in the absence of Mr. Morvillo,"[18] firm in the belief that, if he committed a constitutional violation of the type identified in *Massiah*, the only likely sanction was the suppression of evidence in the government's case-in-chief. In the prosecutor's words, "no indictment has ever been dismissed because of [a *Massiah* violation]." K.Tr. 1114, 1122; W.Tr. 643, 693–94, 709–10.

The prosecutor also testified that he believed it was permissible to interview high ranking employees of an indicted corporate defendant because it was authorized in *Upjohn Co.* v. *United States*, 449 U.S. 393, 101 S.Ct. 677, 66 L.Ed.2d 384 (1981) and because, unlike *Massiah* he was not engaged in acts of "subterfuge."[19] W.Tr. 643, 693–94, 709–10; K.Tr. 1114–15.

When he arrived in Puerto Rico, the prosecutor and another investigator, Victor Torrez Perez, an IRS special agent, appeared without prior arrangement at the branch offices of The Bank of Nova Scotia and proceeded to interrogate several of its representatives. Among others, they questioned Malcolm Haynes' former secretary and his replacement, the branch's controller. They also interrogated other high ranking representatives of the bank—including Douglas Rector, the Puerto Rico area manager of The Bank of Nova Scotia and chief executive officer of the Bank's Puerto Rico subsidiary. W.Tr. 640–42, 696–99.

After leaving the bank, accompanied by Special Agent Torrez Perez, he searched out the school attended by Haynes' two small daughters, ages eight and ten, in order to determine the whereabouts of their parents. At the end of the school day, the prosecutor (who had already elicited information from the school's principal and the girls' teachers) followed the children on foot "by about a hundred yards." His purpose was to have the girls lead him to their mother. W.Tr. 642–45, 699–708.

The prosecutor's visit to Puerto Rico, however, did not end his endeavor to interrogate high ranking representatives of the defendant bank without notice to or leave of defense counsel. Shortly after his interrogation of Mrs. Haynes, he wrote a letter to her requesting that she use her efforts to have her husband speak with the government. Like his previous efforts this approach was made without informing defense counsel. Indeed, the prosecutor asserted that he "would have interviewed Mr. Haynes in the absence of Mr. Morvillo hopefully." W.Tr. 709–10.

G. Mistreatment of Witnesses

Professor Roland Hjorth, a tax law professor who Judge Winner observed "is a recognized expert who was employed by defense counsel" was permitted to testify before the grand jury that returned the indictment. His treatment by the prosecutor on the occasion of his appearance contrasts markedly with the treatment the prosecution afforded its own expert, Roger Schneider, who was passed off as an "agent of the grand jury."

As Judge Winner observed:

> [Professor Hjorth's] views of tax law differed markedly from those of [the prosecutor], who bragged on frequent occasions that he had never taken a course in taxation and knew almost nothing about it. Nevertheless, Professor Hjorth was browbeaten and ridiculed by [the prosecutor], and some of the conversation so out of place for an ethical prosecutor took place during a recess in the hearing of some grand jurors.

575 F.Supp. at 333.

Indeed, the prosecutor's heated argument with Professor Hjorth was also overheard by witnesses scheduled to appear before the grand jury. W.Tr. 334. Moreover, the conduct was so shocking that Richard Slivka, a local attorney formerly employed by the Department of Justice and Colorado United States Attorney's Office, who was representing witnesses scheduled to appear and who himself observed the conduct, wrote a letter to Chief Judge Finesilver shortly thereafter reporting the incident. W.Tr. 317–27, 350–64. Professor Hjorth testified that the prosecutor's conduct was so abusive that he would never again appear as an expert witness in a similar proceeding.

Judge Winner concluded of the prosecutor's conduct that:

> Intimidating witnesses by telling them that their testimony disgraces them and implying that the Tax Division of the Department of Justice will take after the witness and will complain to the University of Washington Law School because an expert testified to his expert opinions does no credit to our

government. . . . [s]eemingly, the professor's testimony isn't seriously contested. I hope that we haven't gotten to the point that disagreement with the legal concepts of the IRS provides grounds for attacks by that bureaucracy because sometimes the IRS is wrong. *U.S.* v. *Sells Engineering,* 463 U.S. 418, 103 S.Ct. 3133, 77 L.Ed.2d 743 and *U.S.* v. *Baggot,* 463 U.S. 476, 103 S.Ct. 3164, 77 L.Ed.2d 785.

575 F.Supp. at 333; *see also* K.Tr. 502-05.

CONCLUSIONS OF LAW

The government's position in this case is reminiscent of the common law defense of confession and avoidance in which, for the most part, the truth of the averments of fact are admitted, but argument is made which tends to deprive the facts of their ordinary legal effect or obviates them. Thus, it is said:

> Just as there has never been a perfect lawyer, a perfect judge, or perfect trial, so has there never been a perfect investigation. Contrary to what one might expect, in view of the defense allegations, the transcripts of the grand jury proceedings do not reveal any conduct whatsoever by the prosecutors seeking to overreach or override the independence of the grand jury.

Government Memorandum, Government Response to The Bank of Nova Scotia's proposed Findings of Fact and Conclusions of Law, filed April 9, 1984, at pp. 3–4. The government's response to the defendant's several proposed findings of facts is mainly a recitation of the number of instances in which its prosecutors did not violate the law.

As I view the present state of the law as it applies to this case, there are four analytical modalities which must be considered. In the first, specific violations of specific rules require dismissal. I view this form of analysis as essentially quantitative. There either is a violation or there isn't and the conclusion is ineluctable depending on the factual premise which is established. The second modality, requires an evaluation of the totality of circumstances extant so that a qualitative assessment may be made. Finally, cases distinguish the third modality, the authority and duty of district courts to supervise the conduct of prosecutions and grand juries, from the fourth modality, the duty to enforce the mandates of the Constitution.

In articulating the conclusions of law I have reached in this case, I shall consider all four modalities in the order in which I have just expressed them. I shall begin with Rule 6, Fed.R.Crim.P.

A. Violations of Rule 6(d)

[7] As noted by Judge Winner, Rule 6, Fed.R.Crim.P. does not authorize grand juries to have agents. The creation of that role and its misleading description to the grand jury is an improper intrusion into the exclusive and independent province of the grand jury by government attorneys and investigators. The most important function of the grand jury is to stand between the government agents and the suspect as an unbiased evaluator of the evidence. *United States* v. *Dionisio,* 410 U.S. 1, 16–17, 93 S.Ct. 764, 772–73, 35 L.Ed.2d 67 (1973). "The purpose of the grand jury requires that it remain free, within constitutional and statutory limits, to operate 'independently of either prosecuting attorney or judge.' *United States* v. *Sells Engineering, Inc.,* 463 U.S. 418, 103 S.C. 3133, 3141, 77 L.Ed.2d 743 (1983).

[8] Rule 6(d), Fed.R.Crim.P., delimits those who may be present in grand jury proceedings by the following explicit language:

> (d) Who May Be Present. Attorneys for the government, the witness under examination, interpreters when needed and, for the purpose of taking the evidence, a stenographer or operator of a recording device may be present while the grand jury is in session, but no person other than the jurors may be present while the grand jury is deliberating or voting.

After his usual thorough analysis of the relevant case law and with characteristic pungency, Judge Matsch, of our Court, stated in *United States* v. *Pignatiello:*

> A review of all of these cases reinforces the conclusion that the only effective sanction for a violation of Rule 6(d) is dismissal without any further inquiry into the effects of that violation.

582 F.Supp. 251, 254 (D.Colo.1984).

> I conclude that events which occurred in the grand jury room while *soi-disant* agents of the grand jury were present and not under oath as witnesses under examination violated Rule 6(d) and therefore require dismissal of the indictment. As Judge Matsch carefully notes in *Pignatiello,* brief intrusions on the proceedings during which no testimony is taken nor questions asked nor statements made about the case by grand jurors such as the delivering of a note to the prosecutor by his secretary or the repair of a switch by a maintenance man are not included within the *per se* rule. In this case, there is no doubt that matters of considerable substance occurred while Rule 6(d) was being violated.

B. Violations of Rule 6(e)

[9] Courts have held that violations of the strictures of Rule 6(e), Fed.R.Crim.P., typically require the sanction of contempt rather than dismissal. *United States* v. *Hoffa,* 349 F.2d 20, 43 (6th Cir.1965). However, where Rule 6(e) is violated recklessly and systematically, dismissal is appropriate. *United States* v. *Gold,* 470 F.Supp. 1336, 1352–56 (N.D.Ill.1979). Where knowing violations of Rule 6(e) prejudice and embarrass targets whose identities the government reveals, the government itself has recognized that the contempt remedy is *"not always . . . wholly adequate."* United States Attorneys' Manual § 9–11.370 (emphasis supplied).

(1) Rule 6(e)(3)—Improper Disclosure and Use

[10] Rule 6(e)(3) provides in relevant part:
(3) Exceptions.

(A) *Disclosure otherwise prohibited* by this rule of matters occurring before the grand jury, other than its deliberations and the vote of any grand jury, *may be made to—*

(i) an attorney for the government for use in the performance of such attorney's duty; and

(ii) *such government personnel as are deemed necessary by an attorney for the government to assist an attorney for the government in the performance of such attorney's duty to enforce federal criminal law.*

(b) Any person to whom matters are disclosed under subparagraph (A)(ii) of this paragraph shall not utilize that grand jury material for any purpose other than assisting the attorney for the government in the performance of such attorney's duty to enforce federal criminal law. *An attorney for the government shall promptly provide the district court, before which was impaneled the grand jury whose material has been so disclosed, with the names of the persons to whom such disclosure has been made.*

(emphasis supplied).

The prosecutors in this case permitted several violations of this rule. They relinquished to the IRS their responsibility to determine the persons to whom disclosure would be made. The IRS agents then failed to provide the "prompt" notification of such disclosure mandated by the rule. Moreover, the IRS representatives, in direct contravention of recent Supreme Court dictates, improperly manipulated the secret material and their novel roles as "agents of the grand jury" to obtain information and data for use during civil litigation that they knew would follow on the heels of the criminal case. *See United States* v. *Sells Engineers, Inc., supra, United States* v. *Baggot, 463 U.S. 476, 103 S.Ct. 3164, 77 L.Ed.2d 785 (1983).*

Rule 6(e)(3) provides that disclosure can be made to "such government personnel as are deemed necessary by an attorney for the government . . ." provided the "attorney for the government . . . promptly provide[s] the district court . . ." with notice of such disclosure. The instant record reveals not only that IRS representatives regularly took it upon themselves to determine to whom disclosure should be made, but also that in some cases the "attorneys for the government" were not notified of such disclosure until after it had occurred, if they were notified at all. Moreover, notices to the district court were not filed promptly but were prepared in some instances substantially after such disclosure, even after the investigation had concluded and the indictment was filed.

With regard to the delegation of the Rule 6(e)(3) responsibilities in this investigation by Department of Justice attorneys, Judge Winner noted:

> I am troubled about testimony suggesting that authority to
> make the disclosure decisions was delegated to the IRS Special

Agent/Grand Jury Agents/Prosecutor's helpers. Under common law rules of agency, this authority couldn't be delegated to a subagent, and especially it couldn't be delegated to an IRS agent whose fellow workers were aiming at the defendants from a different angle. My worry on this score is not lessened by an IRS letter in evidence saying that making a civil tax case under the administrative process would be difficult. *United States* v. *Sells Engineering* and *United States* v. *Baggot,* both *supra,* which settle the question of using a grand jury to collect taxes.

575 F.Supp. at 338 (1983).

The broad delegation to the IRS of control over the course of the grand jury investigation is amply supported by the record. The extensive disclosure of grand jury material to IRS civil employees, the haphazard and *post hoc* method of identifying those to whom disclosure was made and the omission from the disclosure notices of numerous IRS employees privy to grand jury information clearly contravene the rule. It is fanciful to suggest that these IRS and civil employees will erase from their minds that material obtained as part of the grand jury's investigation.

In *United States* v. *Sells Engineering, Inc., supra,* the Supreme Court recognized that it is difficult or impossible to demonstrate the extent of improper disclosure and use of grand jury material made during the course of an investigation. *Id.* 103 S.Ct. at 3142. In the instant case a significant portion of the direction of the investigation was unrelated to the federal criminal goals. As the Supreme Court observed:

> [B]ecause the Government takes an active part in the activities of the grand jury, disclosure to government attorneys for civil use poses a significant threat to the integrity of the grand jury itself. If prosecutors in a given case knew that their colleagues would be free to use the materials generated by the grand jury for a civil case, they might be tempted to manipulate the grand jury's powerful investigative tools to root out additional evidence useful in the civil suit. . . .

Id.

In *Sells* the Supreme Court analyzed the grand jury process and the provisions of Rule 6(e) in deciding whether civil division lawyers in the Department of Justice should have automatic access to grand jury materials to assist them in civil litigation. The court denied such access for three reasons: (1) civil disclosure threatens to subvert the limitations otherwise imposed on the government's powers in civil and administrative discovery and investigation; (2) civil disclosure may tempt prosecutors to manipulate the grand jury investigation to obtain evidence useful in civil litigations; and (3) civil disclosure increases the number of persons privy to grand jury matters thereby increasing the risk of inadvertent or illegal disclosure to others. *Id.* at 3142, 43. The IRS's participation in the grand jury investigation in this case achieved each of these illicit purposes.

As noted by Judge Winner, the genesis of the grand jury's inquiry was a belief by the IRS that it could not effectively investigate the facts underlying the subject tax shelters pursuant to its congressionally circumscribed administrative enforcement powers. Thus, the extraordinary powers of the grand jury were sought and usurped.

(2) Rule 6(e)(2)—Secrecy Violations

Rule 6(e)(2). Fed.R.Crim.P. provides:

> (2) General Rule Of Secrecy.—A Grand juror, an interpreter, a stenographer, an operator of a recording device, a typist who transcribes recorded testimony, an attorney for the government, or any person to whom disclosure is made under paragraph (3)(A)(ii) of this subdivision shall not disclose matters occurring before the grand jury, except as otherwise provided for in these rules. No obligation of secrecy may be imposed on any person except in accordance with this rule. A knowing violation of Rule 6 may be punished as a contempt of court.

Rule 6(e)(2) is a codification of the traditional requirement that matters occurring before the grand jury should be treated as confidential. Courts have consistently recognized that this traditional requirement exists to no small degree in order to protect the name and reputation of the targets during the pendency of the period the allegations are being investigated. *See e.g. United States* v. *Malatesta*, 583 F.2d 748, 752 (5th Cir.1978), *cert. denied*, 444 U.S. 846, 100 S.Ct. 91, 62 L.Ed.2d 59 (1979). Thus, courts have held that Rule 6(e) prohibits the government from publicly identifying the targets of a grand jury's inquiry. *See In re Bart*, 304 F.2d 631, 637 n. 19 (D.C.Cir.1962); *Hawthorne v. Director of Internal Revenue*, 406 F.Supp. 1098, 1128–29 (E.D.Pa.1975).

During the course of this investigation the government repeatedly and systematically disclosed the identity of the targets to individuals and entities that the government acknowledged had a "business relationship" with the targets and to investors identified as customers of the targets. These numerous disclosures adversely affected the business activities of the targets at a time when the grand jury was charged with investigating whether any crimes may have been committed. The abuse of power is evident.

The violations of Rule 6(e)(2) do not end with the improper violations of the secrecy requirements. In order to gain a tactical advantage, prosecutors selected two witnesses and directed them not to disclose the fact or substance of their testimony. As Judge Winner held, this was done in direct contravention of Rule 6(e)(2):

> [The imposition upon witnesses of secrecy obligations] is now verboten because of the language of the rule saying, "No obligation of secrecy may be imposed on any person except in accordance with this rule." This language has been uniformly interpreted to prohibit any instruction to a witness that his testimony is secret. *In re Langswager*, (1975) D.C. Ill. 392 F.Supp. 783; *In re Grand Jury Witness Subpoenas* (1974) D.C.Fla. 370 F.Supp. 1282; *In re Alvarez* (1972) D.C.Cal. 351 F.Supp. 1089; *In re Minkoff* (1972) D.C.R.I. 349 F.Supp. 154; *In re Investigation before April 1975 Grand Jury* (1976) D.C.Cir. 531 F.2d 600; *In re Vescovo Special Grand Jury* (1979) 473 F.Supp. 1335, and many other cases. In spite of this express command of Rule 6(e), secrecy obligations were imposed on several witnesses, and, to make the violation more disturbing, secrecy obligations were imposed on lawyers called to furnish information concerning their clients. That makes the violation gravely beyond the pale, because of the impossible position the lawyer-witness is placed in, but that's what the grand jury transcript discloses. No "oath" of secrecy was administered, but an obligation of secrecy was imposed by instructions from government counsel to witnesses. This foolishness may or may not have been intentional, but ignorance of the law is not a

defense available to a prosecutor. *This misconduct is established by the record, and it will prove difficult for the government to deny,* just as the government had to admit the attempted administration of an "oath" by Mr. Snyder. The government surprisingly defends the proven mishmash of functions of the IRS Special Agent/Grand Jury Agents/Assistants to the Attorney for the Government appointed under Rule 6(e), but maybe it thinks that admitting that this was error would confess the motion to dismiss.

575 F.Supp. at 331, 332 (1983); *see also United States* v. *Radetsky,* 535 F.2d 556, 569 (10th Cir.), *cert. denied,* 429 U.S. 820, 97 S.Ct. 68, 50 L.Ed.2d 81 (1976); *Application of Eisenberg,* 654 F.2d 1107, 1113 n. 9 (5th Cir.1981); *In re Russo,* 53 F.R.D. 564, 570 (C.D.Ca.1971); *In Re Disclosure of Evidence,* 184 F.Supp. 38, 41 (E.D.Va.1960); *Arlington Glass Co.* v. *Pittsburg Plate Glass Co.,* 24 F.R.D. 50, 52 (N.D.Ill.1959).

As Judge Winner suggests, the only issue that could not be determined by the record before him was whether the secrecy obligations were imposed intentionally. The prosecutor's testimony during the hearings before me, however, leaves no doubt that the improper obligation was imposed deliberately, with full knowledge of the witness's relationship to the targets and in violation of the commands of the United States Attorneys' Manual.[20] Moreover, no legitimate explanation for the activity was ever presented.

The numerous violations of Rule 6(e) by the Department of Justice attorneys ignore the rights of unindicted subjects of an investigation and the secrecy and independence of the grand jury itself. As I shall discuss later, a court's supervisory power to dismiss an indictment is appropriately utilized to ensure that governmental impropriety of a similar nature is not repeated in future investigations or prosecutions. *United States* v. *Owen,* 580 F.2d 365, 367 (9th Cir.1978); *United States* v. *Houghton,* 554 F.2d 1219, 1224 (1st Cir.), *cert. denied,* 434 U.S. 851, 98 S.Ct. 164, 54 L.Ed.2d 120 (1977). Dismissal is particularly appropriate in order to hold all government prosecutors acting within this district to the same high standard of conduct that the United States Attorney demands of his own assistants. *United States* v. *Jacobs,* 547 F.2d 772, 778 (2d Cir.1976) (Organized Crime Strike Force attorney operating in the Eastern District of New York); *United*

States v. *Gold,* 470 F.Supp. 1336 (N.D.Ill.1979) (Environmental Protection Agency Staff attorney appointed as Special Attorney in the Department of Justice); *see also United States* v. *Estepa,* 471 F.2d 1132, 1137 (2d Cir.1972).

As previously indicated, however, I hold that where violations of Rule 6(e) are intentional or reckless and systemic, the sanction of contempt is insufficient and dismissal of the indictment is warranted. Under such circumstances, it is not necessary for the defendant to show that he has been prejudiced by the violations. In the instant case, however, such showing of prejudice has been convincingly made.

C. Violations of Witness Immunity Statutes

Earlier in this opinion,[21] I indicated that I believe I was unduly diffident in describing so-called pocket immunity or "Letters of Assurance" as a "damnable practice." I believe I was wrong because I did not then have the benefit of the Supreme Court's opinion in *United States* v. *Doe,* —U.S.—104 S.Ct. 1237, 79 L.Ed.2d 552 (1984).

In *Anderson* v. *United States, supra,* I wrote:

> The government, in this case, made extensive use of informal or "pocket" immunity. This is putative immunity granted to a witness by letter or oral representation of the prosecutor rather than ordered by a judge after satisfaction of the procedures of 18 U.S.C. §§ 6002 and 6003. Such immunity poses serious problems since it circumvents the statute and leaves an inadequate record of the scope of the immunity granted. *See United States* v. *Quartermain, Drax,* 613 F.2d 38 (3rd Cir.1980). The procedures established by Congress in 18 U.S.C. §§ 6002 and 6003 clearly indicate an intent to formalize, standardize and limit the use of immunity. The statute requires approval of a senior Justice Department official as well as application to and order of a United States District Court Judge before immunity is conferred. The procedure leaves no doubt as to the accomplishment of the grant, the particularized need of the witness and the scope of the immunization. It also leaves for Congress and the public a complete and definite record of the frequency, efficacy and reasons for the use of immunity. Informal immunity, apparently in widespread use by the Justice Department, accomplishes none of those goals. It is a damnable practice. No notice need be given to senior Justice De-

partment officials or to a judge. The only record, if any, is a letter by the U.S. Attorney or a transcript of an oral representation, if it was made on the record. Such informality has resulted in confusion over witnesses' rights in the past, *Quartermain, Drax. supra*, 613 F.2d 38, and lends itself to excessive use of unchecked discretion. While the immunity grant is always a matter of prosecutorial discretion, the procedures of §§ 6002 and 6003 subject it to the light of public, congressional and judicial scrutiny and insure that it is not invoked or revoked arbitrarily or capriciously.

In *United States* v. *Doe,* Justice Powell wrote:

> As we stated in *Pillsbury Co.* v. *Conboy,* 459 U.S. 248, 74 L.Ed.2d 430, 103 S.Ct. 608 (1983), in passing the use immunity statute, "Congress gave certain officials in the Department of Justice exclusive authority to grant immunities." *Id.,* at 253, 74 L.Ed.2d 430, 103 S.Ct. 608 [at 612]. "Congress foresaw the courts as playing only a minor role in the immunizing process: . . ." *Id.,* at 254, n. 11, 74 L.Ed.2d 430, 103 S.Ct. 608 [at 613]. The decision to seek use immunity necessarily involves a balancing of the Government's interest in obtaining information against the risk that immunity will frustrate the Government's attempts to prosecute the subject of the investigation. *See United States* v. *Mandujano,* 425 U.S. 564, 575, 48 L.Ed.2d 212, 96 S.Ct. 1768 [1776] (1976) (plurality opinion). Congress expressly left this decision exclusively to the Justice Department. If, on remand, the appropriate official concludes that it is desirable to compel respondent to produce his business records, the statutory procedure for requesting use immunity will be available.

—U.S. at —104, S.Ct. at 1244–45, 79 L.Ed.2d at 562–63.

[11] It thus can be seen most clearly that Congress has vested exclusive authority to grant immunities in a few specified officials in the Department of Justice. Further, Congress has clearly and unequivocally set forth the parameters within which that discretion must be exercised. Ordinary statutory construction employing the principle of *expressio unius est exclusio alterius* and buttressed by the quoted language of Justice Powell leads to only one conclusion: Pocket immunity is illegal; when granting immunity, the Department of Justice must comply with the requirements of 18 U.S.C. §§ 6002 and 6003.

[12] I hold that the repeated use of letters of assurance or so

called "pocket immunity" in the instant case violated the applicable statutes and tainted the grand jury indictment with its illegality.[22]

D. Violations of the Fifth Amendment

[13] Courts have consistently held that it is improper to call a witness solely for purposes of having that witness assert their rights under the Fifth Amendment when the prosecutor is aware of the witnesses' intention to do so. *See Namet* v. *United States,* 373 U.S. 179, 186, 83 S.Ct. 1151, 1154, 10 L.Ed.2d 278 (1963); *United States* v. *Ritz,* 548 F.2d 510, 521 (5th Cir.1977); *United States* v. *Maloney,* 262 F.2d 535, 537–38 (2d Cir.1959). The facts here demonstrated that the prosecutor hoped to take advantage of impermissible inferences that arise from invocation of the privilege. *See United States* v. *Maloney,* 262 F.2d 535 (2d Cir.1959). The prosecutor's ploy "served no other purpose than calculated prejudice." *United States* v. *Samango,* 607 F.2d 877, 883 (9th Cir.1979).

[14] Moreover, the improper efforts to prejudice the defendants by impermissible inferences flowing from the seven witnesses' assertions of their privilege against self-incrimination was compounded by the questioning concerning the payment of the witnesses' legal fees. No legitimate purpose for such questioning exists. Indeed, similar questioning before a grand jury has been held to be improper. *United States* v. *Gold,* 470 F.Supp. 1336, 1352 (N.D.Ill.1979).

Dismissal of an indictment is not required *per se* by the deliberate contriving of a prosecutor to have witnesses invoke their Fifth Amendment privilege. Such conduct is, however, a factor to be considered in the totality of circumstances in determining whether a grand jury has been overreached or usurped.

E. Presentation of Misinformation

[15] The characterization of the testimony before the grand jury and the unidentified use of questionable hearsay information with regard to vital issues intrudes upon the independent role of the grand jury. *See United States* v. *Samango,* 607 F.2d 877 (9th Cir.1979). The court in *Samango* emphasized that such behavior, even if unintentional, causes "improper influence and usurpation of the grand jury's role." *United States* v. *Samango,*

607 F.2d at 882. Such a danger is particularly present where, as here, the misrepresentations could not be expected to be readily apparent to the second grand jury and related to material issues in the prosecution. *See id.* at 883; *United States* v. *Lawson,* 502 F.Supp. 158 (D.Md.1980) (indictment dismissed where prosecutor's examination of witness created a false impression and misled grand jurors as to nature of the evidence); *United States* v. *Gallo,* 394 F.Supp. 310 (D.Conn.1975) (indictment dismissed where grand jurors misled as to hearsay nature of testimony and misstatements).

F. Violations of the Sixth Amendment

[16] It is beyond cavil that, upon indictment, a defendant becomes an "accused" with a right to counsel guaranteed by the Sixth Amendment. *See Brewer* v. *Williams,* 430 U.S. 387, 97 S.Ct. 1232, 51 L.Ed.2d 424 (1977); *Massiah* v. *United States,* 377 U.S. 201, 84 S.Ct. 1199, 12 L.Ed.2d 246 (1964). The guarantees of the Sixth Amendment apply to corporate defendants with the same force as to individual defendants. *United States* v. *Rad-O-Lite of Philadelphia, Inc.,* 612 F.2d 740, 743 (3d Cir.1979); *see also Grandbouche* v. *Adams,* 529 F.Supp. 545, 547 (D.Colo.1982). In order to give meaning to these guarantees, the Supreme Court has held that once a defendant becomes an accused, it is improper for a government official to question that defendant out of the presence of counsel. *Brewer* v. *Williams, supra; Massiah* v. *United States, supra.*

[17] In the instant case, the Department of Justice engaged in precisely the type of interrogation proscribed by the Supreme Court.[23] Without notifying counsel for the indicted bank, the prosecutor along with a federal agent, impermissibly interrogated several high level bank employees in hopes of obtaining incriminating information. In several respects the instant conduct is even more egregious than that which occurred in *Brewer* and *Massiah.* The prosecutor's actions here were premeditated and prompted by the expectation that the worst that would become of his constitutional violations would be a limited suppression of evidence.[24]

The defendants have not, however, demonstrated any prejudice from the interrogations of bank employees in the absence of counsel. The bank's counsel has performed ably and adequately throughout the litigation. Under such circumstances, the Supreme Court has specifically rejected the remedy of dismissal based upon a prosecutor's violation of a defendant's Sixth Amendment rights. "[A]bsent demonstrable prejudice of substantial threat thereof, dismissal of the indictment is plainly inappropriate, even though the violation may have been deliberate." *United States* v. *Morrison*, 449 U.S. 361, 365, 101 S.Ct. 665, 668, 66 L.Ed.2d 564 (1981). *See also United States* v. *Drake*, 655 F.2d 1025, 1027 (10th Cir.1981); *United States* v. *Kapnison*, 743 F.2d 1450 at 1454 (10th Cir.1984). As in *Morrison*, so it is here:

> [Defendant] has demonstrated no prejudice of any kind, either transitory or permanent, to the ability of [its] counsel to provide adequate representation in these criminal proceedings. There is no effect of a constitutional dimension which needs to be purged to make certain that [defendant] has been effectively represented. . . .

449 U.S. at 366, 101 S.Ct. at 669. Accordingly dismissal of the indictment is an inappropriate remedy for the *Massiah* violations in this case.[25]

The Sixth Amendment abuses were, in some instances, undertaken by the prosecutors appearing before the grand jury. Thus, while not directly implicating actions by the grand jury, such actions do reflect upon the general abuses of the grand jury process practiced by the government. The *Massiah* violations must enter into my general qualitative assessments of the prosecutors' and grand jury's conduct.

G. The Totality of Circumstances Test

[18] As I stated in *United States* v. *Anderson*, 577 F.Supp. 223, 230 (1983):

> The Tenth Circuit Court of Appeals has recently articulated the standard to be applied in cases where dismissal of an indictment is sought because of prosecutorial misconduct:
>
> > An indictment may be dismissed for prosecutorial misconduct which is flagrant to the point that there is some significant infringement on the grand jury's ability to exercise independent judgment.
>
> *United States* v. *Pino*, 708 F.2d 523, 530 (10th Cir.1983). While the remedy of dismissal is extraordinary, it may be used

"to insure proper standards of conduct by the prosecution."
708 F.2d at 530. District courts are also empowered to dismiss
indictments because of inherent supervisory powers which
protect the integrity of the judicial system. 708 F.2d at 531.
Isolated errors and improprieties do not require dismissal of
the indictment. It is only when the government engages in
deliberate conduct which interferes with the grand jury's independent function or damages the integrity of the judicial
process that the remedy of dismissal becomes necessary. Because I find that the government engaged in a pattern of
conduct calculated to infringe the grand jury's ability to exercise independent judgment, the indictments must be dismissed.

• • • • • •

The grand jury is more than a symbol of the limitations the
Constitution places on the government's power. When the
government usurps the grand jury and destroys its independence so that it looks and acts like an arm of the prosecution,
the very essence of a government of limited powers is destroyed. *See United States* v. *Dionisio,* 410 U.S. 1, 17, 93 S.Ct.
764, 773, 35 L.Ed.2d 67 (1973); *Stirone* v. *United States,* 361
U.S. 212, 80 S.Ct. 270, 4 L.Ed.2d 252 (1960).

In *United States* v. *Samango,* the Ninth Circuit said:

The Court's power to dismiss an indictment on the ground
of prosecutorial misconduct is frequently discussed but rarely
invoked. Courts are rightly reluctant to encroach on the con-
stitutionality-based independence of the prosecutor and
grand jury.[26] The Court "will not interfere with the Attorney
General's prosecutorial discretion unless it is abused to such
an extent as to be arbitrary and capricious and violative of due
process." *United States* v. *Welch,* 572 F.2d 1359, 1360 (9th Cir.),
cert. denied. 439 U.S. 842, 99 S.Ct. 133, 58 L.Ed.2d 140 (1978).

Nevertheless:

On occasion, and in widely-varying factual contexts, federal
courts have dismissed indictments because of the way in which
the prosecution sought and secured the charges from the
grand jury. . . . These dismissals have been based either on
constitutional grounds or on the court's inherent supervisory
powers. . . . Whatever the basis of the dismissal, however, the
court's goal has been the same, "to protect the integrity of the

judicial process." . . . particularly the functions of the grand jury, from unfair or improper prosecutorial conduct (citations and footnotes omitted.)

607 F.2d at 881 quoting *United States* v. *Chanen,* 549 F.2d 1306, 1309 (9th Cir.) *cert. denied,* 434 U.S. 825, 98 S.Ct. 72, 54 L.Ed.2d 83 (1977).

From the inception of the twenty-month grand jury investigation when the prosecutors divined the office of "agent of the grand jury" on the IRS agents through the time of the agent's improper "summaries" presented shortly before the indictment was returned, the conduct of the Department of Justice attorneys substantially undermined the ability of the grand jury to exercise independence. The numerous abuses and violations of rules and constitutional principles must be considered particularly serious because of the admissions in these hearings that, for the most part, the activity was undertaken knowingly and purposefully.

In addition to the abuses detailed in this memorandum opinion numerous other instances of misconduct are recounted by Judge Winner in his August 25, 1983 Opinion. In sum, the substantial departures of prosecutors in this case from established notions of fairness, from clearly articulated rules of law, from specific rules of procedure and, indeed from the Department of Justice's own manual and operating directives constitute systematic and pervasive overreaching. There is no doubt that the indicting grand jury was usurped and that time-honored constitutional principles were sullied.

Some of the violations, standing alone, require dismissal. Others, while not singularly requiring dismissal, when combined with one another amount to travesty. What is perhaps most alarming is that even in the very last of so many hearings, one of the prosecuting attorneys continued to refer to the challenge to his and his colleagues' conduct as "silly" and "frivolous." K.Tr. 1137. The supervisory authority of the court must be used in circumstances such as those presented in this case to declare with unmistakable intention that such conduct is neither "silly" nor "frivolous" and that it will not be tolerated.

The government attorneys, who replaced the prosecutors whose activities are at issue, reluctantly acknowledge that with regard to *at least* two of the procedures employed in this investigation they were "technically inaccurate" and "should obviously not be repeated in the future." *See* Government Response to Defendants' Opening Brief in Support of Motions to Dismiss the Indictment, filed November 14, 1983, at pp. 11, 15. When all the "technically inaccurate" procedures and abuses which "should obviously not occur in the future" are accumulated, what emerges is a picture of an IRS investigation out of control and a grand jury which was converted into little more than a rubber stamp.

The Fifth Amendment guarantees that no person shall be held to answer for an infamous crime "unless on a presentment or indictment of a grand jury." The Supreme Court observed in *United States* v. *Dionisio*, 410 U.S. 1, 16–17, 93 S.Ct. 764, 772–73, 35 L.Ed.2d 67 (1973) that "[t]his constitutional guarantee presupposes an investigative body 'acting independently of either prosecuting attorney or judge.' *Stirone* v. *United States*, 361 U.S. 212, 218, 80 S.Ct. 270 273, 4 L.Ed.2d 252, whose mission is to clear the innocent, no less than to bring to trial those who may be guilty." As a result of the conduct of the prosecutors and their entourage of agents, the indicting grand jury was not able to undertake its essential mission. That such is a significant and prejudicial deprivation of these defendant's constitutional rights to due process of law and personal liberty should require no further recitation of authority.

ORDER

Based on the foregoing I hold and ORDER as follows:

1. The indictment is dismissed because of the numerous violations of Rule 6(d), Fed.R.Crim.P.
2. The indictment is dismissed because of the numerous violations of Rule 6(e), Fed.R.Crim.P.
3. The indictment is not dismissed solely for the use of "pocket immunity" in contravention of 18 U.S.C. §§ 6002 and 6003.
4. The indictment is not dismissed solely for violations of the Fifth Amendment to the United States Constitution.

5. The indictment is not dismissed solely for the knowing and deliberate presentation of misinformation to the grand jury.

6. The indictment is not dismissed solely for violations of the Sixth Amendment to the United States Constitution.

7. The indictment is dismissed because of the totality of the circumstances which include numerous violations of Rule 6(d) and (e), Fed.R.Crim.P., violations of 18 U.S.C. §§ 6002 and 6003, violations of the Fifth and Sixth amendments to the United States Constitution, knowing presentation of misinformation to the grand jury and mistreatment of witnesses.

FOOTNOTES

1. The facts relied upon in this opinion are taken from voluminous transcripts of hearings before two grand juries, Judge Winner, and me and a trial before a jury. To aid the reader, the following citation form is used: references to the trial to the jury presided over by Judge Winner are cited as "T. Tr."; references to hearings on the motion for a new trial or acquittal and the motion to dismiss before Judge Winner are cited as "W. Tr."; and references to hearings on the motions underlying this order are cited as "K. Tr." Citation of the grand jury transcripts are captioned "G.J. Tr." and recite the relevant witness or declarant, the date and the time of the transcription. Defense and prosecution exhibits submitted on this matter are designated respectively "DX" and PX."

2. The government seeks to absolve the prosecutors of any misconduct by pointing to instances where the prosecutors themselves informed the grand jury of its independent and unbiased mission. *See, e.g.,* G.J. Tr. Remarks of Prosecutor, July 8, 1981, 8:39 a.m. at pp. 9, 11; October 6, 1981, 10:58 a.m., at pp. 2, 3; September 29, 1982, 8:52 a.m., at p. 8. Such admonishments, however, are not curative of actions taken at other times which constitute abuses of the system and impinge upon the grand jury's integrity.

3. Agent Raybin testified that before Mr. Snyder gave him his oath as an agent of the grand jury, he was also sworn in by the foreman of the grand jury. K.Tr. 267.

4. Snyder did suggest that the swearing in of grand jury

agents was practiced in Atlanta, Georgia and the Southern District of Florida. He did not, however, testify as to what grand jury agents did in these other districts or whether the practices employed elsewhere were similar to those used here. K.Tr. 414–15.

5. On some occasions Mr. Snyder referred to Raybin and Mendrop as his agents. G.J. Tr. Remarks of Prosecutor, July 8, 1981, 8:39 a.m., at pp. 9, 15, 18, 21, 23; July 8, 1981, 12:05 p.m., at p. 5; August 5, 1981, 3:50 p.m., at p. 5; September 9, 1981, 8:37 a.m., at p. 2; September 9, 1981, 10:00 a.m., at p. 2; October 6, 1981, 10:58 a.m., at p. 12; May 3, 1982, 9:15 a.m., at p. 5. Such references did not, however, clarify the ambiguous role of the grand jury agents. As noted, the IRS agents were often referred to as agents of the grand jury. The confusion over the agents' role is discernible from isolated statements made by the prosecutors to the grand jury. Snyder, for example, said that he would, "have my agents, when I ask them to be sworn as agents of the Grand Jury, analyze [the documents] and basically figure out what they mean." G.J. Tr. Remarks of Prosecutor, July 8, 1981, 8:39 a.m., at p. 21; *see also* G.J. Tr. Remarks of Prosecutor, July 8, 1981, 12:05 p.m., at p. 5. The agents worked, in form, for the grand jury; but, in substance, they worked for the prosecution.

6. Mendrop and Raybin claim that they never introduced themselves to witnesses as agents of the grand jury. K.Tr. 243; 266–67, 366–67.

7. *See supra* note 5 and accompanying text.

8. The government claims that all prosecutorial decisions made by IRS agents were done in consultation with the prosecuting attorneys. K.Tr. 145–46.

9. The occasional self-serving statements by prosecutors to the grand jury that use of grand jury information in IRS audits is improper does not absolve the improper disclosures but merely serves to highlight the seriousness of the misconduct. G.J. Tr. Remarks of Prosecutor, July 8, 1981, 8:30 a.m., at pp. 12–13; November 4, 1981, 9:12 a.m., at p. 6.

10. For examples, see sections of this opinion entitled "Facts Established by the Record," F. and G.

11. Both government attorney Snyder and agent Mendrop dispute Birchall's testimony. K.Tr. 423–36; 376–89.

12. *See supra* note 20.

13. As discussed later, *see supra* text accompanying note 21, I now believe I was unduly diffident in *Anderson*. The practice is not merely damnable; I believe now that it is clearly illegal.

14. The government's brief, Government's Response to the Bank of Nova Scotia's Proposed Findings of Fact and Conclusions of Law, filed April 9, 1984, at p. 19 provides:

On February 2, 1982, Mr. Snyder advised the grand jury of his negotiations with Mr. Bailor [attorney for many of the witnesses], and again explained to the grand jury the difference between statutory immunity and letters of assurance. 2/2/82 (1:07 p.m.) G.J. Colloquy 5–14.

The transcript for G.J. Tr. February 2, 1982, 1:07 p.m. presents the testimony of Gordon MacManus. The substance of the testimony consists entirely of an inquiry as to whether Mr. MacManus's attorney was being paid for by Realty Inc. and whether Mr. MacManus would invoke his right against self incrimination. Contrary to the government's assertion, the transcript reflects the prosecutor's attempts to prejudice the grand jury. *See supra* text accompanying note 15.

15. *See supra* note 14.

16. The government claims that the doubts about the accuracy of Waters' description did not arise until after Mendrop testified. Nevertheless, even under the government's version, such doubts existed months before the indictment. K.Tr. 1067–68.

17. The government argues that interviewing Haynes does not give rise to *Massiah* violations because he was only "a potential witness who had information as to the bank's conduct concerning the events charged in the indictment." Government's Response to The Bank of Nova Scotia's Proposed Findings of Fact and Conclusions of Law, filed April 9, 1984, at p. 37. The government ignores *Massiah* because Haynes was not individually named as a defendant in the indictment. *Id.* Nevertheless, the government does recog-

nize that Haynes "was the number two man in the Cayman Island branch of The Bank of Nova Scotia at the time of the events in question." *Id.* quoting W.Tr. 653.

18. Mr. Morvillo is the bank's lead defense counsel.
19. *See supra* note 23.
20. The United States Attorneys' Manual provides at § 9–11.362:

> Rule 6(e) specifically prohibits any obligation of secrecy from being imposed "upon any person except in accordance with this rule." Witnesses, therefore, cannot be put under any obligation of secrecy. *Application of Eisenberg,* 654 F.2d 1107, 1113 n. 9 (5th Cir.1981). This, however, should not prevent the grand jury foreman from requesting a witness not to make unneccessary disclosures when those disclosures or the attendant publicity might hinder an investigation.

21. *See supra* note 13.
22. The conventional remedy for illegal use of "pocket immunity" would, in most instances, take the form of a *post facto* grant of statutory immunity or the equitable enforcement of the pocket agreement, for the benefit of grand jury witnesses who relied on the prosecutor's promises. These concerns are not before me here. Still, the use of pocket immunity was so pervasive in this case that it reflects upon the general conduct of the prosecutors and the grand jury.
23. The prosecutor's *post hoc* rationalizations attempting to demonstrate the propriety of his conduct do the opposite. *See supra* text accompanying note 18. *Upjohn* v. *United States,* 449 U.S. 383, 101 S.Ct. 677, 66 L.Ed.2d 584 (1981) established that corporate employees of the kind interrogated here fall within the ambit of the attorney-client relationship and must be considered, in essence, the corporation for purposes of communication. Indeed, while the Supreme Court in *Upjohn* noted that instead of procuring interview notes of the corporation's attorneys, counsel for the government might themselves question employees about relevant events, the facts of that decision give no indication that questioning would be proper if conducted behind counsel's back. Rather, the opinion indicated that questioning would occur with appropriate procedural safeguards. Moreover,

Upjohn, was not a criminal case and the corporation had not been indicted. Thus, *Massiah* and its progeny, of course, were inapplicable. Indeed, the facts and relevance of *Upjohn* are so inapposite as to raise questions as to the sincerity of its invocation.

The prosecutor also relied upon *Diversified Industries, Inc.* v. *Meredith,* 572 F.2d 596 (8th Cir.1977) as support for its position. That case too dealt with civil litigation and the question of attorney-client privilege with a corporate client. The case did not concern post-indictment activity by prosecutors.

The prosecutor's second *post hoc* rationalization that *Massiah* did not restrict his interrogation because he did not employ subterfuge requires little discussion. The Supreme Court did not base its holding in *Massiah* upon the use of subterfuge. Rather, that opinion was premised on an accused's right to counsel. Thus, in *Brewer* v. *Williams,* the Supreme Court specifically noted that the fact that "the incriminating statements were elicted surreptitiously in the *Massiah* case, and otherwise here, is constitutionally irrelevant." *Brewer* v. *Williams,* 430 U.S. at 400, 97 S.Ct. at 1240.

24. Unlike the situations in *Brewer* and *Massiah,* the interrogation of the bank's representatives was conducted not by an investigatory agent, but primarily by an attorney involved in the prosecution also calling into question a possible violation of that attorney's ethical obligations.

Disciplinary Rule 7-104 of the Code of Professional Responsibility provides in relevant part:

Communicating with One of Adverse Interest.

(A) During the course of his representation of a client a lawyer shall not:

(1) Communicate or cause another to communicate on the subject of the representation with a party he knows to be represented by a lawyer in that matter unless he has the prior consent of the lawyer representing such other party or is authorized by law to do so.

See United States v. *Thomas,* 474 F.2d 110, 111–12 (10th Cir.) *cert. denied,* 412 U.S. 932, 93 S.Ct. 2758, 37 L.Ed.2d 160

(1973). *Cf. Ceramco, Inc.* v. *Lee Pharmaceuticals,* 510 F.2d 268 (2d Cir.1975).

25. The prosecutor's interrogation and surveillance here is precisely the type of deliberate governmental impropriety that should be discouraged. *See United States* v. *Owen,* 580 F.2d 365, 367 (9th Cir.1978), citing *Elkins* v. *United States,* 364 U.S. 206, 80 S.Ct. 1437, 4 L.Ed.2d 1669 (1960); *United States* v. *Houghton,* 554 F.2d 1219, 1224 (1st Cir.1977), *cert. denied* 434 U.S. 851, 98 S.Ct. 164, 54 L.Ed.2d 120. Insofar as the prosecutor by his own admission was not deterred by the possibility of other available remedies, dismissal remains the only viable prophylactic tool. The Supreme Court has gone to great lengths to explain that the good faith efforts of law enforcement officials should not be overcome by technicalities beyond their control. *See United States* v. *Leon,* —U.S. —, 104 S.Ct. 3430, 82 L.Ed.2d 677 (1984). The apposing proposition requires that effective sanctions be imposed to prevent deliberate constitutional violations by law enforcement officials. Constitutional protections are of little value if violations are permitted without the imposition of meaningful sanctions. *See Mapp* v. *Ohio,* 367 U.S. 643, 655, 81 S.Ct. 1684, 1691, 6 L.Ed.2d 1081 (1961); *Elkins* v. *United States,* 364 U.S. 206, 217, 80 S.Ct. 1437, 1444, 4 L.Ed.2d 1669 (1960). Here, the prosecutor's premeditated interrogation of bank employees behind the back of the bank's counsel plainly violated the Sixth Amendment protections outlined by the Supreme Court in *Massiah* and *Brewer.*

26. In almost seven years on this bench this case and *United States* v. *Anderson, supra,* are the only two instances out of many cases in which I have felt constrained to dismiss an indictment.